# QUARTERMASTER GENERAL

# OF THE UNION ARMY

# QUARTERMASTER
# GENERAL
# OF THE UNION ARMY

*a biography of M. C. MEIGS*

*by RUSSELL F. WEIGLEY*

NEW YORK

*COLUMBIA UNIVERSITY PRESS* 1959

*To My Mother and Father*

# ACKNOWLEDGMENTS

MUCH of the research for this volume was made possible through the grant of a George Leib Harrison Fellowship by the University of Pennsylvania. For their indispensable cooperation I have to thank the staffs of the University of Pennsylvania Library, the Free Library of Philadelphia, the Historical Society of Pennsylvania, and, above all, the National Archives, especially the Modern Army Section, and the Library of Congress.

Various members of the Meigs family cheerfully supplied me with information, either through letters or in personal interviews. Limitations of space prevented me from using more of the family material. I wish to thank especially Mr. Philip L. Alger, Schenectady, New York; Mr. R. J. Meigs, Basking Ridge, New Jersey; Mr. John F. Meigs, Annapolis, Maryland; and Mr. Henry H. Meigs, Philadelphia.

I feel especially grateful to Harold Langley, who was at the time both my fellow doctoral candidate at the University of Pennsylvania and a member of the staff of the Manuscript Division of the Library of Congress, for all manner of help during my research and particularly for finding Meigs material among the John G. Nicolay Papers. For critical readings of the manuscript I wish to thank Dr. Samuel B. Shirk and Miss Emma

Seifrit. The editorial staff of Columbia University Press has been most helpful with suggestions.

My work on the Quartermaster's Department of the Union army began in the economic history seminar of the late Professor Arthur C. Bining. To Professor Roy F. Nichols, who continually interrupted his incredibly crowded schedule to give me wise and understanding advice, I owe my greatest debt of gratitude.

*December, 1958*                                RUSSELL F. WEIGLEY

# CONTENTS

*The portrait on the title page is a reproduction from a photograph by Mathew Brady.*

# QUARTERMASTER GENERAL

# OF THE UNION ARMY

# INTRODUCTION

ACROSS most of the Virginia Peninsula, the beginning of April, 1862, offered little evidence that the coming of this spring would be a harbinger of the coming of warfare. True, some men were digging new earthworks near the moldering Revolutionary trenches around Yorktown, and others were marching and countermarching in small groups over the low and marshy ground that stretched southeastward from Yorktown toward Hampton Roads. But on most of that long, narrow finger of land bounded by the estuaries of the rivers York and James, fields of brightening green and buds unrolling into leaves were unmindful of the Civil War. The pink-red brick walls of the old manor houses recalled more glorious days when William Byrd and King Carter stood on their wharves to greet the sails from London, and the old colonial buildings of Williamsburg were decaying reminders that it had once been the seat of His Majesty's Governor and Captain General of Virginia.

Only at the eastern extremity of the Peninsula was it unmistakably clear that this spring would be no ordinary one. The frowning old masonry of Fortress Monroe harbored unwonted activity, and the neighboring village of Hampton lay a shambles of charred ruins. Along the shores of the

Chesapeake between Hampton and Old Point Comfort crowded long lines of parked artillery, files of white-topped baggage wagons, clusters of pontoon boats, and behind them marched row on row of shelter tents, alive with soldiers in blue. The troops wheeled and turned in cadence through the quaintly stiff maneuvers prescribed by the drill books, and some whose blue was piped with red performed their rituals amidst the somber beauty of the guns.[1]

In the straitened waters of Hampton Roads and northward up Chesapeake Bay and the Potomac all the way to the Federal city at Washington, steam and sail vessels of all descriptions plied their way: huge three-decked transports, steam tugs dwarfed by the sailing ships they held in tow, canal boats, barges.[2] Major General George B. McClellan's Army of the Potomac was opening the campaign planned to end the war, and to transfer 100,000 soldiers and their supplies and equipage by water to the prospective scene of action, a massive fleet had been assembled: 71 side-wheel steamers; 57 propeller-driven steamers; 187 schooners, brigs, and barks; 90 barges—a total of 405 vessels, aggregating 86,278 tons.[3]

A military operation of comparable magnitude had never before been attempted on the American continent, and rarely anywhere. So that the army might advance overland once it had debarked in Virginia, the vessels carried 3,600 supply wagons and 700 ambulances and spring wagons.[4] Six hundred thousand complete rations sailed with the troops, and a store of 2,500,000 additional rations was being forwarded from New

[1] Robert Underwood Johnson and Clarence Clough Buel, eds., *Battles and Leaders of the Civil War* (4 vols., New York, 1884–1888), II, 189. Cited hereafter as *B. & L.*

[2] *Ibid.*, II, 159.

[3] *The War of the Rebellion: A Compilation of the Official Records of the Union and Confederate Armies* (4 series, 70 vols. in 128 vols., Washington, 1880–1901), ser. 1, XII, pt. 1, 156–61. Cited hereafter as *O.R.*

[4] *Ibid.*

York to Fortress Monroe. Beef cattle were shipped in quantity to Virginia to assure a supply of fresh meats. Each man of the army carried in his haversack six days' rations.[5]

The preparations were by no means excessive. Active campaigning was to find each soldier consuming 3 pounds of provisions per day, and every horse 26 pounds of forage. This meant a total of over 500 tons of subsistence and forage used by the army daily, with other necessary supplies swelling to over 600 tons the total weight which had to be transported to the front and the camps every twenty-four hours. In other terms, the subsistence stores consumed by the army in a day would amount to 150 wagonloads. To move the troops and their supplies by water was a task formidable enough; to keep supplies flowing to the troops by land as they advanced toward the Confederate capital at Richmond would offer perhaps even greater problems.[6]

Nor were the 100,000 men of McClellan's Army of the Potomac the only soldiers wearing the Federal uniform in the spring of 1862. Perhaps 50,000 more were in and around Washington, in northern Virginia, in the Shenandoah Valley, and in the mountains of western Virginia. Some 55,000 were organized into two armies in Tennessee, and similar detachments lay at various points, especially along the Atlantic and Gulf coasts.

All this stood in marked contrast to the condition of the tiny force that had been the United States Army only a year before, an organization which had numbered only 17,113 officers and men.[7] The contrast already had produced certain awkward results, and still more were to come. No officer young and fit enough for active command in the field had ever handled

[5] *Ibid.*, ser. 1, XI, pt. 1, 167.
[6] *Ibid.*
[7] Kenneth P. Williams, *Lincoln Finds a General: A Military Study of the Civil War* (4 vols., New York, 1950–1956), I, 62.

as much as a brigade before the battle of Bull Run in July, 1861; few had seen a single regiment assembled in one place since the Mexican War. Even aging Lieutenant General Winfield Scott, recently retired from supreme command of the Federal armies, had led to the halls of Montezuma a force that was minuscule in comparison to that which McClellan was leading now. For neither the maneuvering nor the administration of the troops rallied to the banner of the Union was anyone prepared by training or experience. The transition from an army of 17,000 to one of half a million in a period short of a year made the task of the services of supply nothing less than staggering.

From the large but not ungainly brick pile of Winder's Building, where the Headquarters of the Armies of the United States looked across Washington's Seventeenth Street to the War Department and, beyond that, to the White House, Brigadier General Montgomery Cunningham Meigs, Quartermaster General, U.S.A., presided over the sprawling system of communications, purchases, and transportation which kept provisions and supplies for the armies stockpiled in the depots and moving along the roads to the front. By the time McClellan landed on the Peninsula, Meigs had been quartermaster general for nearly a year. He was coming to handle his job with a smoothness and sureness of touch which would help to guarantee that, however often the Union army might lose battles because of inept strategy or fumbling tactics, never after the summer of 1861 would a major operation fail because the Quartermaster's Department had not provided food or forage or transportation. The services of supply managed the transition from a shoestring force to one vaster by far than anything of which the old army had ever dreamed with a skill which, given the circumstances, was remarkable. Errors and incompetence in widespread operations, deficiencies and waste, naturally appeared. The clothing which the troops wore in the first months was all too likely to be shoddy. The food was rarely of the best, and sometimes there was little of it at the places where the troops needed it. Yet the glaring abuses of the early months of the war soon were remedied, and for the most part the Union soldier who fought the Civil War probably could count himself better provided for than any soldier ever before in history. The great Union supply depot at City Point near Petersburg in the closing phase of the war and the expedition to reclothe and refit Sherman's armies when they reached Savannah at the end of their march to the sea were fit objects of admiration and even of wonder.

That the effectiveness of the services of supply did much to open the way to ultimate victory for the Union goes without saying. The tremendous superiority in potential material strength which the North held over the Southern Confederacy from the beginning of the war has led many to argue that the Southern cause was doomed from the start. Yet it is essential to remember that for war purposes the material strength of the North was at the outset a potential strength only. It was the ability of the North to translate potential might into strength mobilized on the battlefield, not the potentiality alone, which sealed the decision. Here it was that the services of supply of the Union army played their vital role; their success is underlined by the comparative failure of their Confederate counterparts. In the closing years of the war, and particularly during the siege of Petersburg, the Confederate army was wracked by a crisis in supply which steadily undermined its fighting qualities. In the Petersburg trenches Confederate soldiers at times were reduced to eating rats. The difficulty sprang not so much from a genuine scarcity of food and military material in the South but primarily from a breakdown of Southern services of distribution. A comparable collapse never plagued the North;

the supply services of the Union army kept the flow of goods from Northern factories and farms to the front a dependable one.

In no small measure the success of the logistical support of the Union armies rested upon the talents and experience of men who were soldiers for the duration only. This was particularly true of the United States Military Railroads, on which the cars were assembled, loaded, and moved under the practiced eyes of professional railroaders such as D. C. McCallum and Herman Haupt. Haupt was a West Pointer, but in the war essentially an expert imported from civilian life. In the Civil War, however, as in all our wars, it was the efforts of men who were soldiers by trade that guided and organized the military contributions of those who were soldiers only by temporary necessity. And among the professional military men who directed the supplying of the Union army M. C. Meigs stands in the first place. Few Union officers served so long in one key position; few served with such unvarying competence. This is an account of Meigs's career, of his military service, of his relations with the political leaders of his day, and of the role of the corps he headed in transforming the despair of First Bull Run into the measured triumph of Appomattox.

If Meigs is noteworthy chiefly for his part in the primary political and military crisis of nineteenth-century American history, his life nevertheless has a significance apart from the illumination cast on it by that trial by fire. M. C. Meigs was a nineteenth-century American. And while no man can epitomize in his single life span all the characteristic virtues and values and failings of an epoch, yet there remains in Meigs's career much that helps limn the years in which he lived. The limits of his lifetime mark off a cycle of American development. At his birth in 1816 the Virginia dynasty still reigned in Washington. And if the agrarianism of Thomas Jefferson had already suffered among the sage's followers from a somewhat guilt-haunted fondness for tariffs and internal improvements and a new Bank of the United States, still the independent yeoman farmer almost everywhere held rank as the ideal American and the mainstay of the American economy. By the time Meigs died in 1892 the day of the yeoman farmer had passed. The smoke of crowded factories floated across the Northeast and much of the Midwest; an urban proletariat and an urban middle class were becoming the most typical of American groups.

In some ways M. C. Meigs was a man of the new day, of the materialistic, mechanically and scientifically inclined America born in the second half of the century of industrialization, urbanization, and technological change. The orders he placed with American businesses during the Civil War helped hasten the passing of the old ways and the coming of the new. In his work as a construction engineer he often was a builder in cast iron, that peculiarly symbolic material of the nineteenth-century industrial revolution; the great stone arch which he built over Cabin John Creek for the Washington Aqueduct is a monument of functional design. In his passion for mechanical gadgets and his continual tinkering with new inventions, Meigs was the embodiment of the ingenious Yankee. Yet the spirit of the new age of materialism and realism and the spirit of M. C. Meigs were not always at one. There was in Meigs none of the grasping acquisitive drive which so often darkened the new day, no thirst for wealth and material success for their own sakes, but instead a dedication to service and duty as the great ends of life, which bespoke an earlier and perhaps more gracious era. There stirred in him also a strong element of a characteristically American nineteenth-century Protestantism, with its roots in the Calvinist past. And while Meigs was by all means an individualist, his individualism bore none of that indifference to the welfare of other men which all too often perverted the most applauded of American virtues into an appalling vice.

A nineteenth-century American, Meigs at the same time was a professional soldier. If in this he was atypical, since few of his countrymen had dedicated their lives to the profession of arms, still he belonged to a tradition which for a few years at least dominated his America, and which in our day has climbed to unprecedented influence. Side by side with Meigs's frequent acuteness as an observer of his country and its problems, there existed an occasional myopia which suggests the limitations of a mind trained under a rigid code and in considerable isolation from the main currents of American life.

At the same time, simply to categorize M. C. Meigs as a military man is not enough. For a soldier, he led a life singularly remote from the neighing troop and flashing blade. Only in one emergency did he exercise a field command, and then for no more than a day or two. He saw battle only as an observer. For him an army career meant, before the Civil War, an engineering career, and much of it did not involve military engineering. War translated him to more martial duties, but it was as a staff officer that he served out the civil conflict and what remained of his army life thereafter. The consequence was a measure of detachment in Meigs's views of the army and even of the officer corps. He was critical, for example, of the eagerness he found in many of his colleagues to go to war in 1865 to drive the French out of Mexico; such men saw only the glory to be won by defeating the current European military champion, he said, and they failed to count the cost.

For all that, it was in war that the life of M. C. Meigs reached its climax and Meigs felt his greatest sense of fulfillment. In the war years there shines from the pages which he wrote in letters and diaries and reports a feeling of special achievement, a sense of years of preparation now come to fruition, and a confidence that Meigs's own humble life was functioning as an instrument in the consummation of some inscrutable but certainly glorious divine purpose. To Meigs as to Lincoln the Civil War was a penance which the nation must bear until the last stain of the sin of slavery faded wholly away. With Meigs as with Lincoln the burden of penance brought with it a confident hope that from travail and death would emerge a new birth of freedom, and that a reunited nation would stand stronger than ever as the champion of popular government through all the world.

Beyond his family, on which he lavished pride and affection, it was the nation that was the focus of all that Meigs hoped for. To the nation he had dedicated his own life from the moment he took the oath of allegiance as a cadet on the plains above the Hudson. To the nation he gave her great symbol in granite and stone, the Capitol of the United States. To the nation he sacrificed his first-born son, whose career ended in blood and hatred at the moment of its highest promise. The effort and sacrifice he did not believe to be in vain; even from the depths of the blackest years of war his eye caught a vision of an America purged of her sins and so magnified in strength that she would buttress freedom with a physical power over-shadowing the might of France and England, the great powers of the day, as a giant obscures a pygmy. This was the destiny of America; and the life of M. C. Meigs, by God's grace, was to help make it so. A man could ask no more.

PART ONE

# FAMILY AND FLAG

# I

# PHILADELPHIA

MONTGOMERY MEIGS would remember his boyhood with a warm and happy glow, as nearly all men do whose parents have been kind and good and whose youth has been unscarred by adversity. What is more, he had been a boy when boyhood was a particularly fine and wonderful thing, when for boys America was the sort of place which could produce the epics of Tom Sawyer and Huck Finn. Philadelphia, where Montgomery grew up, was not Hannibal, Missouri, but neither was it yet endless asphalt and mile on mile of compact stores and factories and warehouses. The Delaware and the Schuylkill still flowed clear enough to reflect faithfully the deep blue of an October sky. The old waterworks still marked Center Square, although its successor at the Fair Mount was reaching completion; and now the Greek façades which would delight Charles Dickens looked out over Fair Mount Dam, flanked by the graceful columned pavilion copied from the Temple d'Amour at Chantilly. If New York was leaving the city behind both as port and as metropolis, still Philadelphia was growing rapidly. And yet, "There were still links which bound this restless, fast-growing population to the past, still old habits and customs not easily relinquished. . . . When

things are as good as they can possibly be, what consummate
wisdom in leaving them alone!" [1]

Some 63,000 souls inhabited the city, and the westward
march of concentrated population had not yet reached the
Schuylkill. From the corner of Broad and Arch Streets one
could enjoy a view of Fair Mount uninterrupted by buildings,
and the paving of Broad Street ceased abruptly at Vine.[2] To
grow up here was to grow up in a city to be sure, but
the open countryside was not so distant that a boy might
not occasionally go abroad to hunt for chestnuts and hickory
nuts.[3]

Best of all, there were outings on the rivers, and Montie
Meigs would go up the Delaware with his parents and
brothers and sisters to a farm along the river which belonged
to a friend of his maternal grandfather. Most of the family
would travel upstream on a public boat they boarded at the
Market Street wharf, a large open rowboat with a short sail
that it used in favoring winds. Montie's father would make
the trip his own way, journeying the six miles or so between
the foot of Market Street and the farm in his own light sail-
boat. On one occasion his boat capsized, and he had to spend a
considerable time in the river riding on his upturned craft
until a passing steamboat—still a rarity—rescued him. At the
farm Montie found green grass and a large peach orchard and
a pleasant grove of Lombardy poplars along the clay bank of
the river, and under the shade of the poplars the children played
their summer games. In the river they would go "swimming,"
as they called it, though actually all they could do as yet was
wade, walking into the still water with its foul and muddy

[1] Agnes Repplier, *Philadelphia, the Place and the People* (New York,
1898), p. 327.
[2] Recollections of S. Emlen Meigs in Henry B. Meigs, *Record of the
Descendants of Vincent Meigs* (Philadelphia, 1901), p. 269.
[3] Meigs Letter Book, 1857–1858, p. 97; cited hereafter as Meigs Let. B.

bottom until the water covered their chins and reached their lower lips in a glorious moment of danger.[4]

In town there were relatives, remembered later as gentle and of good humor. There was Mother's brother Joseph Montgomery, whom Montie would associate in memory with churchgoing and the stately old steeple of Christ Church on Second Street and then the splendid new steeple of the Episcopal church on Arch Street. More important was Grandfather Montgomery, Mother's father, with his "portly figure fine face & unwearying love for us boys." Grandfather Montgomery lost his wife in 1819, when Montie was three, and the boy would be able later to recall his grandmother's coffin, surrounded by candles and covered with a black pall, laid out in the second-story front room of her house on Arch Street above Sixth. Grandmother was a Roman Catholic, and Montie's mother would tell him later how Grandfather Montgomery, a Protestant, kept the candles burning around the bier until the priests had left and then hurriedly blew them out. After the funeral Montie and his parents moved into Grandfather's house, and thenceforth Grandfather was an almost constant companion.

He was retired now, but he had been a merchant, and he delighted in extolling the merchant's virtue of thrift. "Who takes care of his pennies, his hands will take care of themselves," he would repeat. Still, thrift was a virtue which he himself sometimes failed to follow, so that when Montie's mother sent him to do the marketing she would nearly always have to scold him on his return for buying more than the family budget would allow. Once when he had indulged in a great purchase of apples and peaches, she threw a whole bushel of the fruit into the street, saying that she simply could not pay for such stuff. Presumably Grandfather had to stand the loss.

[4] Meigs Let. B., 1885–1887, pp. 341–43.

To Montie, however, expeditions to market meant happy early
morning walks at his grandfather's side; and long years later
he would sum it all up by saying of his grandfather, "We were
great friends." [5]

Mother it was who unobtrusively governed and organized
the household, watched the budget, and kept a loving but
penetrating eye upon her ten children. The first five of her off-
spring were boys, then came a girl. The second to last of the ten
was also a girl. With eight boys the house never was lacking
in the noise of jumping from the stairway and excited shouting. The children would remember their mother as invariably
just in her treatment of them. She would impress them too
with a sense of the obligations of duty, a lesson which Montie
learned well. When Montgomery Meigs looked back upon the
family from the years of his manhood, and all that had happened was touched with a wistful romanticism, Mother would
be the quietly smiling woman by the fireplace, her nimble
fingers finishing rapidly the worsted work on which his sister
Emily had spent so many hours only to leave the task undone:
"I can see you now yet picking up stitches counting carefully
the threads but sewing away as if you were hemming a towel.
It was like the rapid touch of an artist . . . after the slow
hesitating work of a pupil." [6]

Father was a physician, Dr. Charles D. Meigs, still a general
practitioner in Montgomery's earliest years, but moving toward
an increasing specialization in obstetrics. In 1826 he became
one of the editors of the *North American Medical and Surgical
Journal.* In 1830 he began lecturing on what was still called
midwifery at the "School of Medicine," and the same year he

[5] Meigs Let. B., 1858–1859, pp. 103–4; 1885–1887, pp. 343–44.
[6] R. J. Meigs, *Register of the Descendants of Vincent Meigs* (Westfield, N. J., 1935), p. 42; S. Emlen Meigs in Henry B. Meigs, *Record of
the Descendants of Vincent Meigs,* p. 269; M. C. Meigs to Mrs. Charles
D. Meigs, March 2, 1863, Meigs Miscellaneous Papers.

completed a translation of a standard French work on the subject, which was published in 1831 as an *Elementary Treatise on Midwifery*. A long succession of professional writings of his own were to follow, and in 1841 he was to become professor of obstetrics and diseases of women at Jefferson Medical College. Charles Meigs wanted to be a conscientious father, and Montgomery would always feel that in his father he could confide and be sure of receiving a sympathetic hearing and sound, temperate advice. But when Montgomery was a boy it was not easy to find time to talk with his father, for Charles Meigs was always busy. Every weekday he would make his rounds from nine in the morning until about ten at night. At midday he would find half an hour to an hour for dinner, and about seven or eight in the evening he would pause for tea; but the meals were always hurried, and often they were interrupted by calls to the office. Nor was it infrequent for Charles Meigs to be away from his home nearly all night, returning in the early morning to snatch a few hours' sleep on a sofa or chair. And on those nights when he did return about ten, it was rare for him to go to bed without first reading a book that would keep him up far into the night.[7]

Many of the Meigs family, including in later years Montgomery, possessed dispositions of marked acidity, to the extent that cantankerousness became something of a family tradition. However, Charles Meigs appears to have been a mild, kindly man, devoted to the right as he saw it, but without the talent for self-righteousness and controversy which other Meigses often displayed. One of his sons would write that he had a "beautiful imagination," [8] and altogether there seems to

[7] *Dictionary of American Biography* (21 vols., New York, 1928–1937), XII, 503, cited hereafter as *D.A.B.;* John F. Meigs, quoted in Henry B. Meigs, *Record of the Descendants of Vincent Meigs*, pp. 234–35.

[8] John F. Meigs in Henry B. Meigs, *Record of the Descendants of Vincent Meigs*, p. 235.

have been a warmth about him which was to be present only in the deeper and usually hidden layers of the personality of Montgomery Meigs.

Charles Meigs had come from a family of ten children, of whom he was the fifth, born in 1792 at St. George in the Bermudas, where his father, Josiah Meigs, was practicing law. The family was of Connecticut Puritan stock, and when Charles was only two they returned to New England. Until the boy was nine his father, a Yale graduate, taught mathematics and natural philosophy at his alma mater, and one of Charles's sons would later believe that to a boyhood spent in New Haven might be attributed the doctor's "honesty, honor, love of country, inflexible uprightness, liberality of mind and love of knowledge." This observation may well be true; yet one cannot but wonder whether even the godly Yale of Timothy Dwight could have had so thoroughly ennobling an influence upon a little boy whose father often was at odds with the rest of the faculty, since Josiah was an outspoken Jeffersonian among outspoken Federalists.

Stubborn Jeffersonianism, combined with a truculent disposition, led to the removal of Josiah Meigs in 1800 from Yale to the infant University of Georgia. Here his Yale scholarship soon advanced him to the presidency of the university. Here too Charles secured a college education, or at least such as was available, and began to read medicine. In early nineteenth-century Georgia a bit of reading in the office of a local practitioner would have been enough in most cases to establish a young man in his own mind and his neighbors' as an adequate physician, but Josiah Meigs was a scholar, and any son of his who thought to practice medicine would be a true doctor. In 1812 Charles journeyed northward to the medical center of the country, the city of Philadelphia, where he enrolled for the lectures at what claimed to be the nation's oldest medical school, that of the University of Pennsylvania. In 1815 he acquired his degree, and in March of that year he acquired also a Philadelphia bride, Mary Montgomery, the pretty daughter of the portly merchant William Montgomery.[9] Despite more than a decade as the seat of the state university, Athens, Georgia, was still small and primitive. Accordingly, Charles Meigs took his bride not to his former home but to the more advanced community of Augusta, a cotton-trading center on the lush green banks of the Savannah River, where he opened his office. Yet even in Augusta the raw and youthful South did not prove congenial to Mary Montgomery Meigs of Philadelphia. Among other things, the blight of slavery was rising to disquiet her. In addition, Charles found himself suffering from repeated attacks of the "bilious fever," a vaguely defined malady supposedly induced by the warm and humid climate.

Within a few short years, then, Charles and Mary Meigs were on their way back to Philadelphia, to a home on Eighth Street, and to a wider career for Charles. With them came their young son, Montgomery Cunningham Meigs, born at Augusta on May 3, 1816, amidst the warmth of a Georgia spring—a warmth which contrasts oddly with certain lines of the life to come.[10]

His family and his country were the two great foci of the loyalty of M. C. Meigs, and the emotional attachments which bound him to both enjoyed careful cultivation in the years of his youth. His father was the preceptor of one's duty to the family name. The name of Meigs was a proud one, he told his children, and each of those who bore it must do all in his power to promote its honor before men. A Meigs dared not disgrace the stock from which he came; his ancestors had been

[9] *Ibid.; D.A.B.,* XII, 506–7; Wm. M. Meigs, *Life of Josiah Meigs* (Philadelphia, 1887).

[10] *D.A.B.,* XII, 503–4; John F. Meigs in Henry B. Meigs, *Record of the Descendants of Vincent Meigs,* pp. 231–35.

men of the highest honor and integrity, and he must be the same.[11]

From his father young Montgomery heard on winter evenings the story of his family's coming to America. Vincent Meigs had sailed from Weymouth in the midst of the great Puritan migration of the 1630's and had settled first in the new Weymouth in Massachusetts, gathering about him the three sons borne by the wife who had died in England, who tradition had it was a Churchill. Charles Meigs consistently used his recitation of the family annals as a springboard for the preaching of moral homilies. He told of Vincent's son John Meigs, who moved with his father from Massachusetts to the more rigidly Puritan colony of New Haven and there demonstrated that duty to conscience ought to hold priority over the claims of any government of men. Into the New Haven colony during his lifetime came two of the English regicides, Edward Whalley and William Goffe, fleeing the Stuart restoration; behind them came the king's warrant and the king's agents to arrest them. But Charles Meigs, telling the story, emphasized that no warrant ought to intimidate a man who has conscience on his side; and he recounted the legend that John Meigs was instrumental in the rescue of Whalley and Goffe, riding from Guilford to New Haven to warn the fugitives that their pursuers were close on their trail.[12]

John Meigs of New Haven was a tanner, currier, and probably a shoemaker. His descendants followed similar unpretentious but respectable occupations for several generations. Josiah Meigs, Charles's father, was the first of the direct line to win a measure of prominence. Quarrels with his trustees over

[11] John F. Meigs, loc. cit.
[12] Wm. M. Meigs, Josiah Meigs, p. 2; Rollin G. Osterweis, Three Centuries of New Haven, 1638–1938 (New Haven, 1953), pp. 54–55.

politics of both the campus and national varieties led him to depart from the University of Georgia as he had from Yale. But since Jeffersonian Republicanism again had helped disrupt his academic career, and such party faith did not in those days go unrecognized, even by an administration whose creed was economy in government, President James Madison presently secured for Josiah an appointment as Surveyor-General of the United States. Soon he became Commissioner of the General Land Office. He died in 1822, and Montgomery saw him only once, through the eyes of a three-year-old on a visit to Washington in 1819.

The career of Josiah Meigs was particularly rich in moral examples of the sort that Charles Meigs delighted to cite. As a lawyer in the Bermudas he had risked his freedom, like John Meigs before him, to assert the claims of conscience against the British crown. He had thought it an honor rather than a misfortune to lose two positions of scholarly prestige rather than compromise his beliefs. He had given the family a heritage of Jeffersonianism in politics which Charles Meigs sought to maintain. Many had considered him a self-righteous curmudgeon, but sometimes such a place in public opinion was the inevitable reward of integrity. Montgomery Meigs appears to have absorbed his father's identification of duty, integrity, and family pride; at least as he grew older he developed qualities strongly reminiscent of grandfather Josiah.[13]

Of all the Meigs family in America, those members who perhaps most captured young Montgomery's imagination were Josiah's brother and nephew. Both were named Return Jonathan Meigs, both were soldiers. The elder, the father, was a colonel of the Continental Army, prominent in Benedict

[13] Wm. M. Meigs, *Josiah Meigs; D.A.B.*, XII, 506-7; E. Merton Coulter, *College Life in the Old South* (New York, 1928), pp. 21-26.

Arnold's march to Quebec and in Anthony Wayne's storming of Stony Point, and the leader of a spectacularly successful commando raid on Sag Harbor, Long Island. The son, as governor of Ohio, figured in the events surrounding the fall of Detroit in 1812 and was one of the few Americans to emerge with credit from that episode.[14] Hearing of the soldiers Meigs, Montgomery doubtless began to dream of soldierly glory for himself.

The time of his boyhood, of course, was the Era of Good Feelings that followed the War of 1812. It was a time of nationalistic exuberance for the young United States, a time to look with confidence toward a future in which national growth would be unbounded, and in which a man of energy might push his own career upward on a course parallel to the soaring flight of the American eagle. It was a time when Stephen Decatur might offer as his toast: "My country—right or wrong!" It was a time when every Fourth of July brought gaily snapping flags and rolling drums and endless gilded rhetoric in which the eagle screamed defiance at the British lion and any other beast of land or sea. It was a time of brightly uniformed militia companies, and on many a summer's day Montgomery Meigs stood on Chestnut Street to watch entranced as the Blues or the Grays with their yellow braided hats, jaunty with cocks' feathers, came strutting by.[15]

For a boy enraptured by military display, Philadelphia's receptions to Lafayette in 1824 and 1825 were days long to be anticipated and long remembered. The very name of the

[14] R. J. Meigs, *Register of the Descendants of Vincent Meigs*, p. 24; Henry B. Meigs, *Record of the Descendants of Vincent Meigs*, p. 200; *D.A.B.*, XII, 508–10; Christopher Ward, *The War of the Revolution* (2 vols., New York, 1952), I, 167, 170, 175–76, 193, 324; II, 598–99; Glenn Tucker, *Poltroons and Patriots* (2 vols., Indianapolis, 1954), I, 149–50, 158, 165.

[15] M. C. Meigs to S. E. Meigs, June 9, 1865, Meigs Let. B., 1864–1866.

foreign visitor caught the imagination with pictures of the bloody boot at the Brandywine, of the storming of Cornwallis's redoubts at Yorktown, and of the return of Louis XVI and Marie Antoinette from Versailles to Paris amidst the shouting of the Parisian mob. Lafayette arrived in Philadelphia in September, 1824. The city cavalry had ridden to Morrisville to meet him, and he rode to the State House in a barouche drawn by six cream-colored horses, cavalry escort at his side, the First City Brigade preceding him, the Second Brigade following. He returned for a final visit the next July; again there were military ceremonies, and at Vauxhall Gardens a throng of boys and girls, each of them carrying a lighted torch, greeted the visitor, while he mounted a stage canopied with red, white, and gold and flanked by the Stars and Stripes and the Tricolor.[16]

Uniform and drum beckoned Montgomery Meigs, a family military tradition spurred him on, and the nationalistic fervor of the day encouraged him to a career of service to his country. Furthermore, from his earliest youth Montgomery had been delighted by anything mechanical, inquisitive about the use of any machine, eager to know how every machine worked and quick to understand when told. An engineering career seemed to be indicated for him, and as he approached maturity he was increasingly certain that this was so. On one institution all the tendencies shaping Montgomery Meigs's career converged: the United States Military Academy at West Point. Active Democratic-Republicans such as the Meigses should not long need to cool their heels waiting for an academy appointment, especially since one of Charles Meigs's sisters was now the wife of John Forsyth, Secretary of State to Andrew Jackson.[17] On July 1,

[16] J. T. Scharf and Thompson Westcott, *History of Philadelphia, 1609–1884* (3 vols., Philadelphia, 1884), I, 608–9, 615; M. C. Meigs to S. E. Meigs, June 9, 1865, Meigs Let. B., 1864–1866.
[17] For Forsyth, see *D.A.B.*, VI, 533–35.

1832, the name of Cadet M. C. Meigs for the first time appeared on the rolls of the academy on the Hudson.[18]

The cadet had prepared himself for the academic tasks of West Point first at a "dame's school," then probably in Samuel Crawford's classical academy at Philadelphia, and finally through a few terms at the University of Pennsylvania.[19] When he left home he was a tall young man, standing about an inch and a half over six feet, with a face just short of being handsome. He was self-willed like his grandfather Josiah, and he had been so since his earliest youth; his mother recorded when he was six that he was "high tempered, unyielding, tyrannical toward his brothers—very persevering in pursuit of any thing he wishes. . . ." With a strong will he possessed also a keen mind. This too had been apparent from early youth, when his mother noted that he "remembers the particulars of many incidents that occurred two or three years ago, and many things that I had not supposed he noticed. He seems to observe every thing that passes. . . ." Though at that date, he "Does not read yet & is not very fond of study." [20]

A family tradition of stubborn self-reliance and implicit devotion to duty, a loyalty to country nurtured by both family and surroundings, these together with a fascination for things military and a deep interest in the mechanical and scientific Meigs carried with him as he began a career in the United States Army, a career which was to span a full half century of the history of the Republic.

[18] G. W. Cullum, *Biographical Register of the Officers and Graduates of the U. S. Military Academy* (3 vols., Boston, 1891), I, 631.

[19] M. C. Meigs probably attended Crawford's school, since his brother John F. did (*D.A.B.*, XII, 505), and we have S. Emlen Meigs's recollections of the school in Henry B. Meigs, *Record of the Descendants of Vincent Meigs*. M. C. Meigs appears on the student roster in the University of Pennsylvania Catalogue, 1831, University of Pennsylvania Archives.

[20] Meigs Sealed Diary, July 15, 1874.

## II

# WEST POINT

THE CADET who had enrolled himself in the United States Military Academy largely because he wanted to become an engineer must have wondered during the first summer whether it was all a ghastly mistake. Montgomery Meigs had other reasons for being there, although the engineering possibilities may well have been primary; but he too must have had his fill and more of the School of the Soldier.

The School of the Soldier consisted of the rudiments of military drill. For the neophyte West Pointer it was taught and practiced and taught and practiced seemingly without end all through the first summer encampment, under the hazy skies and boiling sun of July and August. The manual of arms (performed with muskets trimmed down under their bands to give a sharp rattle when swung) and the simplest evolutions of the line—with these the cadet began, like any infantryman. With these he began, and if often it seemed sheer tedium and humbug, here was the foundation of that smartness of drill which would stir the heart when the full battalion in gray and white streamed across the plain above the Hudson. Here was the genesis of that implicit obedience to orders deemed essential by an army which believed that before one could command, one must learn to obey.[1]

The second summer would be similar, though now to increasingly complex infantry evolutions would be added more extensive drill with artillery. The third summer, if all went well, would bring furlough and the opportunity to go home, but that was too far in the future to be contemplated. Meanwhile you were a plebe, a West Point fourth classman, a pathetic creature not to be regarded seriously by your betters, and in general a fit object for ridicule of all sorts.

While Montgomery Meigs and his fellow plebes stood sentry duty for the first time in their lives, enterprising second classmen such as George Cullum went prowling along the line of posts, flashing powder at the jittery sentries or wrapping themselves in sheets to go about muttering in strange tongues. The sentry would shout his challenge: "Who comes there?" Out of the darkness of the night in sepulchral tones would resound the answer: "Steamboat and file of men," or "Thunder and Lightning with an escort of two plebes," or "The devil's chariot drawn by four mud-turtles." The only relief might come when in desperation a plebe or two would manage nearly to bayonet one of their tormentors.[2]

Summer encampment was disciplined tedium; September brought day after ordered day of disciplined study, from reveille at dawn to tattoo and roll call at 9:30 in the evening. For Montgomery Meigs, product of a Philadelphia classical academy and of a brief sojourn at the University of Pennsylvania, the academic routine cannot have been especially

---

[1] Edward C. Boynton, *History of West Point* (New York, 1863), pp. 304–5; Sidney Forman, *West Point: A History of the United States Military Academy* (New York, 1950), pp. 51–52; Douglas Southall Freeman, *R. E. Lee* (4 vols., New York, 1934), I, 52–55.

[2] W. D. Frazer and G. W. Cullum, letters quoted in Forman, *West Point*, pp. 93–94.

difficult. The prerequisites were a knowledge of reading, writing, and arithmetic. The program catered in part to the requirements of Southern cadets who as often as not arrived with only the sketchiest academic preparation. The plebe and the yearling spent their days principally with mathematics and French. The second year brought an introduction to drawing, carried further in the third. This course Cadet Meigs found especially stimulating, since he discovered in himself a measure of talent for the quickly placed but expressive line. Henceforth he would count sketching among his favorite diversions. Natural philosophy (that is, physics) and chemistry completed the work of the third year, with chemistry giving way to mineralogy in the fourth. Mineralogy would today be called geology, and it had more than merely cultural applications for cadets who as engineers would be builders in stone. In the same year the cadets surveyed rhetoric and moral and political science, in a catch-all course for everything that the academy staff thought it ought to be teaching but could not find time for anywhere else; they utilized texts as various as Lindley Murray's *Grammar* and Chancellor Kent's *Commentaries*.[3]

The capstone of all, crowning the final year and the whole academic experience, was the first classman's course in engineering, the *sine qua non* of his future career, be it in military or in civil engineering. Presiding over the department which conducted the course was one of the great men of West Point, a shy and still youthful professor in Meigs's day, but already a man of mark: Dennis Hart Mahan. Himself a West Pointer, class of 1824, Mahan had caught the eye of Sylvanus Thayer, "Father of the Military Academy." Thayer brought him back to the academy as an instructor in 1826, and when overwork taxed Mahan's frail health and he felt the

[3] Forman, *West Point*, pp. 51–59; Freeman, *Lee*, I, 56–80, *passim*.

need of a trip abroad, with Thayer's encouragement he trans-
formed the journey into an extended investigation of European
military and civil engineering. Now he passed his European
knowledge on to the cadets in the form of lithographed lec-
ture notes, some of them eventually to become textbooks. His
engineering course for first classmen embraced field fortification, permanent fortification, the science of artillery, "grand
tactics" (which included strategy as well as tactics), and
civil and military architecture. West Point was the first
American school of engineering, and until Rensselaer Poly-
technic Institute graduated its first class of engineers in 1835,
it was the only American school of engineering. In Meigs's
day, engineering at West Point meant the teachings of Dennis
Hart Mahan.[4]

Yet if West Point was the only American engineering
school, it was by no means all that could have been hoped
for in a school of the kind, or in a college of any kind. Because the admission requirements demanded so little, a cadet
could begin his academy career on a level far below that of
the freshman at Harvard or Yale. In some ways the gap never
closed. Jacob Cox, an outsider who was to show marked
military ability during the Civil War, estimated that in the
over-all picture, four years at West Point would put a man
abreast of a freshman at one of the old New England colleges.
Others would charge that while Harvard and Yale spent only
one third as much time on mathematics as the Point, they
would carry their students as far in two years as the Military
Academy did in four. Certainly the conglomerate course in
the fourth year offered no adequate introduction to the hu-
manities, yet except for reading *Gil Blas* and Voltaire's *His-*

[4] R. Ernest Dupuy, *Where They Have Trod: The West Point Tradition in American Life* (New York, 1940) and *Men of West Point: The
First 150 Years of the United States Military Academy* (New York,
1951).

*toire de Charles XII* in his French courses it was all the West
Pointer received—though he might well find himself one day
in a position to influence decisively the most important political issues.

Everywhere there was rigidity and an uncompromising devotion to orthodoxy. This characterized the High Church
Episcopalian worship of the cadet chapel, the social code so
reminiscent of the chivalric pretensions of the plantation
South, and the emphasis on respect for authority which faced
the cadet at every turn from the day when he first learned
that as a plebe he had few privileges that an upper classman
need respect.[5] Here was little to encourage flexibility of mind.
And it was some sort of push toward greater flexibility, or at
least toward greater intellectual tolerance, from which in the
light of subsequent events Cadet Montgomery Meigs might
have benefited most. Montgomery Meigs made the rigid code
of life which was West Point's his own. His father's teachings
from family history, particularly the stories of Josiah Meigs,
had inculcated fixed moral principles and encouraged a self-
assured, uncompromising pursuit of those principles; now the
assurances of the academy that its way was a righteous way
reinforced Meigs's conviction that the path on which his family
had set him was a godly one. Meigs emerged from West Point
little inclined to question his moral assumptions and confident
that when he had squared a course with those assumptions it
was the right course. The West Pointer always does his duty,
and duty is a line as straight as a file of cadets, clearly marked
out in the tenets of the academy. Other cadets might question
so simple a postulate. Montgomery Meigs would not; it was
too similar to the premises on which his family tradition
taught him to base his conduct.

[5] For a critique of the academy in the early nineteenth century, see
Lloyd Lewis, *Sherman: Fighting Prophet* (New York, 1932), p. 53.

The final ranking of a cadet on the roll of merit of his class depended upon a somewhat complicated system of merits and demerits, with proficiency in military drill and excellence of conduct as well as academic standing contributing to the final reckoning. Montgomery Meigs placed fifth, which meant that his was among the names of the top cadets inscribed in the army register.[6] Ordinarily his high place would have given him one of the coveted commissions in the Corps of Engineers as well, but perhaps because of insufficient vacancies in the corps that honor was not yet to be his. Instead his commission as second lieutenant assigned him to the 1st Artillery. Not until November 1, 1836, did he receive a brevet as second lieutenant in the Corps of Engineers, to date from July 1; and then, by an order of December 1 he reverted to the 1st Artillery. Final transfer to the engineers came only on July 1, 1837.[7]

Now the scholastic preparation was ended, and Meigs's first goal in life was won. He was both a soldier and an engineer. How far he would advance in his chosen career remained to be discovered; how fit a bearer of the traditions of family and flag he would prove was yet to be seen. For his part, Meigs took confidence in the past record of his line.

[6] Cullum, *Biographical Register,* I, 631.
[7] *Ibid.*

# III

# FORTS AND RIVERS

FORT MIFFLIN in 1836 was an unfinished pile of masonry rising from the sandy surface of Mud Island near the swampy right bank of the Delaware River, just south of the mouth of the Schuylkill. Its purpose was the defense of Philadelphia. Its history as a fortification extended to the colonial period. During the Revolution a wood-and-earth outpost on its site had been the scene of a brave but hopeless stand by some 450 American troops against the combined fire of a British floating battery stationed between Mud Island and the mainland and the guns of five British warships in the main channel, headed by the famous ship-of-the-line *Somerset*.

During the second war with Britain, Admiral Cockburn of the Royal Navy had chosen to remind the American seacoast, with a vividness intensified by the flames of burning Washington, that hasty defenses were apt to be futile. Upon the close of the conflict Congress belatedly set out to erect a chain of strong points along the Atlantic coast from the Florida Keys to New England. This project was the beginning of those masonry fortresses the more southerly of which played so prominent a part in the Civil War. Between the Peace of Ghent and the outbreak of the sectional struggle, appropriations for the new defenses issued from Congress at irregular intervals, construction proceeded at an equally erratic pace, and the year 1861 found the works in various stages of incompletion.

Among them was the new Fort Mifflin, and to the slowly dragging operations at that place Lieutenant M. C. Meigs reported for his first active duty in the summer of 1836.[1] Although his commission continued to be one in the 1st Artillery, from the beginning his duties were principally those of a military engineer. Even the lithographed lectures of Dennis Mahan had afforded him but a limited introduction to the work; he learned most of his craft from study and experience on the job.

It was not unpleasant to be in Philadelphia once more, in close touch with the house on Arch Street, and a center of attention and some admiration in blue officer's coat and the braided shoulder straps of a second lieutenant. Meigs's new sojourn in the city of his youth lasted nearly a year, with ample time to renew old acquantances, to ride once more up the Delaware, and to amble to Fair Mount and beyond. As early as December orders of transfer reached the lieutenant, but not until the summer of 1837 was he able to make his departure. Then he met First Lieutenant R. E. Lee, the son of Virginia's Revolutionary War hero "Light-Horse Harry" Lee, who had come to Philadelphia to complete various purchases. Meigs was now to be his assistant in the surveying of stretches of the Mississippi River with an eye to the improvement of navigation, and more particularly in attempting to avert a danger that sandbars might clog and ruin the port of St. Louis.[2]

Lieutenant Lee was a tall, erect, and remarkably handsome officer, dark of hair and eye. Meigs must have heard earlier

[1] Cullum, *Biographical Register,* I, 631.
[2] Freeman, *Lee,* I, 140.

of the superb record he had compiled at the Point. Graduating in 1829, he had ranked second in his class in total merits, but he had stood first in artillery, had received not one demerit in four years, and while a first classman had served as cadet adjutant, the highest officer in the cadet battalion.[3] Already Lee's superiors regarded him as a young officer of rare promise, and Meigs promptly became another of his admirers.

The Corps of Engineers was now embarking on its long career of peacetime service, and occasional disservice, to the nation as the executor of river and harbor improvements. Commerce on the Mississippi was approaching the noontide of its prosperity, but as yet little had been done to ease the delicate task of the pilots who threaded their steamers between mud flat and snag, around rapid and sandbar, all up and down the length of the great and treacherous river. This was the Mississippi not many years before Mark Twain would be a cub pilot; this was the river he would learn to read in darkness as in light through twelve hundred twisting miles, alert for the faint dimple on the surface which "meant that a wreck or a rock was buried there that could tear the life out of the strongest vessel that ever floated." [4]

Lee and Meigs followed the river improvement pioneering of Captain Henry Shreve. They went first to the Des Moines Rapids and the mouth of Rock River, there to confirm by exact surveys Shreve's estimate that a perfect channel could be dug. They paddled about in a dugout canoe, with Meigs wielding the compass and the level lines, sketching the topog-

[3] *Ibid.*, I, 61–85. Meigs's recollections of his service with Lieutenant Lee were drawn on by A. L. Long, *Memoirs of Robert E. Lee* (New York, 1887), p. 44.

[4] Mark Twain, *Life on the Mississippi* (Author's National Edition, New York, 1917), p. 83.

raphy, and preparing to draw a map. Their base was "the worst kind of small log cabin"; once they had to pause to placate with gifts a party of Chippewa.

From Rock River they proceeded to St. Louis. Here Lee planned a system of dikes which would preserve the port and a deep channel, while Meigs completed the maps of the Des Moines Rapids. This task finished their work. With winter approaching they returned to the East, following the rivers to Wheeling, then crossing the Alleghenies by sleigh along the National Road, moving down the Baltimore and Ohio Railroad in cars drawn part of the way by horses, and finally parting, Lee to return to Washington and his home at Arlington, Meigs to Philadelphia and his parents' family.[5] One wonders about their conversations, for they shared similar ideals of duty to fixed principles along lines suggested by both family and army tradition.

Meigs was an Easterner by heritage and training, but invariably he enjoyed his travels out beyond the Appalachians, and the journey with Lieutenant Lee was no exception. Only once, however, did he dwell long in the West. Now he received again an assignment to military engineering duties on the fortifications below Philadelphia, while Lee returned to St. Louis in 1838 to apply his own suggestions for the preservation of the port. Meigs would be laboring upon works designed to command a bend of the Delaware south of New Castle, Delaware, and north of Salem, New Jersey. Here, where the river flows southeastward, an island called the Pea Patch nestles in mid-channel, and Finn's Point offers a vantage ground from which to control at least half the stream from the New Jersey shore. Meigs found Fort Delaware rising on the

[5] Freeman, *Lee*, I, 142–48; Meigs to Mary Meigs Taylor, Dec. 13, 1871, Meigs Misc. Papers.

Pea Patch; eventually other batteries and walls would guard Finn's Point on the mainland. While Meigs joined in the building of Fort Delaware, he would participate also in the efforts of the Corps of Engineers to improve the harbors of the Delaware and to complete the Delaware Breakwater, a long finger of stone which was beginning to reach south-ward from Cape May in order at long last to afford a measure of safety from adverse tides to mariners who entered the treacherous mouth of Delaware Bay.[6]

Presently Lieutenant Colonel René de Russy departed from Philadelphia and left in Lieutenant Meigs's charge the super-vision of disbursements of funds necessary for carrying on the Delaware works. This was Meigs's first important inde-pendent responsibility, and it was scarcely in his hands before his sense of duty displayed a testy streak which combined with tactlessness to lead him into controversy. His quarrel was with the Moyamensing Bank, the depository of govern-ment funds. The bank refused to meet pay rolls until Meigs had fully certified and receipted them; Meigs argued with much acerbity that to demand this was to demand that he require the workers to sign their names to pay rolls before they had received their money, which he had no right to do. As the issue grew more complicated, both Meigs and the bank appealed to the chief engineer in Washington. Eventually the whole question emerged as largely one of misunderstanding, and the bank agreed to a settlement; but in the meantime Meigs unveiled an uncommon talent for lengthy polemics and self-justification by correspondence. He would not hesitate to scribble across reams of paper rather than leave unanswered a challenge to the rectitude of his conduct; this was the sort

[6] Cullum, *Biographical Register*, I, 631; Struthers Burt, *Philadelphia, Holy Experiment* (Garden City, New York, 1945), p. 137.

of quarrelsomeness which twice had cost his grandfather academic posts.[7]

Semi-independence of status brought Meigs not only controversy but also his first experience in the routines of government management. Somewhat embarrassingly, he found himself without a copy of the regulations of the Corps of Engineers, and headquarters in Washington informed him that they could not supply him with one; how he found his way out of this perplexity we can only conjecture.[8] When the close of the year approached, he was responsible for preparation of the annual report on the progress of the Delaware works, but there were at hand no copies of the previous year's report to guide him in following proper form.[9] These were questions of detail of the sort he would have to master thoroughly in the work that lay before him. He was fortunate to be able to learn the ropes and to make the inevitable early blunders while still a lieutenant of twenty-two.

In 1839 came orders for still another change of station. Meigs was to proceed to Washington to serve on the Board of Engineers for Atlantic Coast Defenses, a place from which he could gain some knowledge of the workings of the central army bureaucracy. He remained for two years; his correspondence suggests that his primary function was to serve as a sort of Washington representative of the Delaware River projects.[10] If the interval was brief, it was nonetheless important for more than the opportunity to observe the top-level direction of a War Department bureau; it was here that Meigs met Louisa Rodgers.

---

[7] Meigs Let. B., 1838–1842: Meigs to Gratiot, Sept. 3, 1838; Meigs to Balin, Sept. 10, 1838; Meigs to Gratiot, Sept. 10, 1838; Meigs to Gratiot, Sept. 13, 1838.

[8] Meigs Let. B., 1838–1842: Meigs to Gratiot, Aug. 31, 1838.

[9] *Ibid.*

[10] Cullum, *Biographical Register,* I, 631; Meigs Let. B., 1838–1842.

Louisa was not an exceptionally pretty girl. She had the high forehead and firm chin of the Rodgers family (her father was the old commodore), and her face could assume an almost masculine sternness. But neither was she unattractive. Meigs began to escort her during the capital social season. The two went riding together on the pleasant paths along the Chesapeake and Ohio Canal, Meigs forgot a certain Miss Hill in whom he had shown some interest, and the lieutenant decided that Louisa Rodgers should be his wife.[11] They were married May 2, 1841.

The wedding coincided with a new milestone in Meigs's professional career; he was about to leave Washington to become superintending engineer of the building of Fort Delaware, for the first time charged with full responsibility for a public work.[12]

Important as it was, the Philadelphia assignment proved briefer even than most of Meigs's tours of duty. By October he had his orders to go westward to Detroit, there to supervise the construction of Fort Wayne on the Detroit River.[13] Part of the winter he spent in Washington making preparations for the journey to the remote Northwest; then, early in 1843, Meigs and Louisa set out for Michigan to establish their first real home. They remained at Detroit for nine years, and it was a time of uncommon contentment and happiness.

The community was new, and the whole Northwest still had a freshness and early-morning brightness; and if a young lieutenant possessed but meager resources with which to support a family, here the demands on his purse were not so

[11] Elizabeth Rodgers to Louisa Rodgers, Nov. 26, 1840, Rodgers Family Papers, Box 2, Library of Congress.
[12] Cullum, *Biographical Register*, I, 631.
[13] *Ibid.*

frequent and insistent as in the more finished society of the East. There were good neighbors to befriend the young couple, there was plenty of land on which to grow vegetables and flowers, there were lakes for boating and winter skating, there were forests for hunting. In short Mont and Louisa could enjoy all that was best in that rural, almost innocent America, the memory of which was to call forth so much nostalgia when at last factories and cities had scattered it away.

Detroit was in the West, its frontier days were not long behind it, the large Roman Catholic population recalled the period when the lilies of France had flown above the settlement, and not infrequently two-wheeled French carts still rolled through the streets. From time to time *voyageurs* would emerge from the forests to the north, men not changed much since the days of Radisson and Groseilliers. Yet as it spread across its level tableland which stretched westward from the river, Detroit was becoming more and more a city fashioned in the image of its older progenitors east of the mountains, distinguished from them chiefly by its wide, straight streets and continued youthful expansion. "Detroit is, in all its peculiar characteristics, an eastern city," wrote a visitor of 1838. "It was peopled and built up by eastern men, in eastern style, and the habits of the east prevail above those of the west." [14] M. C. Meigs, the scion of a staid Philadelphia family, may not have found it so. After all, even many in Michigan were agitating for the removal of the state capital from Detroit, although it is not clear whether these persons believed that the "gross indecency and immorality" of the legislators were contaminating the city, or whether it was the city that was contaminating the legislators.

[14] Quoted in R. Carlyle Buley, *The Old Northwest: Pioneer Period, 1815–1840* (2 vols., Indianapolis, 1950), II, 98–99.

In short, the city was a not uncommon phenomenon of the evolving American frontier, a place of split personality, where "barbaric" politics punctuated by occasional street brawls co-existed with a library, an academy, two theaters, and even something of an intellectual coterie.[15]

Rapid as was the growth of Detroit, no one was in a particular hurry to complete its defensive shield, Fort Wayne, least of all the leisurely United States Army. The customary procedure for an officer stationed at one of these sleepy bastions was to establish an easygoing routine which would fit the tacit wishes of the War Department and entail for himself a minimum exertion of body and mind. Plenty of time was to be allowed for enjoying the woods and the lake shore and the cool, clear air.

Meigs and his bride fell quickly into the routine. Unfortunately, their consciences disturbed them, for both had been bred in the traditions of the hard-working, Protestant America which regarded rigorous effort as the surest road to salvation and idleness as the most damaging of sins. Louisa especially felt disturbed, since she lacked her husband's capacity for self-justification; it was in her nature to be reproachful of self. But if she were indulging too much in the insidious habit of idleness, certainly her relaxed husband was equally guilty. She must do something to mend the habits of both.

So it was that while they sat by the fire on a cold December evening of their second winter at Detroit, Louisa began to remind Mont that he had not kept himself as busy of late as an ambitious young officer should, and that both his career and his mind—to say nothing of his character—probably would benefit from increased application to duty during the after-

[15] *Ibid.*, II, 98–99, 340, 564, 574; C. F. Hoffman, quoted in Walter S. Tryon, ed., *A Mirror for Americans; Life and Manners in the United States 1790–1870 as Recorded by American Travelers* (3 vols., Chicago, 1952), III, 548.

noons and to a self-improvement program during the rest of
the day. Even Mont was not so self-satisfied as to be able to
deny her point. He had to acknowledge that he had been often
idle of late; and the training of his youth whispered that this
was not good, that indeed it was likely if continued to effect
degeneration of moral fiber. The Calvinism of his background
rose to the challenge, and he decided straightway that the
snares of the devil should entangle him no longer. He must
break the habit of idleness before it became engrained in his
nature; the method he selected was to keep a journal. In this
he would note each evening his plans for the following day
and, by way of assessment, the success or failure of his plans
for the day past. Thus he would subject himself constantly
to self-criticism, and always he would have before him a record of his achievements and shortcomings to guide him, to
challenge, and perhaps to reproach.

He would abandon even his gun and his hunting for the
rest of the year—unless by exemplary conduct he should gain
Louisa's permission to indulge for a few days after Christmas.
Immediately he made his first entry in his journal; he was
embarking on a lifetime as a diarist.[16]

If she had stirred her husband to renewed moral endeavor,
Louisa manifestly dared not neglect herself: "I was forced to
consider that I had myself been so prodigal of those precious
minutes which make up hours, days & months as to have no
right to assume the position of censor." Therefore she too
determined to become a critical diarist, and after Mont had
gone to bed she set down her own first entry:

Not having in the year that is now concluding one act in my
remembrance that entitles me to any degree of self approbation
or one day that I can distinguish as having fully & satisfactorily
employed, We have both come to the conclusion that there is a

[16] Meigs Diary, Dec. 13, 1842.

necessity for a change in our plan of life, and we hope to commence and conclude another year in a manner which will afford us the testimony of better consciences than this has done. I fear that I shall find it very difficult to adhere to any regular system of conduct. I have in my life formed numerous plans & resolutions for "*the future*" & I am sorry to add that I had never perseverance to continue for any length of time the systems I had marked out for my self government. We must each remember that we can do "no good thing"—trusting in our own strength & look to a higher source for the power to resist temptation. I have been too self indulgent—too negligent of those duties which it has become necessary for me to fulfill. . . . I must rise earlier, and be more active in the discharge of my household duties, so as to have more leisure for the enjoyment of my husband's society and the cultivation of my own mind. . . . After tea I hope we shall enjoy the reading of some pleasant books together. And at 10, We shall have *prayers invariably*—excepting when prevented by the presence of visitors.[17]

Alas, worthy resolutions proved as difficult as ever to keep. The next evening Louisa felt compelled to inscribe further self-reproach:

Rose earlier this morning than I have done for some time and yet did not get down stairs until after 8. I hope to be earlier tomorrow. I have not spent the day as systematically as I had wished but the presence of visitors was some apology for my remissness. Have not yet got a new book to read.

Mont met only slightly better success:

I succeeded in rising this morning at the intended hour. And was able to make some preparations for my drawing. . . . The morning I devoted to my drawing. Though visitors interrupted me and I did not make so much progress as I wished. . . . I drove to the Post Office and attended my wife to church. Visitors during the afternoon prevented (though they should not have done so) any reading. Tomorrow Rise 6½—till dinner work.[18]

[17] *Ibid.*
[18] *Ibid.*, Dec. 14, 1842.

From the second entries onward, the diaries began to follow a pattern. Louisa suffered constantly from what she interpreted as a somewhat sinful weakness of the flesh; never could she quite adhere to her daily schedule, always that snare of Satan, idleness, was thrusting itself upon her. Mont, while he possessed an acute sense of duty, displayed remarkable adeptness in rationalizing his lapses, viewing them with considerable complacency. The Meigs conscience was likely to be self-righteous. If he did not each day fulfill the schedule he had prepared the previous night, still Mont was likely to regard his progress as satisfactory. One night Louisa regretted that that morning she and her husband had not breakfasted until nine, and that she had left undone many things which she had hoped to do; that same evening Mont recorded that he had "Passed the day with more satisfaction to myself than before I attempted the reform. Tho my time is not perfectly well employed yet." [19] After all, who achieves perfection?

Louisa might record: "This morning I rose late, and did not breakfast until ½ 9. There is some excuse for me in this case as I did not feel well. I passed the day industriously, but I do not effect as much as I wish. I hope to improve." [20]

While Mont could write on December 27, with no trace of self-reproach: "Yesterday and today I have given myself a holiday in consideration of Christmas tomorrow will endeavor to rise early & work well." [21] Was not Christmas worthy of a three-day holiday?

Louisa's self-improvement program included regular attendance at choir rehearsals: "I hope these meetings may prove advantageous to my music." For Mont this generally meant squiring his wife to the meeting place: "We went tonight,"

[19] *Ibid.*, Dec. 16, 1842.
[20] *Ibid.*, Dec. 21, 1842.
[21] *Ibid.*, Dec. 27, 1842.

he recorded on December 30, "to the choir practising at Col Whitings, Where owing to the cold air & exercise of that day & the music of the evening I had like to have gone to sleep." From this point what purports to be Meigs's entry for the day continues in a suspiciously feminine hand: "Of this want of musical taste I am much ashamed. I hope to improve by taking every opportunity of listening to music. I should inevitably have shot that deer or *one of those* deer to day—if the bullet had pierced him as I intended." Unfortunately for posterity's impression of Meigs's devotion to music, over the ink of these last lines a bold hand has scrawled in pencil, "*Not mine. M C M.*" [22]

Not until late in life would Meigs fully reconcile himself to the sedentary existence which his duties often entailed, and now that he had time to hunt and at his doorstep great stretches of forest still scarcely touched by man, he took gun in hand at every opportunity. Whether by Louisa's indulgence or not, he was hunting again within a week of his first diary entry. Even when he failed to shoot anything—and success was notably infrequent—Meigs returned from a hunting expedition to describe it in his journal with zest.[23]

Louisa was less enthusiastic:

Spent another solitary day in consequence of Mr. Meigs's absence on a hunting, not shooting expedition. This passion for passing a whole day tramping through snow and sleet, or mud and mire— beating bushes, ransacking thickets, through highways & byways, now here, now there, hungry & solitary, splashed, muddy & forlorn, from day break until nightfall—leaving a smiling wife, a prattling *babe*, a plentiful board and cheerful fire side for the companionship of a dog and gun, all these domestic enjoyments for the pleasure of seeing a deer whisk his tail or a quail run out of sight—appears to my womanly mind quite incomprehensible! [24]

[22] *Ibid.*, Dec. 30, 1842.
[23] For example, *ibid.*, Dec. 21, 29–30, 1842.
[24] *Ibid.*, Dec. 30, 1842.

"A prattling *babe*"—for by now there was one, born in
Washington on February 9, 1842,[25] just before the departure
for Detroit. It was a boy, and inevitably a man as proud of
family—and self—as M. C. Meigs would envision a noble
future for him. And to spur the boy on, and to remind him
of his heritage, they gave him a proud name, attaching to
the patronymic the name of Louisa's father, the hero of the
Old Navy, which was also the name of the promising young
naval officer who was Louisa's brother: they called the boy
John Rodgers Meigs.

As he grew he promptly demonstrated his inheritance of the
Meigs willfulness. On January 23, 1844, before Johnny was
two years old, Louisa noted:

I was obliged to punish Johnny severely this morning. He refused
to obey me and exhibited a great deal of temper. He shows in such
encounters great obstinacy and determination, and it is already
difficult to conquer him. His disposition I fear will make him very
difficult to manage, and his temper promises to give much trouble
to himself and others if not properly controled. On the Mother
rests great responsibilities—and I pray that my influence may be for
"good." And I must pray to be strengthened for this duty. It is
not a light one, but one which requires great attention.[26]

If he was self-willed, the boy also gave early evidence of
being the sort of son his father expected him to be. On the
same day Louisa wrote in her diary:

In a few days Johnny will be 2 years old, but in character he is
already 3 or 4 years old. He is very intelligent and exhibits great
fondness for books. He knows already all his letters, which he has
learned as an amusement, and points them out on all the scraps of
paper he picks up.[27]

[25] Meigs Journal, March 16, 1851.
[26] *Ibid.*, Jan. 23, 1844.
[27] *Ibid.*

The first-born, and the son who Meigs somehow felt confident would make a great name for himself, John occupied always a special place in his father's heart. But other children followed in the rapid succession that had been characteristic of Meigs's father's family and his grandfather's. During the Detroit years a girl and two brothers joined Johnny. Mary Montgomery Meigs, named for her grandmother, appeared in 1843. "My little Mary," Louisa wrote in 1844, "is very sweet and gentle, perfectly healthy and good."[28] In 1845 came Charles Delucena Meigs, named in honor of his grandfather, and in 1847, another Montgomery Meigs.[29] Always, of course, M. C. Meigs felt the satisfaction expected of a father on these occasions; to Louisa's mother he wrote when Charles was born:

This morning at 20 minutes before six she [Louisa] gave me a son, a famous large fellow with dark hair, and as yet invisible eyes. He is strong and heavy, sucked his thumb as hard as Johnny does, before he was an hour old. And announced his arrival in this world of care by a cry which I at first attributed to a baby two or three months old in the street.[30]

Nor did the father's satisfaction diminish with the years; in 1851 he wrote a sober assessment of his four children:

They are . . . I think not particularly handsome except the youngest who in the eyes of Lou's friends is a beauty—and a very engaging lovable child. But they all seem intelligent and have the material if well trained to grow up into useful and honorable men and women.[31]

Meanwhile Meigs delighted in his children and in their playmates among the neighbors. There were days such as that on

[28] Meigs Journal, March 16, 1851; Meigs Diary, Jan. 23, 1844.
[29] Meigs Journal, March 16, 1851.
[30] Meigs to Mrs. John Rodgers, June 5, 1845, Rodgers Family Papers, Box 2, L.C.
[31] Meigs Journal, March 16, 1851.

which he "took Johnny and the little Trowbridges down to the river for a frolic on the ice. I fixed on Tads skates and he tumbled about with the ease natural to a beginner but did very well for the first time." [32]

Christmas especially was joyful among the Meigses, perhaps even more than is usual on that gayest of holidays. The first Christmas in the West, to be sure, could not but bring certain misgivings: "Christmas day. Spent far from my Parents brothers and sisters." Yet even remoteness from Arch Street could dim only slightly the glow of the occasion:

I presented Louisa this morning with a looking glass in which she can see her whole figure thus reviving in her the knowledge of her own appearance which she declares she had forgotten from the long use she had made of the little 10″ by 12″ mirror the only one we have had in the house heretofore. The present to me was a beautiful copy of the prayer book with red Rubricks. Johnny received a bit of mint stick, and Mother Hubbard's diverting life. Which he has shown a prodigious intellect in studying [he was now less than one year old], having learned already to point out the dog and Mother Hubbard in the splendid embellishments of the volume. I wrote to Father this evening.[33]

Louisa remembered the delight of her own girlhood in the visits of Kris Kringle, and she cultivated the legend of the kindly old gentleman among her children—though by now his name was Santa Claus. The children spent December 24 waiting in great anxiety and anticipation. For Johnny as his fourth Christmas approached, anxiety was uppermost, since he had been lazy and more than a little irritable of late, and he feared that Santa Claus would pass him by. He spent all afternoon of the 24th writing a letter to Santa Claus, beseeching him to leave some tokens of his good will. He sealed the note, addressed it clearly, and placed it on the bureau just over the place where

[32] Meigs Diary, Dec. 27, 1842.
[33] *Ibid.*, Dec. 25, 1842.

his stocking hung. Mary, Charles, and Montie hung their stockings beside Johnny's. Then all went to bed, hoping to go to sleep as quietly as possible, since they knew Santa Claus would never appear so long as they were awake.

Now Mont and Louisa began their hurried but silent Christmas Eve's activity. They strung together books and toys and hung them above the stockings. Into the stockings Louisa inserted the sweets she had bought; with much care she dressed a large and handsome doll that was to be Mary's. Johnny's letter to Santa Claus they removed from its place, and for it they substituted a reply written by Saint Nick himself (in the person of their cook's husband). The letter gave Johnny much good advice, but also assured him his toys would not be denied him.

At daybreak Mont and Louisa awakened to Charles's beating of reveille on his big drum. Now the children "made a rush to their stockings and deafening was the din that ensued." They hurried into their parents' room to open their treasures, and all were most gloriously and noisily delighted. From neighbors such as the Sibleys and the Trowbridges came additional gifts. And the reassured Johnny announced: "I think Santa Claus is the kindest man that ever lived."

Louisa was well content, even if a little melancholy, when she described it all in a letter to her mother:

We live our childish pleasures over again in our childrens joys, but I confess I always feel a tinge of sadness at the recollection that such happiness is so limited in its existence, and that to us of more mature years, "those joys never come again." My memory always carries me back to my own childhood and I feel a vain longing to be at home, and among my own kindred and people, and yet no one ever had kinder friends than I have here.[34]

[34] Louisa Rodgers Meigs to Mrs. John Rodgers, Dec. 27, 1845[?], Rodgers Family Papers, Box 2, L.C.

The years in Detroit slipped by, and the decade of the forties approached its close. The regular army of the United States marched off to conquer Mexico under Rough and Ready and Fuss and Feathers. Meigs chafed restlessly at Fort Wayne through all of it, for he was not among the young lieutenants who won their first fame along the old route of Cortez. Gradually the resolutions to encourage more purposeful living by keeping diaries faded; as the children arrived, Louisa abandoned diary writing altogether, while Mont's journals suffered a period of neglect.

Slowly Fort Wayne came to look more like a fort. By November, 1849, the defensive works were in place, two barracks for officers stood completed and a third needed only to be furnished, and quarters for enlisted men were going up. Meigs did not wish to leave the fort before the last nail was driven home; but when orders arrived for a new change of station, he knew that thanks to his direction, a fort now stood where none had been before. Neither did he wish to part from the friends of nine years' residence, but such was the way of the army. In 1849 he and Louisa packed their possessions and prepared to return eastward.

The journey to the Atlantic seaboard enabled Meigs to again visit Philadelphia, where he found his father moved from Arch Street to a smaller and more economical house at 324 Walnut Street. Charles Meigs was helping to build the reputation of the Jefferson Medical School, and his practice and his lectures combined to make him financially comfortable; already he was looking forward to an early retirement. Meigs found his mother looking well and happy. Her children had scattered across much of the United States, but none of them had disappointed her.

Of Meigs's brothers, Charles, the second son, was farming in

Indiana, blessed, thought Montgomery, with a charming wife
and several children, but with little of worldly wealth. John
Forsyth Meigs had always been the most studious of the boys;
it was he who followed his father's career, studying at the
University of Pennsylvania, at the Philadelphia Hospital, and
in Paris, and now beginning a prosperous medical practice of
his own. Vincent Montgomery had died in childhood. Henry
Vincent had married a cotton factory heiress at Columbus,
Georgia, and was managing the factory. Reports traveled north
that he was already worth $50,000; he was by far the most
prosperous of the family. His return to the old Meigs territory
in Georgia would bring in time other differences as well.
Emily, the first of the girls, had married well; her husband was
a lawyer and a Philadelphia Biddle. William now worked
briefly as Montgomery's clerk. Emlen was employed in a
Philadelphia countinghouse and lived at home. Franklin was
to be among the family's wanderers and would settle finally in
Indiana; now he was with a commercial firm. Mary—or Molly
—was still going to school.[35]

Lieutenant Meigs's new assignment was that of assistant to
the chief engineer in Washington.[36] Thus he worked directly
at the side of Brevet Brigadier General Joseph G. Totten, an
old man, like nearly all the bureau chiefs of the somnolent
little army, but one of competence, integrity, and dignity.
He could tell of the days of the second war with Britain, when
as a captain he had built the fortifications at Plattsburg on
the shore of Lake Champlain, helping halt the invading army
of Sir George Prevost and thus helping save the American
negotiators at Ghent from accepting an Indian buffer state.
Meigs formed a deep and lasting respect for the quiet general in
frock coat of blue lined with black velvet. The general for

[35] Meigs Journal, March 16, 1851.
[36] *Ibid.;* Cullum, *Biographical Register,* I, 631.

his part decided that the young lieutenant was a man the army should watch: high achievement might one day be expected from Lieutenant Meigs, with his conscientious attention to duty and detail, his precision of mind, and his skill in reducing all that he undertook to orderly method.

Always Meigs found the Federal capital stimulating. Louisa and he renewed their acquaintance with Washington social life, meeting the President and cabinet members at receptions and balls and dining often with General Totten and other army officers. He seized the opportunity to learn of the latest scientific developments, viewing the exhibits at the Patent Office, purchasing a microsope, studying how to metalize a plaster cast for electrotyping, and examining at the Ordnance Bureau a breech-loading Sharps rifle with a Maynard self-priming apparatus.[37]

Again the stay in Washington was a short one. In October, 1850, Meigs left the capital to take charge of the construction of Fort Montgomery at Rouses Point, New York, on the west shore of Lake Champlain where the lake begins to funnel into the Richelieu River, just south of the Canadian border. Here was a station without even the social opportunities of Detroit. From time to time Meigs relieved the monotony of isolated existence by traveling to New York City on financial business and detouring through New England on the way. Again there was hunting, though again Meigs bagged few victims. Winter was bitterly cold, but it brought good sleighing; often the whole family would bundle itself in a sleigh and go gliding across the frozen surface of Lake Champlain.

The natural setting was among the finest in America, especially when the weather turned warm and green mountains set off the blue of the sky and the deeper blue of the lake.

[37] Meigs Diary, 1851, *passim.*

Sometimes Meigs paused to sketch what he saw: Mount Mansfield (where the cold even of early April froze his brushes to the paper), Lake Dunmore, or, ranging farther, the solitary peak of Monadnock. In Washington he had met Captain Seth Eastman, on duty in the Indian Bureau preparing sketches for a government publication on Indian manners and customs. Eastman lent him some of his own drawings to copy by way of practice, and when Meigs went to Rouses Point he discovered he had progressed far enough to make a fairly accurate transcript of a landscape.[38]

On September 12, 1851, Louisa gave birth to a fifth child, the fourth boy, Vincent Trowbridge Meigs.[39] An added burden fell upon the limited financial means of the lieutenant, and while the baby was on the way Meigs felt himself unable to reject an offer of assistance from his father. The doctor wrote that he cared for money only for his children, and he authorized Montgomery to draw upon him for $100 yearly on Louisa's account and $200 yearly on his own. If the lieutenant fell into genuine financial difficulty, he might draw still further from his father without notice. Meigs found it mortifying to accept the aid, but he could not deny that he needed it. Soon the first payments were arriving; Meigs was pleased to note that Louisa's was in gold: "So that whenever she wants any little thing she has no change and I am called upon to supply it. I think it will last her a long time." [40]

Presently the Rouses Point interlude was one with almost all the others that had marked Meigs's army career since his graduation from the Military Academy: a fleeting sojourn in a seemingly endless succession of changes of station, with no tour

[38] *Ibid.*
[39] *Ibid.*, Sept. 12, 1851.
[40] *Ibid.*, June 16, 1851.

of duty save that at Detroit lasting long enough for Meigs and Louisa to put down new roots in place of those they had broken in Philadelphia and Washington.

At last all that was to cease, the years of preparation were over. M. C. Meigs was about to embark upon the first of those enterprises by which he would seek to inscribe still more deeply in his country's history the family name of which he was so proud. On October 15, 1852, he received orders to proceed to the Philadelphia-New Jersey area, there to assume charge of three public works recently voted by Congress. He reached Philadelphia about a fortnight later and discovered that General Totten, the chief engineer, had been inquiring after him at his father's house. He found Totten the next evening. The general informed him that Congress had appropriated $5,000 for a survey of possible sources of a public water supply for the city of Washington, hitherto dependent upon springs and wells; that Captain Frederick A. Smith, Corps of Engineers, had barely begun the survey before he fell ill and suffered an untimely death; and that Totten proposed that Meigs should be Smith's successor.

The Secretary of War had yet to confirm Meigs's appointment; thus the lieutenant was to remain in Philadelphia until he heard further from General Totten. He might profitably employ the interval in the study of all the material he could find on waterworks. Philadelphia's own system would provide an excellent starting point.[41]

On November 2 the new orders arrived. Lieutenant Meigs was to report immediately to Washington, there to take charge of "Surveys, projects and estimates for determining the best means of affording the cities of Washington and Georgetown an unfailing and abundant supply of good and wholesome

[41] *Ibid.*, May, 1853.

water." A broader, an almost new career was opening. Never again would Meigs leave for long the city of Washington.[42]

The lieutenant took with him his sense of a family background rich in honor, integrity, and devotion to country. His married life and his children had mellowed him in a measure, but domestication could not soften the resolve with which, the example of Josiah Meigs before him, he trod the path of duty. More than that, Louisa brought to their partnership a conscience as firmly rooted in middle-class Protestant ethics as Meigs's own, with a far greater capacity for self-criticism; from this source there would never be encouragement to compromise issues of principle. With the coming of his children Meigs had the future as well as the family's past with which to keep faith. For his children he dreamed of accomplishments in pursuit of honor and duty still finer than his ancestors' or his own. Especially did he look with gratitude and pride on the accumulating evidence that John Rodgers Meigs was a youth of considerably more than ordinary intelligence and ability.

As he traveled southward to Washington, the lieutenant could reflect that he had chosen his career wisely. His life in the army had been a pleasant life, and he had found ample opportunity to develop and demonstrate his abilities as an engineer. He was entering upon what easily might prove a rare path to distinction. The army had done well by him, and his increased dedication to the army reflected upon and strengthened his devotion to the flag which he and the army served.

[42] *Ibid.*, Nov. 2–3, 1852.

PART TWO

*AQUEDUCT AND CAPITOL*

# IV

# WASHINGTON

THE CAPITOL of the United States stood high on its hill, dominating the scene below it and majestically facing the wrong way. From its west front, which was really its rear, the broad sweep of Pennsylvania Avenue stretched grandly past proud hostelries and bedraggled markets, where pigs wallowed in the garbage, to the point where the outbuildings of the White House obstructed the view which was supposed to reach to that mansion.

Due west of the Capitol the incredible brick towers of the Smithsonian Institution, sanctum of American science, watched stolidly over the mud and effluvia which stagnated in the neglected canal between the Potomac and the Eastern Branch. Farther on, where the canal joined the main river, a truncated shaft of granite rose startlingly from a scattering of cut stone blocks to testify to the ingratitude of republics; even the hallowed memory of the Father of His Country could not cast a spell strong enough to keep financial subscriptions flowing for the Washington Monument. Northward and just east of the White House loomed the Ionic façade of the Treasury Building; still east of that, facing each other across F Street at Seventh, were the similar temples which housed the Post and Patent Offices. In these structures and in the capital at large it was intended that visitors should see embodied the grandeur of the American Republic. Unfortunately, if the capital, like the Republic, occasionally achieved grandeur, like the Republic it suggested more often a grandiose dream scarcely beginning to be realized. Therefore it was likely as not to impress the alien as reflecting merely absurd pretensions.[1]

Between the scattered temples and palaces of white which sheltered the Federal government there sprawled a Southern village, churning thick dust from its unpaved streets when the weather was dry, cursing its way through quagmires when the rains fell, dozing lazily in the shimmering heat of summer, turning out gay in crinolines and dignified in frock coats under bright candelabra on the long evenings of winter. As in a Southern courthouse village, all became quiet and languid when the government season had ended, and only the buzzing of the malarial mosquitoes remained to disturb the loungers on the sere lawns in August. But like a Southern courthouse village, when the government returned Washington awoke to the sounds of an oratory so turgid and rotund that few bothered about the meaning when the mere sound of the words offered so deep a satisfaction.

Much there was that was crude about the town: the houses were mostly low, rambling, and wooden; outbreaks of criminality in the warrens of poor whites and Negroes which cluttered "the island" between the canal and the river regularly troubled the respectable citizens. Even on the main streets a man walked after dark at the risk of life and purse; police protection was absurdly inadequate, and there was less of it at night than during the day. When the moon was expected to shine the

[1] Margaret Leech, *Reveille in Washington* (New York, 1941), pp. 5–9; Allan Nevins, *Ordeal of the Union* (2 vols., New York, 1947), II, 51–58; Roy F. Nichols, *The Disruption of American Democracy* (New York, 1948), pp. 2–3.

city did not light its street lamps; vice was rampant in all its forms; the fire companies were controlled by the local toughs and often chose to battle each other rather than the fires which called them out. In general the place had a raw, youthful, devil-may-care atmosphere which Northerners were likely to consider more suitable to the cotton frontier of Mississippi and Arkansas than to the capital of the United States.[2] Nevertheless, even Henry Adams could find it in himself to love the city; he was to notice that among its inhabitants, "No one seemed to miss the usual comforts of civilization." [3]

By 1852, however, there was one comfort of civilization which even Washington missed. For half a century the city had subsisted without a municipal water supply, and even in the national capital there were those who on occasion felt the need to bathe. If few seem to have experienced any particular longing for drinking water, since other beverages were plentiful, the fire hazard was constant. And late in 1851 the Capitol dome itself, a highly combustible structure containing much wood and tar paper, had been in a fair way to go up in smoke when the Library of Congress just below it did in fact burn. It was this incident as much as anything which appears to have inspired Congress to appropriate $5,000 for the investigation of possible water sources.

Hitherto Washington had relied for water on what Robert Mills in a fit of optimism had called the "rich gifts of nature of underground springs, which rise up whenever a well is dug." There were also a number of small streams, not all of them likely to please the nostrils of a modern sanitary engineer. And in 1831 the Federal government had constructed pipes for the transmission of water to the public buildings from a spring two

[2] Leech, *Reveille*, pp. 8–13; Nichols, *Disruption*, 140–42.
[3] Henry Adams, *The Education of Henry Adams* (Modern Library Edition, New York, 1918), p. 245.

miles north of the Capitol. The citizens promptly had formed the habit of tapping the pipes.[4]

Washington lacked the comforts of civilization in part because it was a sort of stepchild of the Federal government, an annoying distraction to which Congress had to turn its attention reluctantly in the intervals between more engrossing debates on tariffs and slavery. If the capital was a stepchild of the government, so was the United States Army; for few Congressmen could pretend to any pressing interest in an institution which apparently had no earthly use beyond that of keeping an eye upon Indians on the remote frontiers. This being true, why not find employment for one stepchild in the improvement of the other? Why not allow at least one army officer to give the government some return for the education bestowed upon him at public expense by turning him to the useful task of examining possible water sources?

The problem called for an engineer, the army presumably was full of engineers, and such persons could employ their talents far more constructively in contemplating the water question than in building coastal fortifications which probably would never be used. Some such line of reasoning the administration of Millard Fillmore seems to have followed, and so it was that on November 3, 1852, Lieutenant M. C. Meigs reported to the headquarters of General Totten, there to receive his instructions for his survey.[5]

Meigs plunged into the hardest three months' work he had ever undertaken; the contrast was particularly great after the languid months at Fort Wayne and Fort Montgomery. He roamed the wooded banks of Rock Creek, he rode the towpath up the Potomac to the Great Falls, and on February 12 he

---

[4] W. B. Bryan, *A History of the National Capital* (2 vols., New York, 1914–1916), II, 305.
[5] Meigs Journal, Nov. 3, 1852.

turned in a report describing three possible water systems. The city might draw upon the entire flow of Rock Creek, or it might tap the Potomac by erecting a dam at the Little Falls, or it might construct an aqueduct all the way from the Great Falls. Meigs strongly recommended the third solution, which offered a far greater and more dependable flow of water at a comparatively small increase in cost. He buttressed his recommendation with a detailed analysis of the problems to be confronted in building each of the possible systems and of the methods he would employ in solving them. From the Great Falls, he said, Washington might secure 31,015,400 gallons daily at an initial cost of $1,921,244; for an additional cost estimated at $350,000, it might increase the supply to 67,596,400 gallons daily.

Meigs did not hesitate to pass beyond recommendations based on scientific findings to a plea to patriotic sentiment:

Let our aqueduct be worthy of the nation; and, emulous as we are of the ancient Roman republic, let us show that the rulers chosen by the people are not less careful of the safety, health, and beauty of their capital than the emperors who, after enslaving their nation, by their great works conferred benefits upon their city which, their treason almost forgotten, cause their names to be remembered with respect and affection by those who still drink the water supplied by their magnificent aqueducts.[6]

Having received Meigs's report and a concurring recommendation from the Secretary of War, the Finance Committee of the Senate unanimously instructed its chairman, R. M. T. Hunter of Virginia, to move an amendment to the Civil and Diplomatic Appropriation Bill providing $150,000 for beginning work upon such a waterworks as the President might approve. A House-Senate conference committee cut the

[6] 32 Congress, 2 session, Sen. Ex. Doc. 48 (serial 665); Meigs Journal, Nov. 30, 1852.

amount to $100,000, and in this form the bill passed both houses, amidst the turmoil of the final day of the session.[7]

Grateful Washingtonians, delighted at the prospect of bathing, drinking, and effectively fighting fires, credited Meigs's report and his lobbying on its behalf with the victory of the waterworks bill. They presented to him a silver water kettle and stand, appropriately symbolic of his achievement.[8] Meigs obviously hoped the executive would choose him to carry his own proposals into effect; and when the new President, Franklin Pierce, assigned the waterworks to the War Department, it was to Meigs that Secretary of War Jefferson Davis entrusted the task. The most ambitious of Meigs's suggestions, the aqueduct from the Great Falls, was the one adopted. Nor was this all; on the same day in late March on which he became superintendent of the Washington Aqueduct, Lieutenant Meigs was placed in charge of the extension of the United States Capitol and the wings of the Post Office.[9]

Here was opportunity indeed—and challenge too. In Meigs's eyes the Washington Aqueduct was to be no ordinary public monument, but a limitless blessing to the people of Washington in his day and for centuries, a work which must be approached with a sense of dedication. He expressed his feelings in his journal two years later, when Congress approved a new annual appropriation for the Aqueduct:

God make this people grateful for the blessing thus bestowed upon them.

God grant to me a grateful heart for the high priviledge [sic] bestowed upon me in being an humble instrument in his hand

[7] 32:2 *Congressional Globe*, XXVII, 380.

[8] Bryan, *National Capital*, II, 306.

[9] Meigs Journal, March 29, 1853; 58:2 House Rep. 646 (serial 4585), *Documentary History of the Construction and Development of the United States Capitol Building and Grounds*, p. 586; cited hereafter as *Doc. Hist.*

for the outpouring of this great blessing. One that does not stop in the brief space of one mortal life, but flowing on down the long stream of time for a thousand years will to still increasing thousands aye in their course to millions yet unborn carry life health comfort and happiness. Making more healthful the dwelling of the poor more grateful the heart of the humble as of the high.[10]

And the Capitol—to join the list of the builders of the Capitol was to merge one's name with the history of the nation at its very heart, to create a monument for oneself which at the same time would be a part of the great national monument of the Republic. Here too was a task that called for dedication and, to a man of Meigs's views, for heartfelt thanks to the God who made him the instrument for this work, as well as for a plea for strength and skill to be worthy of the task.

The Capitol of the United States as it stood in 1850 was a comparatively small building, but it was not without dignity. Thomas Jefferson's concern that the infant American Republic forsake the effeminate architectural niceties of England under the Adam influence for a sturdy, pure, and masculine mode inspired by republican Rome had determined that the building should have symmetry, balance, sturdiness, and restraint. The French architect Etienne Sulpice Hallet, after coming to the United States known as Stephen Hallet, had turned from Jefferson's suggestion of a temple form for the Capitol to a design based upon a central dome and wings. The amateur architect Dr. William Thornton had then won the competition for the Capitol design by carrying out Hallet's idea on a grander scale. Hallet in turn had begun actual construction of the building and turned Thornton's plan somewhat back toward his own in the interests of practicality, and perhaps of vanity. Finally Benjamin H. Latrobe and Charles Bulfinch had restored the Capitol from the lugubrious ruins left by General Ross's

[10] Meigs Journal, March 4, 1855.

redcoats and had created the building essentially as it stood
now, pilastered façades of Virginia sandstone, low wings
topped by small cupolas, central rounded dome of wood covered with copper.[11]

If the over-all effect was one of grace, unfortunately the
details sometimes jarred. If the interior was not yet the artistic
delirium tremens which Mark Twain would one day find,
a beginning had been made; and flanking the main stairway
entrance on the east was the quaint statuary of the Discovery
group and the Rescue group. Furthermore, the Capitol presented unfortunate features which from the Congressional
viewpoint were more serious than artistic eccentricities. For
one thing, there were the baffling acoustics of the House of
Representatives, which made it virtually impossible for anyone
short of a circus barker to make himself heard, except by the
happy gentleman who occupied the charmed spot where he
could hear even a whisper from across the room. Worse still
was the ventilation, which in both chambers would threaten
the members with suffocation after a few hours, and which in
summer weather could perform the rare feat of producing an
atmosphere even more oppressive than that of Washington
outdoors. Even worse was the heating, which in wintertime
might as well have been nonexistent, except for those Congressmen who were able to huddle on the very edges of the
fires.

The result of all this was that since the first sessions of
Congress in Washington many of the lawmakers had felt convinced that their place of business was deliberately contrived
to thwart all efforts toward intelligent legislative activity. As if
bad acoustics, bad ventilation, and bad heating were not enough,
by the mid-nineteenth century the Capitol was also too small.

[11] Glenn Brown, *History of the United States Capitol* (2 vols., Washington, 1900–1903), I, 1–73.

Devotion to economy and fears of what constituents might think of the luxury of grander chambers imposed overlong delay, but at last Congress could endure its quarters no longer. On September 30, 1850, it voted $100,000 for the construction of two new wings, one for the Senate, one for the House.[12]

Again a competition for designs was announced, and among the four winners of premiums was Thomas U. Walter of Philadelphia, pupil of William Strickland and architect of Girard College. To Walter, President Millard Fillmore assigned the drafting of working plans for the new wings and the supervision of construction, with the title of Architect of the Capitol. The cornerstone was laid July 4, 1851, with appropriately bombastic oratory by Daniel Webster.[13]

Little more than a year elapsed before Architect Walter was under fire for alleged peculation. A Congressional investigating committee could find no conclusive evidence of wrongdoing, but it did uncover curious practices among the contractors. Confidence in Walter could not but suffer. As a result, when Congress passed the deficiency appropriation bill of 1853, among the clauses was a provision that unexpended funds for the Capitol Extension as well as all subsequent appropriations should be disbursed through a new agent appointed by the President.[14] President Pierce chose to limit the powers of Walter still more narrowly by elevating the disbursing agent to the position of supervising engineer. The man he named was M. C. Meigs.

Meigs was a captain now; he had been a first lieutenant since 1838, and on March 3, 1853, he received his second bar in recognition of fourteen years' continuous service.[15] On March

[12] Brown, *Capitol*, II, 119.
[13] *Ibid.*, II, 120–21; Helen Nicolay, *Our Capital on the Potomac* (New York, 1924), pp. 168–70. For Walter, see *D.A.B.*, XIX, 397.
[14] Brown, *Capitol*, II, 119–26; *Doc. Hist.*, pp. 569–77, 583–85.
[15] Cullum, *Biographical Register*, I, 631.

29 came his assignment to both the Capitol and the Aqueduct.
Six days later he received detailed instructions from Jefferson
Davis, Secretary of War. At the Capitol Extension, Meigs was
to hold full powers to make any changes in the work he
might deem necessary. He was to turn his attention particularly
to the foundations of the Capitol Extension and to Walter's
arrangements for heating, ventilation, and acoustics; on these
points heavy criticism had hit Walter. Captain Meigs might
consult freely with the War Department, and he would report
directly not to the chief engineer but to the Secretary of War.[16]

Meigs moved into his new tasks with vigor and assurance,
and he promptly displayed the hand of a firm and skillful
administrator. Whatever the shortcomings of West Point
training in engineering, Meigs had acquired through experience
the knowledge to perform his technical duties with a relaxed
competence. He was to work with smoothness and adroitness,
and he was also to work hard. Now that a genuine challenge
was facing him, he drove himself unsparingly, rising early in
the morning to visit his office on the Capitol grounds, wander-
ing among the workingmen at the Capitol and checking their
performance, consulting with Walter, poring over diagrams,
considering problems of employment and personnel, then in the
evening perhaps riding almost to Great Falls to examine some
distant operations on the Washington Aqueduct.

When the annual battles for appropriations raged through
Congress, Meigs could often be found in the corridors, persuad-
ing and cajoling and winning the friendship and respect of
many of the leading men of both houses, so that in later years
when he would quarrel with the executive, he could count on
firm support from Congress. For the present he enjoyed the
implicit confidence of the executive as well. President Pierce
often remarked upon his high abilities, and he became a par-

[16] *Doc. Hist.*, pp. 585–87.

ticular favorite of the Secretary of War; henceforth anyone who challenged the merits of Captain Meigs would have to answer to the acidic displeasure of Jefferson Davis.

His new responsibilities coupled with the stimulating atmosphere of the national capital pushed Meigs toward a development of his capacities which routine engineering duties on the fortifications and harbors had never accomplished. Meigs possessed a keen intelligence, albeit of a practical rather than a speculative bent. But at Fort Wayne or Fort Montgomery that intelligence had found little to arouse it, and Meigs had long been drifting into mediocrity, an officer competent enough in the unexacting duties that fell upon him, but growing lethargic under tasks which were wholly without urgency, and turning intellectually stale for lack of stimulus in surroundings and often in companions. An ideal day had come to mean merely a hunting trip through the woods with perhaps time out for a bit of sketching. Even Meigs's scientific curiosity, always active, had become less so in the monotonous years of garrison duty.

Now Meigs's alertness and the wide range of his interests were to impress nearly all he met. His Saturday evenings he devoted to a scientific club, reading and discussing scholarly papers with men such as Joseph Henry of the Smithsonian Institution, Alexander Dallas Bache, the founder of the Coast and Geodetic Survey and possessor of an inquiring mind reminiscent of his ancestor Benjamin Franklin, and Meigs's quick-witted fellow officer, Andrew A. Humphreys. A Philadelphia visitor to the capital was soon to write Dr. Charles Meigs:

I returned from Washington thursday after forming there the acquaintance of your son Captain Meigs, and engrossing a good deal too much of his time in examining his plans for the Capitol. He is one of the most striking men it has been my fortune to meet with. He has more breadth, of design, capacity of minute detail, and refined artistic taste, than I have ever known united in an individual:—and I was delighted, as I thought of you, to learn that this was also the judgment of men, whose praise is synonymous with merit, but who valued him much more for his scientific attainments and his admirable social worth.[17]

Through the summer of 1853 the condition described by Meigs as "the extreme sickliness of the Potomac shores" prevented active operations on the Aqueduct;[18] meanwhile Meigs examined possible stone quarries and busied himself at the Capitol. At last, on October 31, a bright blue day, the captain rode up the river banks to Great Falls, where one of his foremen had gathered a small force of workers and begun clearing away brush. The foreman awaited Meigs's coming in the expectation that the captain would strike the first spade into the earth; this Meigs did, with each of his principal civilian assistants following him. "Thus quietly and unostentatiously," he wrote in his journal that evening, "was commenced the great work. Which is destined I trust for the next thousand years to pour healthful waters into the Capital of our union. May I live to complete it & thus connect my name imperishably with a work greater in its beneficial results than all the military glory of the Mexican War." [19]

As the Aqueduct set out on its course through tunnels, over bridges, and down the valley of the Potomac toward Georgetown and Washington, the Capitol of the United States began to assume the sprawling form familiar today. Here Meigs began with the problems noted for special attention in his instructions. Walter's foundations he found somewhat lacking in hydraulic

---

[17] J. K. Kane to Charles D. Meigs, Dec. 23, 185?, Meigs Misc. Papers.
[18] Meigs Journal, Oct. 24, 1853.
[19] *Ibid.*, Oct. 31, 1853.

lime but nevertheless adequate. Heating, ventilation, and acoustics he regarded as crucial to the success of the extension; these were the problems which had most plagued the old Capitol. On acoustics especially he found little reliable information to guide him, and his task demanded originality of thought.

In an effort to discover reliable principles of acoustics Meigs toured the principal auditoriums of the East, taking with him Joseph Henry and Alexander Dallas Bache; for his final plan he secured the approval of the two scientists. The twin problems of heating and ventilating the chambers he sought to solve by driving air into the rooms with a steam-powered blowing engine, warming the air as it entered by means of hot water pipes. While Walter had placed the Congressional chambers at the extremities of the new wings, with windows opening from them to north and south, Meigs set them in the centers of the wings, surrounding them with retiring, conference, and committee rooms and business offices. A corridor circling each chamber would give free access from the subsidiary rooms; and at the same time the public could be excluded from the corridor in order that members might be spared the constant interruption of visitors and lobbyists who habitually assaulted them as they moved from committee and conference rooms to the legislative halls in the old Capitol.[20]

Meanwhile Meigs pushed construction with a dispatch unusual for public projects. By the close of his second year upon the Capitol Extension he was able to report to Secretary Davis that he hoped the chambers of Senate and House might be ready for occupancy by the next meeting of Congress. Already

[20] *Ibid.*, April, 1853; Meigs Let. B., 1857–1858, pp. 140–45; *Doc. Hist.*, pp. 585–90, 703–6. For a report of the Senate Public Buildings Committee in 1864 sympathetic to Charles B. Anderson's claim that he should be compensated because the idea of placing the chambers in the centers of the wings was his, see 38:1 Sen. Rep. 39 (serial 1178).

the walls of both chambers had reached the height of the ceilings, most of the interior walls were at the height of the spring of the roofing arches of the attic story, and construction of the iron roofs of the wings had begun. The question mark was the marble supply. Marble came to the Capitol by a tedious route from a quarry in Berkshire County, Massachusetts. There were indications that its shipment might fall far behind schedule, and Meigs feared that a shortage of marble might slow all his operations and prevent early occupancy of the chambers.[21]

His fears proved well founded. Marble did come in only slowly and irregularly, and Meigs had to postpone the opening of the wings. When Franklin Pierce's administration ended, Congress still met in its old quarters. By that time, however, both chambers were roofed over, the ceilings of both were completed, and interior decoration was under way. A few committee rooms were finished, and others needed only to be painted; already Congress was using some of these rooms.[22]

By now Meigs had turned also to the task of erecting a new dome. As the Capitol more than doubled its original length, stretching out across 751 feet, the old dome faded pathetically out of proportion. Architect Walter had known all along that this would be the result of erecting the wings, but apparently he had not pressed the point upon Congressmen lest they evade the difficulty of paying eventually for a new dome by forgetting about the new wings. By the close of 1854 the absurdity of keeping the original dome was apparent to all; now Walter was ready with a project for a dome of lofty magnificence. With much grumbling about the tendency of appropriations to perpetuate and enlarge themselves, Congress approved on

[21] Doc. Hist., pp. 616–18, 627.
[22] Ibid., pp. 627, 629–30, 663–64.

March 3, 1855, an initial appropriation for removing the old dome and building the new.[23]

Walter and Meigs set to work to refine Walter's original drawing into a practical working plan. In the course of this task Walter modified the proportions of his dome, producing a structure somewhat less lofty than he had first contemplated, but one with considerably more dignity of line. And the new dome was to be lofty enough; its pinnacle stands today 307½ feet above the esplanade below.

The old dome had consisted mainly of wood and copper. Most of the great domes of Europe were of stone. The new dome of the Capitol was to be fashioned entirely of cast iron, the strongest construction material then available, offering a combination of lightness and strength which masonry could not match. Meigs pointed out that few of the domes of the Old World had not begun to show symptoms of decay; their foundations settled irregularly and the result was the cracking of their masonry. Sometimes even wrought-iron bands which reinforced the masonry broke under the tremendous strains imposed by shifting foundations. Thus the dome of St. Peter's at Rome had had to be reinforced with iron hoops, and the dome of the Pantheon of Agrippa displayed threatening cracks.

All this Walter and Meigs expected to avoid with the use of cast iron. Each course in the construction of the Capitol dome would be so united as to form a continuous chain, capable of resisting any thrust that it might receive from above. Furthermore, the application to the old principle of the dome of a modern use of cast iron would effect a great reduction in cost over a masonry dome; there would be no need to consume months in carving elaborately the columns and cornices, but instead these could be repeated indefinitely from the original

[23] *Ibid.*, p. 993.

pattern. The machine age was applying its techniques to the architecture of the Caesars; technology changed, but architecture remained derivative.

While the conception of the dome was Walter's, the difficult engineering problems of its construction appear to have been solved principally by Captain Meigs. In order to demolish the old dome and erect the new, Meigs raised in the center of the rotunda a scaffold in the form of a triangular tower, 18 feet square at its base and 100 feet high; this rose a little above the eye of the old dome. Upon the tower he installed a derrick built of two sticks of timber, mast and boom, each 80 feet long, so that the derrick commanded a circle 160 feet in diameter. To stabilize the tower he commissioned John A. Roebling to fashion for him special stays of wire rope. The derrick was to remove the materials of the old dome and to lift into place all the iron of the new. A steam engine placed upon the roof of the Capitol near the base of the dome furnished power for hoisting castings and other materials into place; another steam engine drove a crane which lifted the materials from the ground and deposited them on a platform beside the first engine. The whole mechanism had to be planned so that it could lift safely a single casting weighing ten tons. It was an elaborate and a delicate scheme; but it was also ingenious, for it obviated the need for the elaborate scaffolding usually used in building a dome.[24]

Meigs was an engineer by education and long experience; to make himself now an art critic required laborious study. But the decoration and adornment of the Capitol were his to supervise as well as the construction. And an inquisitive Congress, sometimes hesitant to assert itself on engineering questions, felt no compunctions about its artistic judgment and waited to greet with ridicule any misstep by Captain Meigs.

[24] *Ibid.*, pp. 993–97, 1008–9.

Meigs's self-confidence rose to the occasion. He read widely in art books, visited the galleries of New York and Philadelphia on every possible occasion, and consulted amateur critics such as Edward Everett and Gouverneur Kemble; then he plunged boldly forward. If the results of his commissions in sculpture and in painting are not what the twentieth century would desire, the fault lies less with any special obtuseness on Meigs's part than with the tastes of his times and the talents he could command. Among the works he commissioned were Thomas Crawford's Senate pediment and doorway and his statue of Armed Freedom crowning the dome. Among the artists he hired was Constantino Brumidi, whom he set to work painting in fresco the committee room walls, and who ultimately would execute most of the famous frieze encircling the rotunda wall at the base of the dome.[25]

Brumidi always remembered gratefully the Captain Meigs who first hired him—so much so, in fact, that once Meigs had to call on his successor at the Capitol to make Brumidi remove from his Commerce group "the Blue Uniform with my head on it." Meigs thought its presence would make him look ridiculous.[26]

By the close of the Pierce administration Captain Meigs was becoming a Washington institution. He was a familiar sight as he prowled about the scattered blocks of marble and unfinished statuary which gave the Capitol grounds the appearance of some decayed city of antiquity. Washingtonians

[25] For a detailed discussion of Meigs's contributions to Capitol sculpture, see Charles E. Fairman, *Art and Artists of the Capitol of the United States of America* (Washington, 1927), pp. 140–58, 174, 191–93. On American art of the period, see especially Oliver W. Larkin, *Art and Life in America* (New York, 1949). For Brumidi and the Capitol, see Myrtle C. Murdock, *Constantino Brumidi, Michelangelo of the United States Capitol* (Washington, 1950).

[26] Meigs Diary, Sept. 3, 1865.

and Congressmen pointed him out to their visitors as "Captain
Meigs among the ruins of Carthage." [27]

The first year in Washington had brought tragedy to the
captain's family life: his eight-year-old son Charles—the happy,
drumming Master Charles of Christmas in Detroit—had died,
and with him had gone two-year-old Vincent Trowbridge
Meigs, born at Rouses Point. But the following year, 1854,
offered the consolation of a new daughter, Louisa Rodgers
Meigs. With the family circle brightened again, Mrs. Meigs
enjoyed the companionship of her mother and sisters, and
occasionally even Louisa's brother Captain John Rodgers of
the navy came home, bearing tales of explorations in the far
north Pacific. Captain Meigs had provided his family with a
comfortable house, on H Street near Twelfth. The winters now
were not the bitterly cold seasons of Rouses Point and Detroit,
but with them came snow and ice and even sleighing to the
Potomac valley. The summers brought holidays in Maryland
and western Virginia for Louisa and the children, with long
rides up the green river banks and rural weekends with his
family for the captain.

To domestic content Meigs could add the satisfactions of a
man whose achievements won the esteem of his fellows. In
January, 1854, he learned of his election to the American
Philosophical Society, his name having been presented for
nomination not as was customary by some friend, but by the
officers and council of the society.[28] From Congress, to be
sure, Meigs learned to expect a measure of criticism and
ridicule; some members saw in his presence on the civil works
the specter of militarism, while others simply could not escape
the temptation to exhibit at his expense their talents as critics of

[27] Leech, *Reveille,* pp. 12–13.
[28] Meigs Journal, Jan. 23, 1854.

art and engineering.[29] But Congress included faithful friends as well as opponents, and the friends were both more numerous and more influential.

Senator James A. Pearce, Democrat of Maryland, was Meigs's most constant confidant and ally. But generally at his side were James A. Bayard of Delaware, chairman of the Senate Committee on Public Buildings and a power in the Democratic inner circle; the noisy and erratic but gifted and eloquent Robert Toombs of Georgia; hard-working, conscientious R. M. T. Hunter of Virginia; and the only Northerner and, with the change of party alignments, the only Republican among Meigs's close Congressional friends, the shrewd little New Yorker William H. Seward.

To President Pierce, Meigs could feel confident in turning for any aid he might ask. More important, the captain could count always on the unqualified support of the dominant figure of the administration, the lean and precise Jefferson Davis. Davis "would be ready to carry the war into Africa," Meigs told his diary during one of his early struggles with Congressional detractors.[30] And to have won the confidence of the Secretary of War was doubly reassuring in the light of Meigs's increasing conviction that Davis was a great man.

The confidence of friends was heartening. But M. C. Meigs relied most heavily upon his inner resources, and it was a personal conviction of accomplishment and of duty well and faithfully performed that he valued most highly. He had ample reason, he thought, for satisfaction. His military rank might still be merely that of captain, but in the engineering profession he had risen high. After a visit in the summer of

[29] For examples of Congressional attacks on Meigs's management, see *Doc. Hist.*, pp. 598–604, 633–41, 643–59.
[30] Meigs Journal, Dec. 22, 1853.

1857 to new construction on the line of the Baltimore and Ohio
Railroad, he could write to his father:

> I met some engineers examined some of the best works & have
> come back feeling that I too am capable of all that I have seen
> of doing it as well or better.
> I do not find any man to whom in conversing upon our profes-
> sion I feel any call to vail [sic] my bonnet. I find some of elder
> standing to whom I stand as an instructor.[31]

Under Meigs's direction the Aqueduct and Post Office were
proceeding smoothly. Under his watchful eye the new Capitol
was becoming a more sturdy and useful building than Walter's
plans had contemplated. Not only had Meigs improved
acoustic, heating, and ventilating arrangements, but he had
substituted larger and more durable marble blocks in the outer
walls; was planning to replace sectional marble columns with
monoliths on the porticos; had substituted encaustic tiling for
Walter's plan of brick floors; had installed iron rather than
wooden door and window dressings; had erected fireproof
iron roofs and ceilings instead of wooden; and through careful
economies in construction methods had accomplished all this
at little increase in cost.[32] With good conscience he could
report through Secretary Davis to the House of Representatives:

> I have labored faithfully and diligently to construct this build-
> ing in such a manner that it would last for ages, as a creditable
> monument of the state of the arts at this time in this country.
> I have spared no labor to secure economy in its administration,
> faithfulness in the agents employed, and justice and kindness to
> the mechanics and laboring men by whose hands it was raised.[33]

[31] Meigs Let. B., 1857–1858, p. 23.
[32] See Meigs's various reports, reprinted in Doc. Hist., pp. 585–91,
607–8, 650–59, 663–64, 707–9.
[33] Ibid., p. 659.

The great dome of the Capitol was the conception of Thomas U. Walter. But it was Captain Meigs whose skill in engineering guided its construction; and if the dome displays a grace of line which is the mark of the architect of Girard College, it possesses also a sturdy dignity and reassuring stability which reflect the mind and character of its chief engineer.

# V

# THE SECRETARY AND THE PRESIDENT

"ENTER THE VILLAIN," Captain Meigs might have penned in his diary on March 4, 1857. He did not. The significance of the day for his personal and professional fortunes he could not foresee, and he was preoccupied with the crowded final moments of the Thirty-fourth Congress, which witnessed the eleventh-hour passage of a $1,000,000 appropriation for the Washington Aqueduct.[1]

This was the inauguration day of President James Buchanan, entering into office under the darkening clouds of sectional crisis, narrow victor in the November canvass over glamorous John C. Fremont and the Black Republicans, conservative politician who must somehow hold together the mutually suspicious wings of the Democratic party upon whose concord now depended the preservation of the Federal Union itself. To conciliate all factions was Buchanan's initial and primary purpose, and he chose his cabinet with this aim in mind. Conciliation called for geographic distribution of cabinet seats, which in turn called for representation of the upper South, specifically Virginia. To this end the none too decisive President turned to the Virginia electors for a suggestion. They named a recent governor, a man whose principal political asset

[1] Meigs Diary, March 4, 1857.

was the service of his father as governor of Virginia before him, but the man most widely acceptable to all leaders of the Virginia Democracy. His name was John B. Floyd; Buchanan made him Secretary of War and hence the new superior of Captain M. C. Meigs.[2]

Meigs realized that he could not expect from the new administration at the outset the ready confidence which Pierce and Davis had extended to him,[3] but with discouraging suddenness he began to divine that the change of pilots entailed more than a need merely to demonstrate anew his engineering capacity. John B. Floyd was an ambitious politician whose success had followed from a capacity to win influential friends by demonstrating what pleasant consequences could ensue if so obliging a gentleman as John B. Floyd were in a position to dispense public patronage and government contracts. He had a weakness for those who approached him bearing the claims of good fellowship; and if occasionally this weakness led him into actions of dubious merit from the viewpoint of the common good he swore to serve, always he could excuse himself on the ground that the violation of a few technicalities of law was as nothing compared to the obligation of a gentleman to his friends. Moreover, there was the Democracy to be served; and what was the winning of elections for, if not to ensure further victories and the continuance of good government and sound administration by holding the allegiance of the party rank-and-file through the distribution of suitable government posts?

With such attitudes, Floyd was scarcely in office before he clashed with Meigs in an effort to confer Aqueduct contracts upon a syndicate of the politically deserving, including John

[2] Allan Nevins, *The Emergence of Lincoln* (2 vols., New York, 1950), I, 71, 78; Nichols, *Disruption*, pp. 57, 62, 67.
[3] Meigs Let. B., 1857–1858, p. 2.

W. Forney, a prominent Pennsylvania Buchanan man for whose contentment the administration felt concern. Meigs reacted with outspoken opposition, and he was able after a difficult fight to turn back Floyd's political foray into the Aqueduct contracting. But Floyd concluded that the captain was "too damned honest," and there are indications that he began already to consider seeking a more docile substitute.[4]

Sources of new friction between Meigs and Floyd seemed to appear almost daily. Floyd presently asked Meigs for copies of his monthly pay rolls, and the captain took them to him and went over them with him as though the object were to study how the rolls were kept. The Secretary asked to hold the rolls for a time so that he might examine them more carefully, whereupon Meigs concluded that Floyd's real object was not the same as the ostensible object: "Pleasant reading some 2 or 3000 Irish German French Italian & American names. Useful occupation of the valuable time of a member of the Cabinet. I presumed that he wished some member of the Jackson club or some such person to read them for him & point out the names of any Know-nothings who might be on the work."

Word soon came from Floyd that Meigs should dismiss from the rolls a Mr. Burton, a canal foreman conscientious and experienced in work for which competent men were difficult to find, directing the construction of secure embankments to hold back the Potomac. Into Burton's place was to go a Mr. Chandler, named by Floyd with no knowledge of what would be required of him. Soon Floyd was openly announcing his intention to drive all Know-Nothings from the public works. Meigs sourly observed that there might exist some chance that Chandler's pay would not prove a mere robbery of the Treasury.

[4] Meigs Let. B., 1857–1858, pp. 3–4, 9–12, 13–16, 21–24, 27–28, 45–48; 1858–1859, pp. 67–70; Meigs Diary, May 6, 20–23, July 29, 1857. On Forney, see Nichols, *Disruption*, pp. 59, 61–63, 86–87.

The man too knowing that he is appointed by the Secretary cannot be expected to pay much respect to the orders of my subordinates or of myself. To the dismissal of any man by the Secretary I do not much object. It is clear that I ought not to assume that the world does not furnish men enough to whom he can make no objection & it is my duty & my interest to employ men not obnoxious to my masters—but he ought not to appoint & to employ them where he does not advise himself of those who are employed. If I am responsible for the execution of the work I should have the selection of the agents. I have no power to compel obedience except by fear of dismissal or by gratitude for employment. If these are taken out of my hands I should no longer be held responsible.[5]

Continued similar conduct on Floyd's part led Meigs to resolve firmly: "I shall carefully keep the actions of such a Secretary distinct from mine—Doing right myself & leaving to him the responsibility for his own outside actions." As a citizen and patriot Meigs found Floyd's methods appalling. "A man who gratifies personal or party prejudice at the expense of the public funds entrusted to him by the representatives of the people is below the level of the honest workman as his station is apparently higher." [6] For all the admirable integrity of Meigs's position, there is in his view, of course, a certain naïveté of the soldier confronting the political partisan.

Architect Thomas U. Walter and the marble contractors, whose slow deliveries were delaying Meigs, complicated relations with Secretary Floyd. Walter was proud and sensitive, and through four years he had nursed the bitterness of losing his command of the Capitol to an upstart engineer from the army. After all, Walter stood in the first rank of the American architectural profession, and in 1857 he played a leading part in establishing the American Institute of Architects. Striking

[5] Meigs Let. B., 1857–1858, pp. 74–77; Meigs Diary, Oct. 18, 21, 1857.
[6] Meigs Let. B., 1857–1858, pp. 74, 77, 89–90, 109; Meigs Diary, Nov. 2, 4, 6, 14, 1857.

abilities had carried him from his father's brickyard and stone masonry business to the studios of William Strickland and eventually to the commission for Girard College. If Walter's college had flaws as a school building, they were flaws inherent in its Grecian design; with its chaste and noble colonnade it loomed as the very climax of the Greek Revival in America. Nor was that all. Walter had dotted eastern Pennsylvania with his structures, mostly Greek Revival; and more than one of them, especially Nicholas Biddle's Andalusia, were among the outstanding buildings of the New World. The commission for the Capitol he regarded as the merited crowning honor of a distinguished career, and he did not fancy the ignominy of bowing to a mere West Point civil engineer.[7]

Walter happened to be a close friend of another Philadelphian, John Rice, of the firm of Rice, Baird, and Heebner, the marble contractors. Slow deliveries offered one of several grounds of friction between Meigs and this firm, and their dealings tended to become acrimonious when Meigs's interpretation of the contract for marble columns for the porticos threatened both to disrupt the firm's schedule and to cost it money. The fact that Meigs's interpretation was substantially correct embarrassed Rice, Baird, and Heebner all the more. They were not even sure that meeting Meigs's reading of the contract was possible. Lest they lose their contract, they began to consider how pleasant it would be to deal with a more pliable superintendent of public works. Such musings gave them common ground with Walter. It seems probable that John Rice played upon Walter's bitterness toward Meigs to urge upon the architect a show of independence of the captain. Rice could point to Secretary Floyd as a likely ally of anyone who opposed Captain Meigs, and he could remind Walter that his brother, William Rice, exercised a certain political influence as editor of the Democratic journal, *The Pennsyl-*

[7] *D.A.B.*, XXII, 397–98; Larkin, *Art and Life*, pp. 157, 166.

*vanian.* Perhaps Walter could force a showdown which, given Floyd's annoyance with Meigs, would lead to the departure of the captain from the scene.[8]

Confident of a new strength in his position, Thomas Walter announced that as Architect of the Capitol he could claim certain "usages of the profession" and need not obey certain orders if issued by the engineer Captain Meigs. In particular he refused to transfer to the captain certain drawings which Meigs claimed he needed, and instead he accused Meigs of tampering with the original plans of the Capitol Extension to make them appear the work of M. C. Meigs rather than of Thomas U. Walter.

To Meigs, trained in the ways of the army, Walter's new attitude was nothing less than insubordination. If Walter had his way, Meigs would be reduced to the role of a disbursing agent, and the Capitol would once more be Walter's. Meigs appealed to the War Department to remind Walter of the true proportions of his position; he prevailed upon Jefferson Davis to address a letter to Secretary Floyd explaining that in 1853 Walter clearly had ceased to be independent and had become subordinate to Meigs, that indeed Walter had retained any place whatever only on Meigs's insistence. Davis sent the letter, but Floyd did not respond; Walter's conduct had the vexatious opponent of politics in the public works squirming, and Floyd was enjoying the spectacle far too much to drop the curtain upon it.[9]

The grandson of Josiah Meigs would not refuse a fight; he had no intention of yielding prerogatives rightly his to Thomas U. Walter. His answer to Floyd's silence was a direct appeal to the President. He had observed Buchanan long enough to be

[8] *Doc. Hist.*, pp. 607–8, 707–9; Meigs Let. B., 1857–1858, pp. 115–18, 148, 171–74; 1858–1859, pp. 143–46; 36:1 Sen. Misc. Doc. 29 (serial 1038), pp. 5–6, 63–70, 164–65.

[9] Meigs Let. B., 1857–1858, pp. 205–6; Meigs Diary, Jan. 20, March 19–20, 1858; 36:1 Sen. Ex. Doc. 20 (serial 1031), pp. 113 ff.

sure he was honest and just; the question was whether the
President had enough backbone to control his Secretary. Meigs
asked Buchanan to settle clearly the issue of Walter's relationship to the supervising engineer, and he put Buchanan upon
notice that he would have no incentive to continue his work
if the system established by the Pierce administration were to
be changed; in that case he would hope to be relieved. Buchanan
by no means desired an explosion from Captain Meigs. Not only
did he feel confident of the captain's technical abilities, but the
Meigses carried enough weight in the Philadelphia Democracy
to be able to worsen an already somewhat unpleasant party
situation there. Beyond all that, something inside Buchanan
probably continued to remind him that in dealing with a
Meigs of Philadelphia a country boy from Lancaster had better
step gently.

Presently Buchanan informed Meigs's friend Senator Pearce
that he considered the captain's view of his authority correct
and Walter in a state of rebellion. But when he broached the
matter to Secretary Floyd, said Buchanan, the Secretary argued
that with Capitol, Post Office, and Aqueduct Meigs had too
much to do. The Senator told Buchanan that Meigs's most
difficult work on the Capitol was done and that he was entitled
to finish what he had started, but where this left Buchanan's
feelings was uncertain. No discernible result followed from
Meigs's appeal to the President; there was no word from the
White House, and Floyd also was uncommunicative. Months
later Meigs was to hear a rumor that Buchanan had sent to
Floyd a message endorsing Meigs's viewpoint, but that Floyd
had chosen to ignore it.[10]

Meanwhile Meigs continued to ply Walter with orders which
Walter persistently ignored, while both men complained to

[10] Meigs Let. B., 1857–1858, pp. 210–11, 213–14, 220; Meigs Diary,
March 20, 1857.

the War Department in terms of growing acerbity. Meigs gave new offense to the Secretary of War by combating Floyd's award of the Post Office heating contract to ludicrously unqualified political friends. Heating and ventilating the Post Office Building called for no small engineering skill, but Floyd bestowed the task on Dr. Charles Robinson of Virginia, who was a dentist, not an engineer. Robinson then subcontracted with a Baltimore firm who claimed to be experienced boilermakers but who apparently were not.[11]

Of course Floyd reacted with new resentment, and his dissatisfaction with Meigs now took the form of constant petty harassment. Late in the summer of 1858 Floyd forced Meigs not only to retain but to promote a lazy, drunken, careless worker whom one of the captain's assistants had fired; the worker, naturally, was one of Floyd's friends. Meigs believed that incidents of this kind were intended to provoke him into an outburst which would justify his dismissal. Informants told him Floyd was swearing he would be damned if he did not foil Captain Meigs yet.

If I could work in his way [Meigs wrote], he & I would in a very short time be so wound up in intrigues & improper contracts that the aqueduct would stink in the nostrils of the people.

While supported by the sympathy of those above me [he told his father], it was a pleasant toil to conduct the work of the Capitol Extension. When that is withdrawn or not so plainly shown it becomes a task, a heavy responsibility a great labor without a corresponding recompense.

I feel as though I was a plug which filthy rats & mice were gnawing at all the time in order to increase the flow from the Treasury—Contractors architects & Secretaries all against me.[12]

Because he wished to protect his works from mismanage-

[11] 36:1 Sen. Ex. Doc. 20 (serial 1031), *passim*, especially pp. 94–103; Meigs Diary, Dec. 29, 1857, Jan. 9, 11, 16, 1858.

[12] Meigs Let. B., 1857–1858, pp. 204, 208, 215–16, 285–87; 1858–1859, pp. 22, 45–49.

ment, and because his ambition called him to finish what he had begun, Meigs strove to retain his post, placing every feasible roadblock in Floyd's path but avoiding outright insubordination. He believed that Floyd was not an evil man, but only a weak and misguided one; and thus he clung to the hope of a change in the Secretary's attitude. "He is a violent tempered man but of a kind heart too and disposed to gratify his friends[;] at present it is certain that he loves me not yet he is not without generosity and may yet change his inclination when he comes to see better the character of those he deals with." [13]

More than that, Meigs believed that the President held something of a checkrein upon Floyd and that despite the Walter affair he could appeal in a crisis to the White House, with hope of receiving justice. In November he concluded a crisis had arrived. Floyd ordered Meigs to forward to the War Department his duplicate copies of the pay rolls for the Capitol Extension and dome. When Meigs failed to comply promptly he received a second order, rather rudely phrased and signed by Floyd's chief clerk. For Meigs, this was too much entirely. Small in itself, the incident seemed to him symbolic. He had already furnished the War Department with the official copies which were all the department had a right to ask, and these were on file in the Treasury. To transmit to the Secretary the duplicates would have left Meigs with no evidence whatever that he had expended faithfully and properly two or three millions in wages and thus without means of refuting malicious attacks, for which there existed by this time ample precedent. More than that, thought Meigs, the Secretary had no more claim to these duplicates than he had to the captain's watch; they were Meigs's property.[14]

[13] Meigs Let. B., 1857–1858, pp. 262–64.
[14] Meigs Diary, Nov. 10–12, 1858; Meigs Let. B., 1858–1859, pp. 53–55.

At the headquarters of the Corps of Engineers Meigs confirmed his opinion that the papers legally were his; then in exasperation he marched to the White House to call on President Buchanan. If there was anything that the President wished to avoid above all else it was undue controversy. He must have blanched in despair when Captain Meigs, whose encounters with Floyd had won him a reputation for truculence, came storming into his office. It was Buchanan's reception hour, and he asked whether Captain Meigs would not like to call again at some other time so that the President might work through the mob that was thronging the halls. The captain would not. Nor would the captain like to moderate his words. He told Buchanan that he had concluded that the Secretary of War no longer held such confidence or such regard for him as would enable him to carry on his works usefully to the country, the administration, or himself. He demanded that the President read Floyd's order about the pay rolls, and he characterized that order as only one of a long series of unfriendly official acts. Buchanan alone could advise him: was the administration to support him, or must he resign?

This was the gist of a long tirade which must have left Buchanan feeling somewhat limp. Squinting at Meigs above the wrapper which swathed his wry neck, the President attempted to soothe him with expressions of sympathy. He had no doubt, he said, that any misunderstanding could be straightened out; he would talk with Governor Floyd about the whole matter. He invited Meigs to return at seven the next evening.[15]

Buchanan had no desire to lose or antagonize Captain Meigs, but he desired even less to quarrel with a Virginia Democrat as influential as John B. Floyd. Not only was it his natural inclination to avoid contention with anyone, but also he had dedicated himself to holding together the Democratic party.

[15] Meigs Diary, Nov. 11–12, 1858; Meigs Let. B., 1858–1859, pp. 53–55.

What with the Lecompton furor in Kansas he could scarcely afford to make new political enemies. He spoke with Secretary Floyd; and for what it was worth—this was a ritual he had performed before—he probably tried to persuade Floyd to take a more charitable view of Captain Meigs. He accomplished nothing in particular.

When he saw Meigs again, he tried to persuade Meigs in turn to adopt a more charitable view of Floyd; but again he accomplished nothing. When Buchanan spoke of how fine a fellow Governor Floyd really was, Meigs refused to be drawn aside. The Architect of the Capitol was insubordinate, he said, and pleas to Floyd evoked only encouragement for that insubordination. Meigs hoped to complete the public works, but he could not do so against the opposition of the War Department. He would not ask to be relieved, but if the department did not intend to support him it ought to relieve him.[16]

Despite the apparent futility of Meigs's visits to the President, there was a lull in the skirmishing with Secretary Floyd as 1858 came to a close. In December, 1857, Meigs had opened the House chamber, and now with the New Year of 1859 he turned over the Senate chamber to its occupants. At the same time he watched the first water from the Washington Aqueduct pour through the lower pipes near Georgetown into the capital. "I wish you could see," he wrote his father, "my jet d'eau in the Capitol Park. I look upon it with constant pleasure for it seems to spring rejoicing in the air & proclaiming its arrival for free use of the sick & well, rich & poor, gentle & simple, old & young for generation after generation which will have come to rise up & call me blessed." [17]

It was one of the great occasions of Meigs's life. "The weather was snowy & bad, but these two events the occupation

[16] Meigs Let. B., 1858–1859, pp. 56–59.
[17] *Ibid.*, p. 99.

of the new hall & the opening of the aqueduct gave great satisfaction." "Thank God who has given me strength & health to go this far, & made me grow daily a wiser & I hope a better man." [18]

As the fifties moved forward, Meigs rejoiced to find that his children continued to give every promise of being worthy of the name they bore. The tragedies of the early years in Washington, the deaths of Charles and little Vincent Trowbridge Meigs, were fading in memory; and now there was Loulie—young Louisa Rodgers Meigs—to give joy to the captain's heart. When Mrs. Meigs was absent, Meigs reported faithfully to her upon their daughter's activities:

I reached home about 5 p m having had time in Baltimore to see the Bridge. . . .
Loulie rushed into my arms with her usual impetuosity & will share my room to night. She counted out the six gum drops to each of the children in a manner which seemed to give entire satisfaction. . . .
Loulie heard your letter with satisfaction only equalled by that derived from the gum drops.[19]

Or again:

Loulie tonight declined having the gas to go to sleep by because, thogh she enquired anxiously of her sister whether it looked like bears in the room with the light coming in from the Library only, she said it would cost her father a handfull of money to burn the gas. So she has heard some of our economical resolutions in regard to waste of gas.[20]

Young Montie was a bright little boy, and Mary was becoming an attractive young lady. But Captain Meigs's great-

[18] Meigs Diary, Jan. 4, 1859; Meigs Let. B., 1858–1859, p. 95.
[19] Meigs Let. B., 1858–1859, pp. 150–51.
[20] *Ibid.*, p. 165.

est pride and his fondest hopes for the future centered in the tall, erect young man named John Rodgers Meigs. It was for John's future that he endured much of the annoyance and backbiting which since Floyd's accession accompanied the building of the public works; he must be worthy now not only of the Meigses of times past, but of his splendid son. We can be sure that on long evenings John Meigs had listened while his father recounted the tales from the family archives, the stories which Captain Meigs had heard in his own boyhood at the knee of Dr. Charles Meigs. Now also there were tales of the doughty old commodore whose name John carried, of *Constellation* and *Insurgente*, of *President* and the British blockading squadron in the War of 1812. In the career of his maternal grandfather as in the annals of the family Meigs there was much that Captain Meigs would have had his son remember; and the young man might look also to the swiftly rising career of his uncle, Commodore John Rodgers II.[21]

With good reason Captain Meigs anticipated a notable future for his son. John Rodgers Meigs was not a handsome young man; but he was tall, like his father, carried himself well, and had clear eyes, a strong chin, and a heartening directness of look and manner. In school he ranked consistently near the top of his class, taking first honors in mathematics. He shared his father's interest in the physical sciences, and as he approached maturity he announced his intention to follow his father's career: he hoped to enter West Point. Here was double cause for Captain Meigs's gratification, and John's West Point ambitions had a practical aspect as well: the army pay scale was low even for the builder of Aqueduct and

---

[21] For the Commodores John Rodgers, see *D.A.B.*, XVI, 75–77; Dudley W. Knox, *A History of the United States Navy* (New York, 1936), *passim*.

Capitol, and Captain Meigs could not afford to send his son to a private college.[22]

As the son of an army officer, unfortunately, John Meigs was not eligible for appointment to the Military Academy from a Congressional district. Captain Meigs would have to approach the President for an appointment at large, and approach him through Secretary of War John B. Floyd.

Few prospective cadets have sought entrance into the Military Academy with a recommendation comparable to that which reached the desk of Secretary Floyd in December, 1857. The document praised John Meigs's high martial and physical qualifications for the military service, mentioned his fondness for scientific pursuits, called attention to the illustrious service of his grandfather in the navy and the distinguished career of his father, and expressed the certainty that his appointment would give much satisfaction to the numerous friends and admirers of Captain Meigs. But the most impressive part of the letter consisted of the names attached to it. Its writer and principal signer was Senator Jefferson Davis. A cordial concurrence was attached over the signature of Senator Stephen A. Douglas; another over that of R. M. T. Hunter; still another over that of William M. Gwin. Finally, a further concurrence was signed by Alfred Iverson, James A. Bayard, Albert Gallatin Brown, William Bigler, Zachariah Chandler (in strange company here), Charles E. Stuart, John M. Mason, John Slidell, and Judah P. Benjamin.[23]

Secretary Floyd ignored the recommendation.

The following year Captain Meigs tried again. This time he called first upon the President. "Pres$^{dt}$ looked as if it was a bore," was the only notation he entered in his diary.[24]

[22] Meigs Let. B., 1857–1858, pp. 158–59, 167–69.
[23] Photograph in *Pennsylvania Magazine of History and Biography*, XXV (1901), opposite 77.
[24] Meigs Diary, Nov. 20–21, 1858.

The next spring, 1859, Buchanan sent his list of cadet appointments to the War Department; the name of John R. Meigs was not on it. Louisa attempted to see the President, but she could not get in. It looked like failure again, and Meigs consoled himself by recording his confidence that in the end God would do better for John. Soon the word spread abroad that the President's list included his own nephew and several persons connected with Floyd: "All appears to be Floyd's work. John of course gets nothing[,] which leaves me the more independent." [25]

Hope rose again toward the end of June, when Meigs learned that two of the cadets appointed by Buchanan had failed their entrance examination. The captain called on Senator Davis, heard his advice, and then hurried to the President to hand him a new application for John. Buchanan said he was disposed and anxious to appoint Meigs's son, but that he had been prevented through the captain's dispute with one of his secretaries about "this damned Capitol Extension and waterworks." Governor Floyd was his friend, said Buchanan, and he did not wish to lose him. ("He evidently is governed by him," Meigs told his diary.) However, if Meigs spoke to Floyd personally, Buchanan was sure John would have the appointment.[26]

Thus Meigs undertook a none too hopeful pilgrimage to the office of the Secretary of War. Floyd claimed he had not approved John's appointment earlier because Meigs had not asked him for it, and he said that if there were a vacancy not already filled John would have it. Meigs could not feel much confidence in this, but he could do nothing more. As he expected, no appointment appeared; on July 9 the deficient cadets were restored.[27]

[25] *Ibid.*, March 16–18, 1859.
[26] *Ibid.*, June 23, 1859.
[27] *Ibid.*, July 9, 1859.

There remained one chance. The deficients would have to be examined again, and Meigs sent to Major Richard Delafield, the superintendent of the Military Academy, a request that he be informed by telegraph if any of the cadets appointed at large should fail his second examination. On the evening of August 31, Delafield sent word that one of them had.[28]

At last Buchanan gave John a conditional appointment. He told Meigs that he took great pleasure in awarding it—but he wished that henceforth the captain would be more courteous in his dealings with Governor Floyd. Already John had missed the summer encampment, and Meigs hurried him northward. The appointment appeared on September 5; on the evening of the 6th Captain Meigs was in Major Delafield's office introducing his son to the superintendent. The next day John took the entrance examination, and the results made his father swell with pride: he turned in the best paper the academy had received in three or four years. Captain Meigs stayed to see John regularly entered and beginning his first drills. Then he turned homeward; his dreams for John R. Meigs were coming true.[29]

Before he left John he gave him a letter which sheds a warming light upon the strict sense of honor which Captain Meigs carried beneath his shell of truculence:

5th Sepr '59

My dear son:

Inclosed is a letter which I have addressed to Govr Floyd Secretary of War.

I wish you to read & keep it & ever after to remember that while Govr Floyd & I have had much difference not always conducted in good grace . . . he has in the matter of your appointment acted with a gracious disregard of these differences of which few men would have been capable. Had he not spoken favorably to the President you would not have had this career opened to you

[28] *Ibid.*, Aug. 24, 31, 1859; Meigs Let. B., 1859–1860, pp. 11–12.
[29] Meigs Diary, Sept. 1, 5–7, 1859; Meigs Let. B., 1859–1860, p. 18.

& I trust that you will always bear in mind the fact however my differences with the Secretary may terminate that to him you are under lasting obligations & that you should always hereafter stand ready to acknowledge them & to act as they require for him & his.

From your affec Father

M C Meigs[30]

A letter to Floyd expressed Meigs's own gratitude to the Secretary and assured him: "My son shall know that while there have been official differences between us, you have not allowed them to prejudice his claims for this appointment and I trust that he may at some future time be able to show his gratitude to you & yours." [31]

In moments like this the character of M. C. Meigs took on a genuine nobility.

John Meigs had his appointment; but the late summer and early fall of 1859 saw the long smoldering quarrel between Captain Meigs and Secretary Floyd flame up again and leap toward a climax. For various political reasons the Buchanan administration had broken with the Rice brothers, newspaper editor and marble contractor, and the roles of Meigs and Floyd in relation to the Rices were now reversed. After much difficulty the firm of Rice, Baird, and Heebner was now delivering marble on schedule, so that Meigs could see no legitimate grounds for voiding their contract, whatever his personal feelings. But the new turn of politics left Floyd wanting to squelch the Rice contract, find marble columns in his own way, and break the last connection between the Rices and the Buchanan administration. The upshot, of course, was more friction and hostility between Floyd and Meigs.[32]

[30] Meigs Let. B., 1859–1860, pp. 21–22.
[31] *Ibid.*, p. 20.
[32] *Ibid.*, 1858–1859, pp. 1, 72, 74; 36:1 Sen. Misc. Doc. 29 (serial 1038), pp. 5–6, 87–88, 90–92, 108–9, 111–12, 119–37; *Doc. Hist.*, pp. 707–8; Nichols, *Disruption*, p. 204–7.

Meanwhile Meigs was tossing sarcasms at the engineering pretensions of Floyd's dentist friend and his Post Office sub-contractors, while the latter were complaining of loss of money because Meigs would not give them the plans for the Post Office boilers. Meigs replied to this charge that he could not send the plans because their current holder was Thomas U. Walter, still claiming independence and refusing to pass documents to Captain Meigs. Floyd did nothing effective about Walter's disobedience, since apparently he felt that the controversy between the architect and the engineer might eventually give him the pretext he needed for ridding himself of Captain Meigs.[33]

With tempers rising with the thermometers, in early August Thomas U. Walter addressed to the War Department a serpentine letter disclaiming responsibility for delay in transmitting the boiler plans and filled with venom for Captain Meigs. Much of the phrasing consisted of subtle but damning indirection. Walter alleged that Meigs had duplicate copies of the plans which were better for everyday work than the originals, he argued that all the drawings were rightfully his, and he closed by suggesting that the real difficulty lay in Meigs's incompetence to design a heating apparatus, a task he himself would gladly undertake if it were desired.[34]

When Meigs saw Walter's letter his anger surpassed anything which even Floyd had induced. Walter had gone beyond insubordination to insult. Meigs had the talent of the self-righteous for hating his enemies, and now he proceeded to demonstrate a nice skill in impaling an enemy upon an acid pen. The missive which he addressed to William Drinkard, Floyd's chief clerk and for the moment Acting Secretary of War, is a minor masterpiece of its genre; but it went too far.

[33] 36:1 Sen. Ex. Doc. 20 (serial 1031), pp. 113–19, 158–61.
[34] *Ibid.*, pp. 158–61.

It was intended to compel the War Department to choose between Walter and Meigs, yet Meigs aimed his barbs not at Walter alone, but also at the War Department.

The insulting letter now referred to me for report [he said], is only one of a long series of acts, the natural consequences of the toleration which his conduct has received from the department. This question originated in an attack upon me by Mr. Walter in January, 1858, and it was referred by me at once to the department. . . . It was evident that injury to the public service must result from any delay in settling the question [of Walter's status]. I have lost no proper opportunity to urge upon the War Department and upon the President a decision of the question. By the War Department I have been put off at every interview, with promises to take up the papers and settle the matter upon a just basis in a few days. My written communications remain not only unanswered, but unacknowledged. I am compelled, therefore, to believe that my appeals have not been read.

This was true; but was it not also verging upon the very insubordination of which Meigs was accusing Walter?

Mr. Walter [Meigs continued], to pass over for the present what he says in regard to working drawings, &c., is highly indignent [*sic*] that I should say he abstracted from my office certain drawings. I used the word advisedly, a harsher one would have been just, but respect for the department prevented its use. His whole argument rests upon the assertion that he is the architect of the public buildings of which I am the superintendent, and that the custody of the drawings belongs properly to him.

The implications of the next paragraph could scarcely have pleased the War Department:

I am weary of sending to the War Department copies of its orders and instructions to me. Instructions which it appears to have forgotten, and the copies of which it never notices; but I must here quote the orders of the Secretary of War, under which all persons engaged upon the Post Office building have been employed.

Herewith Meigs presented the original orders of Secretary Jefferson Davis giving him full authority over the public works. He pointed out that Walter had long acquiesced in his custody of the drawings to which the architect now claimed Meigs had no right; he hinted at Floyd's encouragement of Walter in this sham. Walter had argued that the architect could not discharge his duties properly if deprived of them.

The plain truth of the matter [Meigs rejoined] is that a proper discharge of the duties of the office is impossible so long as a divided authority is permitted. There was no difficulty in the use and consultation of the drawings so long as they and Mr. Walter remained in their proper place, my office. We could and did both consult and use them, but the moment he deserted it and took them with him, the operations of the office became embarrassed, and the proper conduct of the work impossible.

As for Walter's statement that Meigs possessed the duplicate drawings, which might even be preferable to the originals, these, said Meigs, were "the working drawings made for the use of the foremen and workmen." Walter now wished him to attempt to collect from the hands of the workers "the soiled and dilapidated fragments, which may or may not be in existence. . . . I decline the task, the offer of which is an insult; and again call upon the department to punish the insolence and insubordination which it has tolerated so long by its neglect to act upon this question."

Finally, Meigs preferred to dispose in the briefest way of Walter's offer to design the heating apparatus of the Post Office: "Mr. Walter's entire unfitness for such a work is well enough known to all men of science who know him at all." But the captain could not resist the opportunity for a dig at the Robinson contractors and thus at Secretary Floyd:

Yet I doubt not that he [Walter] will be able to make plans satisfactory to the persons pressing for the work, whose object, I presume, is less the most perfect and economical mode of heating and ventilating the building than the expenditure of a certain liberal portion of the public money.[35]

Thus Meigs challenged the War Department to choose between Walter and himself. On Monday, October 31, he received a visit from a colleague in the Corps of Engineers, Captain William B. Franklin, West Point, 1843, and lately an instructor at the Military Academy. Floyd had ordered Franklin to take charge of the Capitol Extension, the dome, and the Post Office immediately; the question of Meigs's removal was to come before the cabinet Tuesday at noon. At eight on Wednesday morning Meigs received his orders of dismissal.

That afternoon he notified General Totten, chief of the Corps of Engineers, that he was returning to the sphere of his appropriate duties in the corps. "I have I trust so done my duty that I retire from this detached command having in nothing lowered the reputation of the corps to which I am proud to belong." [36]

He was confident that in fact he had upheld the reputation of the army's corps d'elite, and in that confidence he found his strength. He had long anticipated dismissal; he had been sure that when Floyd struck against him, and the issue for the President became a choice between Captain Meigs and his Secretary of War, Buchanan, however reluctantly, would have to choose Floyd. But Meigs had completed the most challenging and interesting features of the public works. The dome of the Capitol remained open and jagged against the sky, but the captain had established the principles of construction on which it would be completed. Upon the wings all that

[35] 36:1 Sen. Ex. Doc. 20 (serial 1031), pp. 162–73.
[36] Meigs Diary, Oct. 31, Nov. 1–2, 1859; Meigs Let. B., 1859–1860, pp. 68, 71.

remained unfinished were four or five out of hundreds of rooms and halls and the erection of the superstructure and columns of the porticoes. The Post Office was only slightly less advanced; all the rooms were roofed in, the columns were up, and much of the entablature of the porticoes was complete. The work that remained, then, was largely routine; and in itself Meigs did not greatly regret losing it—though he admitted a lingering wish to have been able to place the statue which he had commissioned from Thomas Crawford upon the high pedestal of the Capitol dome.

More important than his loss of the works was his adherence to principle: "It is not a fall to be removed from a contest in which I have not been defeated in which I have maintained the right successfully & from which I am removed because not supple enough for the purposes of the War Department."

The Aqueduct remained, but to complete the Aqueduct while doing nothing else would be a work of leisure. Seven years before, when he first came to Washington, Meigs would have considered the Aqueduct a great burden. "Now the mountain seems a mole hill a thing to play with." [37]

At the Aqueduct Meigs could distract himself from his fall by watching the Cabin John Bridge complete its leap across its great ravine. The bridge would be the great monumental work of the Aqueduct, the largest masonry single-arch bridge in the world and destined to remain so for years to come, a granite span of 220 feet, sturdily graceful and smoothly functional. When there was talk of planning ornamentation for the bridge, Meigs announced his belief that it should be as bare of embellishments as possible; its beauty would be the functional beauty of the arch. If he could remain as superintendent of the Aqueduct until Cabin John Bridge were com-

[37] Meigs Let. B., 1859–1860, pp. 72–74.

pleted, not to finish the rest of his works would not be so severe a disappointment: "Upon the bridge I want to inscribe my name & the Aqueduct must always be attributed to me as its author, who ever completes it." [38]

Meigs took pleasure, too, in the fact that at the Capitol Captain Franklin was soon enmeshed in the same old difficulties with Secretary Floyd. The only difference was that Franklin was not quite so stout in defiance of the Secretary as Meigs had been, and together Floyd and Walter soon had him well on his way to becoming a mere disbursing agent. As Meigs wrote, "F[ranklin] feels this but if he speaks out he may have a Tortugas pill to swallow or a Utah cathartic to improve his digestion." [39]

Nevertheless, Meigs was sure that he had been removed simply because he had chosen to defend the right; he was the victim of an injustice, and he hungered for public vindication. In such circumstances he was not a man to wait idly for the day when vindication might find him of its own initiative. When the executive government denies common justice, he thought, the recourse of the citizen must be to the grand inquest of the nation, the Congress. Like the British Parliament, Congress bore the duty of inquiring into every step of public action to ensure that nothing was amiss; and to Congress the aggrieved citizen was in duty bound to turn. Therefore Meigs laid his troubles before his friends on Capitol Hill. [40]

He turned first to the upper chamber. Of his influential friends there, all save William Seward were Democrats, the Senate majority was Democratic, and what Meigs as a Demo-

[38] *Ibid.*, 1857–1858, 100–101; W. T. S. Curtis, "Cabin John Bridge," *Collections of the Columbia Historical Society*, II, 299; Meigs's Aqueduct reports in annual reports of the Secretary of War.

[39] Meigs Let. B., 1859–1860, pp. 251–59, 281; 1860, pp. 54–57; Meigs Diary, March 7–9, 22, 1860; 36:1 House Rep. 566 (serial 1070).

[40] For a reference by Meigs to the elder Pitt's characterization of Parliament as the "grand inquest," see Meigs Let. B., 1860, p. 246.

crat desired was an investigation sponsored by Democrats, therefore free from charges of partisan motivation, and aimed specifically at the conduct of the Secretary of War. He believed that such an investigation might serve not only his own cause but that of the Democratic party and of the nation as well. Unpleasant odors were arising not only from Secretary Floyd's management of the Capitol Extension, but also from his financial dealings involving fortifications at Willett's Point, Long Island, and Fort Snelling, Minnesota. Ugly rumors of nepotism and contract favoritism centered on the Secretary. What right, asked Meigs, had Buchanan to saddle the Democratic party with the burden of Floyd's mismanagement? The party could not support that burden, and it must do all that was possible to cast it off.[41]

Impelled by Meigs and his misfortunes, the Senate called upon the War Department for the relevant papers in the question of the Post Office heating contracts. Senator Jesse Bright's Public Buildings Committee unearthed a lugubrious story of carelessness, favoritism, and incompetence on the part of the Secretary of War.[42] Meanwhile the Republican House established a committee to unravel the tangled history of the Capitol marble contracts. Since Meigs's departure Floyd had negotiated a new contract to replace that of Rice, Baird, and Heebner; but the House committee concluded that the new instrument was in accordance with neither good faith nor fair dealing, nor in conformity with law, and that, as Meigs had maintained, the Rice contract remained in effect.[43]

The revelations did not topple Floyd from his post. Instead they probably helped impel him to efforts to banish Captain

[41] *Ibid.*, 1859–1860, pp. 169–72; Nevins, *Emergence of Lincoln*, II, 199; Nichols, *Disruption*, pp. 190, 285–86.
[42] 36:1 Sen. Ex. Doc. 20 (serial 1031).
[43] 36:1 House Rep. 566 (serial 1070).

Meigs from the Washington scene. Apparently only the President stood between Meigs and orders for what would amount to an exile to Fort Jefferson on the Dry Tortugas.[44] When the War Department estimates for fiscal 1861 went to Congress, furthermore, they included no request for funds for the Washington Aqueduct. Lack of funds would mean a suspension of work; and if Aqueduct operations were not to be resumed, why should not Captain Meigs be assigned to another post, preferably a distant one?

By now Meigs's close relations with Congress had combined with his confidence in his own rectitude to give him a sense of independence which in an army officer was highly singular. The captain proceeded to call the attention of the chairman of the Senate Military Affairs Committee, Jefferson Davis, to the presence of an Aqueduct estimate among the estimates of the Corps of Engineers; Meigs himself had supplied this figure, and it stipulated $500,000 as the amount required to complete the work. Meigs submitted, "with all deference to the opinion of the Sec of War," that if the government could not afford to expend his original estimates for both the public buildings and the Aqueduct, then true economy and the advantage to the public would be consulted by voting $500,000 to the Aqueduct, so that the people of Washington and Georgetown might enjoy an adequate water supply; the Capitol required only decorations, and these could wait. An intelligent argument; but what it amounted to was a suggestion from a captain of engineers that he knew better than the Secretary of War how the War Department might best allocate its funds, and that Congress might better follow his recommendations than the Secretary's.[45]

[44] Meigs Diary, June 20, 22, 1859, Jan. 13, 1860; Meigs Let. B., 1859–1860, pp. 163–68.
[45] Meigs Let. B., 1860, pp. 1–3.

Given the low repute of the Secretary and the unique position of Captain Meigs, to follow the captain's recommendations was precisely what Congress proceeded to do. An Aqueduct appropriation of $500,000 began to move through the proper committees of Senate and House. But Captain Meigs had to consider the possibility that even should Congress appropriate enough money to finish the Aqueduct, nevertheless Secretary Floyd might remove him from superintendence of the work. After all, there was already much talk in the department of sending Meigs to the Tortugas. The captain thought it only fair to his countrymen who would have to pay the public bills that his own continuance on the Aqueduct be ensured, so that the public might enjoy the guarantee of an honest and economical administration.

To this end he suggested to Robert Toombs that the Senate Finance Committee add to the Aqueduct appropriation a proviso that the money should be expended by "the Chief Engineer of the Washington Aqueduct who shall be as heretofore an officer of the corps of Engineers not below the rank of Captain and having experience in the design & construction of Bridges & aqueducts." Such wording described only one man: Captain Meigs. It raised the issue of the President's power as Commander-in-Chief to reassign army officers at will, but Meigs's Congressional friends accepted it and went even further: as finally passed, the Aqueduct appropriation contained Captain Meigs's name, stipulating that the funds might be expended only under his supervision.[46]

To Meigs, this was all the vindication he could have asked. He had the army officer's common habit of regarding Congress rather than the executive as the true fountain of the popular will; and thus to him the Aqueduct appropriation

[46] *Ibid.*, pp. 102–6, 166–67; 36:1 *Congressional Globe*, pt. 4, 2868–70, 3199–3213.

was an endorsement springing virtually from the people themselves, against an executive department that had lost touch
with the popular will. "This is an encouragement," he wrote,
"to all who faithfully do their duty even when against the
wishes of their superiors in authority. . . . The debate & the
votes are equivalent to votes of confidence of the highest order,
& as we get no blue ribbons & crosses these are our evidences
of good service & our badges of merit." [47]

Yet Meigs's triumph was not secure. The President signed
the Aqueduct appropriation with its proviso because it was
embedded in the miscellaneous appropriations bill, upon which
numerous government activities depended. But the President
did not sign happily. He regarded the naming of Meigs as an
insult and a rebuke to his administration, which of course it
was; because of Meigs's part in securing it he lost his sympathy
for the captain. Furthermore, he questioned Attorney General
Jeremiah Black on the binding quality of the Meigs proviso
and secured the opinion that Congress's naming of Captain
Meigs to superintend the expenditure of the appropriation
was merely a recommendation to the executive, not a compelling condition. It could be no more than a recommendation,
said Black, since Congress did not possess the power to name
a public officer under the Constitution, least of all to impinge
upon the prerogatives of the President as Commander-in-Chief
of the army. Buchanan retained the power to transfer Meigs
to any station he chose.[48]

In the opinion of the administration, then, there existed no
compulsion whatever to retain Captain Meigs upon the Aque-

[47] Meigs Let. B., 1860, pp. 127–28.
[48] Meigs Diary, June 20–21, July 18, 20–26, 1860; Meigs Let. B., 1860,
pp. 130–40, 142–43, 153–55, 178–79, 197–200, 239–48; John Bassett Moore,
ed., *The Works of James Buchanan* (12 vols. Philadelphia, 1908–11), X,
452–55; copy of Black's opinion, July 31, 1860, with marginalia by
Meigs, Meigs Misc. Papers.

duct. With Buchanan no longer of a mind to defend the captain, one more clash between Meigs and Floyd was likely to send Meigs packing for the Tortugas, Utah, or the Pacific coast.

A new passage of arms was not long in brewing. The Aqueduct appropriation stipulated that the funds were to be expended under the superintendence of Captain Meigs; Meigs regarded them as having been committed to his personal trust. The Secretary of War ordered him to pay from the Aqueduct account the cost of the visit of another Aqueduct officer to fortifications at Sandy Hook, New Jersey. Since the assignment of the officer was to the Aqueduct, Floyd professed to believe he was ordering a legitimate expenditure from the appropriation; since the visit to Sandy Hook had nothing to do with the Aqueduct, Meigs thought otherwise. He argued that the expenses of the New Jersey trip should be paid by the quartermaster general out of the military appropriations; he refused to make the payment.[49]

The refusal was patent disobedience of the orders of the Secretary of War, and Meigs's friends disagreed on the wisdom of it.[50] Colonel J. G. Swift, who had been chief of engineers during the War of 1812, wrote to the captain from retirement that his course was right, that it was the duty of every officer as a citizen to take the responsibility of refusing to violate the law at the command of the executive.[51] Dr. Charles Meigs was not so sure; he feared a court-martial and the ruin of his son's career. General Totten, "grown old in subordination," urged the captain to obey the Secretary's orders; he held that Meigs had no right to question their legality.

This was the crux of the matter: could Captain Meigs take

---

[49] Meigs Let. B., 1860, pp. 310–12.
[50] *Ibid.*, pp. 257–58, 260–61, 271.
[51] *Ibid.*, p. 311.

it upon himself to decide whether an order of his superior accorded with law? General Totten said not. "What," Meigs asked him, "would you do if the Secretary ordered you to cut your own throat?"

"Oh," said Totten, "that is an extreme case!"

"Should he order you to head a detachment to turn Congress out of doors, would that be lawful?"

"Oh, another extreme case."

"Well," said Meigs, "Becket died under an extreme case, and Cromwell's and Napoleon's careers have both illustrated the second instance. Had Hampden bowed to the opinion of the attorney general, England had perhaps been a despotism." [52]

As Meigs saw it, the primary principle of military law in this case was that illegal orders are not obligatory. The standard treatise on military law stated: "To disobey an unlawful command of a superior is undoubtedly lawful." If an officer were guilty of an insubordination merely because he declined to obey an order of his superior, without regard to its legality, why bother with courts-martial?

Meigs turned to the decisions of the Federal courts. In *Greely v. Thompson* the Supreme Court had ruled:

The orders as well as the opinions of the Heads of Departments are entitled to great respect and will always be duly weighed by the courts. But the laws are to govern and not the opinions of the Heads of Departments on them. . . . [Thus] The removal of the appraiser must be deemed valid or not according as the collector possesses legal power to make it on the facts of the case, and not with reference to the orders of the Secretary of the Treasury.

Again in *Teal v. Tiller* the court declared: "The laws and not the instructions of a Department furnishes the guide to officers." True, these cases involved civil officers; but there

[52] *Ibid.*, p. 267.

were also military precedents. In *Colonel Mitchell v. Henessy* the court announced:

The officer who made the seizure cannot justify his trespass by showing the orders of his superior officer. An order to commit a trespass can afford no jurisdiction to the person by whom it is executed. [Further, said the court:] Upon a principle independent of the weight of judicial decision it can never be maintained that a military officer can justify himself for doing an unlawful act merely by producing the order of his superior. The regulations require all officers to obey the "lawful command" of their superiors. The oath is to obey orders of superiors according to the rules and articles of war.[53]

It was not for nothing that Captain Meigs had been raised to a stern conception of individual moral responsibility. It was not for nothing that he imbibed a rigid code of family honor. M. C. Meigs might be forbiddingly self-righteous, but when the question became one of duty, his stern integrity would ensure that his decision would be his and his alone, and that its foundation would be nothing less than his conception of the ultimate right.

I take issue on the broad principle. The congress made a condition which was my judgment & superintendence. Havg exercised that judgment I decline to act against it by order & this whether it be good or bad. I must decide. I must say to Congress you have given me a trust an order you had no right to do so, or to the Presdt you gave me an order you had no right to do so. Which master shall I obey? Who shall decide for me? The Atty Gen? a court martial? Myself alone.[54]

A heavy rainstorm struck Washington on the night of September 19, 1860. The next day Captain Meigs rode out along the Aqueduct to the distributing reservoir in order to assess the effects of the storm. He discovered that rain had injured

[53] *Ibid.*, pp. 278, 267–69.
[54] *Ibid.*, p. 270.

some new banks being built for the reservoir, and he returned
to his office to prepare suggestions for correcting the damage.
While he sat writing at his desk he received an order from
the Secretary of War. He opened it. It removed him from
the waterworks and instructed him as soon as possible to proceed to the Dry Tortugas, there to assume charge over construction at Fort Jefferson.[55]

From President Buchanan's summer retreat, where the waters of Bedford Springs trickled from the Alleghenies to course
toward the Juniata, had come word that the President did not
know what to do with Captain Meigs, whether to send him to
a court-martial or to allow Governor Floyd to banish him.
He had wished to befriend the captain, he said, but Meigs had
assumed so extraordinary an attitude that he could shield him
no longer. He wished to treat him with leniency; but he
thought a court-martial would certainly cashier him. Perhaps
the better course would be banishment.[56]

Meigs reconciled himself to his exile. He did not expect to
stay long; for he was sure Congress would make the administration uncomfortable, and in any event Buchanan's days in
the White House were numbered. As Meigs interpreted the
law, no funds could legally be expended upon the Aqueduct
in his absence. He notified Captain H. W. Benham, his successor as superintendent, that the property of the waterworks
was in his charge, and to Benham he transferred his drawings.
The Secretary of War had directed him to turn over to Benham also the money that was in his hands; but this he did not
believe he could rightfully do. He deposited the money,
$3,276.68, in the Treasury. And he notified the Secretary of
the Treasury that the unexpended balance of the Aqueduct
appropriation, about $475,000, was in the Secretary's custody,

[55] *Ibid.*, p. 288.
[56] *Ibid.*, p. 276.

and that any bill, draft, or requisition paid out of it in Captain Meigs's absence and while the captain was prevented from superintending the expenditure, would be paid in direct violation of law.[57]

He then made preparations to depart. Louisa wanted to go with him, but he did not expect to stay long enough to make it profitable to break up his home. Besides, it might be of benefit to his cause if his wife remained in the capital: "A wife if silent is a living protest against a good citizens exile. . . ." [58] He was confident that all would turn out well, as he wrote to Louisa's sister, Mrs. John Macomb:

Washgtn Oct 1, 1860

My dear Nannie,

Do not trouble yourself about me. You know you used to say with Lou that I was a most self-righteous fellow, & I find this approval of one's own conscience whether proper or not is "mightily convenient."

It amuses me to see very good people & very kind friends look at me with a sort of air as thogh they thoght [*sic*], why did you not bend just a little, it would have been safe to bend to the storm. . . . A very honest fellow . . . but obstinate, a leetle. Had the Secretary lost his hold upon the affection or fears of the Presd[t]. & been driven out of the field, Had I retained command of the aqueduct, they would have been loud in approval. Now they suspect that Meigs is honest, firm, but obstinate & foolish.

. . . still I shall be content I shall occupy my mind with study of the rare & beautiful forms of life with which God has bedecked those tropic shores, I shall amuse myself with yachting, fishing hunting. I shall study & try to increase my store of knowledge & make myself more able to be useful to a people whom Washington & Adams, Jefferson & Clay thought worthy of their highest efforts, their most unselfish devotion.

And I shall conceitedly rest contented in the conviction that I have striven to do my duty & that in the end God will consider it.

[57] *Ibid.*, pp. 288–89, 310–13.
[58] *Ibid.*, pp. 310–13.

. . . Lou has told you that Gen Scott volunteered the assurance
that he approved my conduct.

My time of departure is so uncertain that I do not think you
should trouble yourself with the idea of changing your plans.
Nurse yourself lay in a good stock of strength & health to take
care of this family until I return to support Louisa again with
my presence. She will depend much upon you. . . .

God bless you dear Sister

Ever your affec

M. C. Meigs[59]

The battle was fought; and if in the eyes of the world Captain Meigs had met defeat, Meigs knew that his was a victory
of honor. John B. Floyd may not have been a corrupt man.
There is nothing in Meigs's quarrels with him to indicate that
the Secretary sought or derived personal profit from the irregularities which he foisted upon the public buildings and the
Aqueduct. Yet certainly Floyd was a weak man, a petty politician unable to set the public welfare above considerations of
personal and partisan advancement and a pliable individual too
eager to oblige his friends. His administration of the War
Department was less dishonest than merely careless, yet at the
same time Floyd could be devious; he appears plainly to have
used Thomas U. Walter as an instrument for thwarting Captain Meigs by indirection. And if Floyd was a pliable and
obliging personality, he was nevertheless strong enough to
mold the even more pliant putty of James Buchanan to his
will.

Buchanan nursed a stricter sense of personal and public honor
than Secretary Floyd. While we never glimpse Floyd strug-
gling with problems of conscience, Buchanan struggled often
and painfully. The President was conscientious, but his was
a conscientiousness plagued by doubts and unwilling to reach

[59] *Ibid.*, pp. 326–29.

clear-cut decisions. The President possessed a generous heart; he wished to treat Captain Meigs with kindness and justice. But Buchanan was so eager to retain the friendship of all, and so fearful of giving offense, that he could scarcely bring himself to assert his own will against anyone's; and this policy could well lead to injustice. When at last the President had to choose between Meigs and Floyd, his decision rested less upon the merits of the case than upon his unwillingness to break with his closer, and more powerful, friend of the two, Governor Floyd.

Buchanan trembled as he watched the Democratic party collapsing around him. And he could not afford to add further to the woes of the party by breaking with Floyd and his Virginia following, especially since it was to the South that he now had to look for his principal political strength. To be sure, to support Floyd against Meigs meant to clash with powerful Southerners like Davis and Toombs. But this was not so direct a break as the disavowal of the Secretary of War would have been. And so long as Buchanan's administration hewed to a policy of conciliating the South on the slavery issue, the President could count on Davis, Toombs, and Meigs's other Southern friends to back him on more vital matters than the fate of a captain of engineers. The picture that emerges of Buchanan, then, is not particularly a favorable one: an honorable, conscientious, generous old gentleman beset by insecurity in his personal relationships and by disaster in his political life, fearful of offending others and thus bowing to whatever stronger personality was closest to him at a given moment.

The guiding thought of Captain Meigs throughout his battle with the Secretary had been to do what was honest and right. No consideration of fame or reward, no threat of punishment or disgrace could sway him from his family and personal code of honor. He could be bumptious. He struck a jarring note when he wrote, "I have beaten the administration," [60] or when he stated categorically in a letter to Buchanan that it was his assurances that induced Congress to vote the Aqueduct appropriation in 1860. He cultivated Congressmen and lobbied tirelessly on his own behalf—on behalf of the works under his charge, and thus of the people, he would have said—with small regard for tact and courtesy toward his superiors.

But he did it because he believed his superiors were no longer deserving of the ordinary amenities, and he did it because he believed it was necessary for the public welfare. If he sometimes grew arrogant, he was never cowardly. He would do the right; he would not kowtow, he would not crawl. He was a man of rigorous conscience who could be complacent only because he did not make excuses to that conscience. He was a man of utter integrity, and this is no small thing.

[60] *Ibid.,* p. 130.

PART THREE

*THE CIVIL WAR*

# VI

# THE FLORIDA FORTS

ALL THROUGH Meigs's quarrel with Secretary Floyd the sectional controversy had sounded an increasingly insistent background note in his diary and correspondence—at the moment a background note for Captain Meigs, but for the nation a crisis of the first magnitude. From that soil of Kansas which the newspapers covered with blood had risen the issue of the Lecompton Constitution to drive a wedge into the last great intersectional political instrument, the Democratic party, the party of Captain Meigs and his fathers.

The captain and Dr. Charles Meigs followed Douglas and the anti-Lecomptonites, and accordingly Buchanan's attempt to push the Lecompton Constitution down the unwilling throats of the Northern Democracy was another source of ill feeling between the captain and the Federal executive. When rumors of an impending collapse of the cabinet floated through Washington, Captain Meigs rejoiced not only because this might mean the fall of John B. Floyd, but also because he believed that the loss of public confidence in the administration demonstrated the futility of its attempt to dragoon the party into support of an iniquitous measure.[1]

The Meigses were anti-Lecomptonites, but they were still Democrats, and certainly they were not antislavery crusaders.

[1] Meigs Let. B., 1858–1859, pp. 24, 28.

Meigs's closest supporters in Congress remained for the most part the Southerners, with Jefferson Davis in the forefront. When John Brown seized the arsenal at Harpers Ferry in October, 1859, and proclaimed with gleaming eye his intent to arm the slaves of the South for a black revolt, Captain Meigs recognized at once that the men of the North must assure the South without fail that Brown acted only for himself, a canting fanatic, and not for the leaders and people of his section. Meigs wrote to his father urging the doctor to work for a mass meeting in Philadelphia which would demonstrate not in favor of John Brown but against him. Political schemers in the South had already aroused the fury of the section; now the South saw only the mad abolitionist in the engine house and his abolitionist supporters, not the hundreds of Northerners who denounced Brown and his folly. A Philadelphia meeting well attended and well conducted, without angry speeches but calm and cool in its resolutions, this Captain Meigs was sure would help curb angry passions.[2]

Late in January, 1860, Meigs received a visit in Washington from his brother Henry, who had married in the South and become a mill owner at Columbus, Georgia. The visit gave the captain his first opportunity to discuss the sectional crisis at length with a man to whom he could speak with complete freedom, and what he heard was in part encouraging, in part disheartening. Henry preferred to adhere to the government of the Union, even though he considered the prospects for the South increasingly hopeless; this at least was something. On the other hand, if against his wishes Georgia should secede, then he would cast his own fortunes with those of his adopted state.

Captain Meigs could not believe that a brother raised in the principles of the Meigs family could take such a view unless

[2] *Ibid.*, 1859–1860, pp. 104, 110.

he had abandoned principle entirely; never could he comprehend the viewpoint of secessionists, least of all when his brother was among them. Of Henry he wrote,

I cannot persuade myself that he is thus determining from principle, from high & lofty patriotism in so great a question. I fear recent contiguity & the almighty dollars which he has invested in Columbus Mills are the arguments which unknown to him move him. But the eternal blot of slavery defiles all the . . . thoughts of men on this question even when to the manner born.

The captain was willing to admit that slavery had done some good, "as all that God permits on this earth does." But the principal good, the conversion of the Negroes to Christianity, was long since accomplished, and no man mindful of the American tradition of liberty could regard fellow human beings as mere property.

Recite all the arguments for slavery imaginable, and still "it is not a thing which men brought up to look upon liberty of action speech thought & conscience should be called upon to worship, under penalty of dissolution of their political organization & society." This much was clear. Meigs was neither abolitionist nor Republican, but he would not bow the knee to the apologists for human slavery. When the South moved toward a demand that even moderate men such as Captain Meigs do what seemed to them to be bowing just so, then the nation moved toward the culmination of crisis.[3]

In April, 1860, the Democratic national convention met in Charleston and divided in bitterness and anger on the issue of protection of slave property in the territories—and on the loathing of the administration and the Southern chieftains for Stephen A. Douglas. In May the Republicans shouted and cheered above the blare of brass bands in the Chicago Wig-

[3] *Ibid.,* pp. 176–79.

wam; and in their search for a candidate who could unite
their disparate factions, ex-Whig and ex-Democrat, East and
West, moderate and radical, they settled upon Abraham Lincoln of Illinois. In June the Democrats attempted to reunite
in Baltimore; but the gulf between Northern and Southern
wings had grown, not narrowed, and two candidates emerged,
Douglas representing most of the North, John C. Breckinridge
most of the South and the Buchanan administration.

The split in the Democracy ensured a victory for the Republicans, and election day approached to raise louder the
threats of the South that Lincoln's election would mean disunion. Pennsylvania cast her ballots in the second week of
October, just before Meigs's departure from Washington for
the Tortugas; and in his diary the captain recorded the result:
"The defeat of the administration in Penn is complete 20 to
30 000 majority. A crushing rebuke to the corrupt cabinet."
That day the granddaughter of Secretary of State Lewis Cass
told the captain that all the cabinet had concluded that Lincoln's election was sure—and that consequently the Union
would be dissolved.[4]

Meigs traveled southward by the overland route, departing
on October 22. He passed through Lynchburg, Knoxville,
Columbus, Georgia, and Montgomery, reaching the Gulf at
Pensacola. Along some parts of the route he found a strong
feeling of hostility toward the Union, if the Union were to
be in the hands of Republicans. Men reported to be sober,
careful, conscientious citizens expressed regret for the danger
to the Union but advanced the belief that its bonds could not
endure much longer. Many of them felt that since the struggle
must come, it might as well come at once.

Around Montgomery and Columbus, where Meigs lingered
to visit his brother Henry, disloyalty to the Union was par-

[4] Meigs Diary, Oct. 11, 1860.

ticularly rife. Between Montgomery and Pensacola the portents were more encouraging: this was an area of pine forests remote from markets, and to the tillers of its infertile soil the slavery question was not vital. Among these people Meigs believed that secession and disunion found no favor. But he could not forget the talk he heard around Columbus and Montgomery, and especially in his own brother's house. For it was more obvious than ever that even Henry would willingly forsake the Union.[5]

In Washington, Meigs had been preoccupied with his own problems, and he had sloughed off the secession threat. His journey through the South awakened him to the depth and imminence of the danger. For all that, the trip was a pleasant one; and the journey by sea from Pensacola via Key West to the Tortugas was delightful. The sky was clear, the sea calm, the temperature pleasant. The schooner moved along under "a good full rigged sailing breeze." At night the water was splendid with phosphorescence, waves of fire breaking away from the bow of the vessel, her track a fiery foam. By day the sea was wondrously clear; Meigs called a man to spear him a fish by a wharf where the water was fifteen feet deep, and the spearman killed at the word a grampus twenty-three inches long, gliding ten feet below the surface.[6]

The Dry Tortugas presented a scene desolate enough, and Meigs would not have relished the prospect of a prolonged stay there. There were five or so islands, nestled in an isolated corner of the Gulf some seventy-five miles west of Key West. The only place of any consequence was Meigs's station, Fort Jefferson, begun in 1846, still far from complete, and destined to become in the next few years a Federal prison—"America's Devil's Island." Remote and isolated the fort was, but in the

[5] Meigs Let. B., 1860, pp. 368–73, 480–83.
[6] *Ibid.*, pp. 363–64, 376–98.

exuberant years of Manifest Destiny—note the date, 1846—
the Tortugas had acquired a strategic importance: with Fort
Taylor at Key West, Jefferson commanded the Straits of
Florida; and it guarded the northwest approaches to Havana.
If the disunion talk in the South meant war, the fort would
take on a new significance: it commanded the northern outlet
for Mobile, New Orleans, and the other ports of the Gulf.

The ominous talk he had heard on the way southward gave
Meigs reason to be less idle than he had expected, for he hurried to bring Fort Jefferson into as strong a condition for
defense as possible. Unfortunately, so neglectful had Congress
been, and so timid was the administration, that he could accomplish little. Fort Jefferson was one of five United States
coastal defenses in the state of Florida. At Key West was Fort
Taylor; at Pensacola were the other three: Fort McRee, the
Barrancas, and most important, Fort Pickens. None of them
were in much more readiness to hold off attack than Fort
Jefferson, and his own post Meigs believed could be taken
with ease by a dozen men. At Key West on his outward voy-
age he had heard rumors of a possible demand by the government of Florida for possession of the United States property,
and accordingly he knew that an attempt to seize the fort was
not out of the question.

Even before the meeting of the Florida secession convention,
even before definite word arrived of the secession of South
Carolina, Meigs slept uneasily; the forts offered too great a
temptation to Southern adventurers.

Well I hope that no hot headed South Carolinian will head a dozen
fire eaters some bright night through the open gaps in the wall
of what ought to be Fort Jefferson to astonish me in bed by demanding a surrender in the name of the Great Moloch & the
Southern Congress. He might safely make himself an Ethan Allen
Gain recognition . . . & be elected Senator or Vice President or

ambassador to Timbuctoo . . . with full authority to negotiate a peaceful commerce in blue beads & horn handled knives on the one side & captives of the bow & spear on the other.[7]

As they were, the forts offered an invitation to Southern hotheads to light the powder of civil war. But if they could be armed and garrisoned adequately, they might demonstrate to the South the earnestness of the national government, and the effect might be to discourage the secession of Florida, or at least to head off warfare. Meigs considered writing to Buchanan or Floyd, but he rejected the idea: "I do not believe that one drop of patriotic blood flows in eithers veins, & I believe it useless." Then perhaps a letter to Winfield Scott? This struck Meigs as a more likely thought. Pompous old Winfield Scott, the lieutenant general commanding the army, was a Virginian by birth, but after a military career of more than half a century, he was as loyal to the Union as any man alive. And if he had grown fat and dropsical, he nevertheless possessed a keen military mind that would perceive instantly the requirements of the Florida situation. Meigs would have to address Scott unofficially, but the case was extreme enough to justify it.

He wrote on November 10, almost immediately after his arrival. He began by describing the dangerous temper he had found in his trip through the South, but he held that a wise discretion and preparation by the authorities might prevent a general outbreak. He showed how easy it would be for a few desperate men to seize the forts at Pensacola, Key West, and the Tortugas. The Barrancas, Fort McRee, and Fort Pickens contained guns, but Meigs doubted whether more than one man occupied any of them; the few troops at Pensacola were outside the walls of the Barrancas. Fort Taylor was partly armed, but it possessed little else. A clerk and perhaps

[7] *Ibid.*, pp. 388–89.

a few laborers lived within its ramparts; a single company of artillery occupied pasteboard barracks two miles away. At Fort Jefferson there was not a single gun; and Meigs doubted whether among the seventy or eighty persons, white and colored, who dwelt on the island he could have found a half dozen fowling pieces. The embrasures of the lower tier of the fort were ready for guns; magazines were ready to receive ammunition. The walls had reached thirty feet in height. If the flanks were armed with a few carronades or howitzers, and if one or two heavy guns were placed on each curtain, then with a proper supply of ammunition and small arms a single company of artillery, aided by a few volunteers from the island and the Gulf fishing fleet, should be able to hold the fort against any Southern filibustering expedition. Such preparation probably would suffice to prevent a hostile attempt.

Similarly, said Meigs, Fort Taylor ought to be occupied and a few more guns sent to the place. At both Jefferson and Taylor the climate was such that troops could encamp in the casemates with shelter from the sun and rain and in greater comfort than in the barracks of a colder climate; for the officers of a small garrison the quarters already erected were enough. Already Meigs was not neglecting the problems of a quartermaster. Finally, the captain cautioned that the commanders of the exposed forts should be men carefully selected, known to hold their allegiance to a state or section subordinate to that due the Federal government whose commissions they bore.[8]

While he hoped for action from General Scott, Meigs did what he could on the scene. Toward the end of November he induced the commander of the artillerymen at Key West to move into Fort Taylor, on the pretense of drilling his men at the guns. Two navy steamers were in the area, and he pre-

---

[8] *Ibid.*, pp. 368–73. For Scott, see Charles Winslow Elliott, *Winfield Scott, the Soldier and the Man* (New York, 1937).

vailed on them to take station at the forts: *Wyandotte* off Fort Taylor, *Mohawk* off Fort Jefferson. He expected Buchanan's cabinet to fume at this. So pusillanimous was that body that with treason abroad in the land it had not yet sent a single military or naval officer on Florida station instructions for the care of the government property or fortresses. But if the cabinet must fume, let it; once official reports from the officers on the spot had exposed Washington's neglect, then the cabinet would hardly dare to order the forts back to their defenseless state.[9]

At Key West meanwhile the citizenry had formed the "Island Guard," a new militia force of about one hundred men of secessionist leanings; it drilled under the eyes of the United States commander with ammunition "borrowed" from United States stores.[10]

At the beginning of December, Captain Craven of the *Mohawk* received from Secretary of the Navy Isaac Toucey, a Connecticut doughface whose personality resembled Buchanan's, a dispatch stating that the Secretary knew of nothing to make the captain's presence at the Tortugas desirable; he should return to his station. Meanwhile Meigs heard nothing in reply to his letter to Scott, and he concluded that the administration had rendered the general-in-chief helpless. At least his own record and Craven's would be clear: "Personally I think that the President ought to be impeached & convicted of treasonable weakness in leaving such temptations in the way of the excited & desperate of the South." The South was more excited and desperate than ever; Lincoln was known to be the President-elect.[11]

On the lonely island Meigs had much time to think, and he

[9] Meigs Let. B., 1860, pp. 417–18.
[10] *Ibid.*, p. 439.
[11] *Ibid.*, pp. 451–54.

reflected upon the national government to which he had sworn allegiance, to which he owed his career, and to which he had dedicated his life.

To us on this dot of earth [he wrote] how small the states & state quarrels appear compared with the Great National Confederacy which alone gives value to this sand bank & this reef encircled Harbor. The states are but the bunches of coral millions of which each made up of millions of individual insects make up the reefs which united defend a harbor capable of sheltering the fleets of the world from the assaults of the ocean.[12]

The more he considered the conduct of the Southern secessionists, the angrier he grew.

Am I to be the officer of some contemptible little state republic, some Bolivia or *Keittania* or Calhounia? or Georgia or Pennsylvania[?] instead of the servant of a people stretching their empire from ocean to ocean & touching the confines of the Arctic as they do of the torrid zone a people great in enterprise, science arts commerce & in arms & this because they are free.

Is all this to end in order that slavery not freedom may have greater sway?

Is slavery stronger than freedom? or does the Almighty who punished Israel for desiring a king punish us for boasting of freedom & yet encouraging upholding or tolerating even slavery?

My heart grows sick as I think of this prospect, & yet I believe that even in greatest political trouble there is peace & happiness for those & those only who each hour & minute endeavor to do their duty & I hope to be able to do mine.[13]

In M. C. Meigs the spirit that would sweep across the North in 1861, the almost mystical reverence for the Union, already was rising. But in December, 1860, the spirit still battled with frustration; it scarce received encouragement from the very government it sought to defend.

[12] *Ibid.*, p. 438.
[13] *Ibid.*, p. 457.

> Now is the winter of our discontent
> Made glorious summer by this sun of Scott
> And all the frowns that hovered over our House
> In the deep bosom of the ocean buried.

Yesterday morning a large steamer was reported to me coming from the West.[14]

Thus M. C. Meigs to his father on January 19, 1861. He reported the arrival of the *Joseph Whitney*, out of Boston, carrying to the Tortugas a company of artillery. Meigs's efforts since early November had brought the fort to readiness except for guns and a garrison. Now it had these, and no Ethan Allen would rouse the captain from his sleep.[15]

Few if any of the commanders of fortifications along the Southern coast had responded to the threat of secession with the vigor of M. C. Meigs, but Meigs would have been as helpless as any of those whose posts fell one by one to the seceding states through December and January had he not been rescued by special circumstances. Most important was his isolation. Florida seceded on January 10, 1861, but she lacked the means to mount an expedition over the water to Fort Jefferson. Yet this was not all, for even Fort Pickens in Pensacola harbor remained in Federal hands. The Florida forts were of special importance because they watched over the outlet of the Gulf of Mexico, and at the beginning of January the authorities in Washington took steps to reinforce and hold them.

It was not only General Scott, to whom Meigs's paraphrase of the bard gave credit, who initiated this turn of events. Scott had been aware of the condition of the Southern forts, and he had urged reinforcement even before he received Meigs's letter of November 10.[16] But until the close of 1860 the administra-

---

[14] *Ibid.*, p. 512.
[15] *Ibid.*, pp. 516, 522–24; *O.R.*, ser. 1, I, 346–47.
[16] "Views" of Winfield Scott, Oct. 29, 1860, Scott Papers, L.C.

tion had feared to take any step which might stir antagonism
in the South. The reason was not difficult to find: the voice
of the administration was not that of James Buchanan, but a
synthesis of the strongest voices about him; and through most
of 1860, as through all the preceding years of Buchanan's term,
those voices were chiefly Southern. Howell Cobb of Georgia,
Secretary of the Treasury, John B. Floyd of Virginia, Secretary of War, Jacob Thompson of Mississippi, Secretary of the
Interior—these could carry with them the timid Toucey of
Connecticut, and then Buchanan himself, to overrule Lewis
Cass and Jeremiah Black, the two other Northern members,
and if necessary the border-state Postmaster General, Joseph
Holt of Kentucky. Then the end of 1860 brought a decisive
change.[17]

Howell Cobb resigned on December 9; he had become a
rabid secessionist, and he hurried south to make certain that
Georgia would not waver when the time came to forsake the
Union. Meigs's old nemesis John B. Floyd followed on December 29. The pretext he advanced was Buchanan's failure
to honor a promise that he would do nothing at the forts in
Charleston harbor to injure South Carolina or excite undue
alarm among the Carolinians, who since mid-December were
claiming to be an independent republic. What angered Floyd
was Buchanan's countenancing the transfer of the Charleston
harbor garrison by its commander from Fort Moultrie to the
more defensible Fort Sumter in the middle of the harbor.

The actual reason for Floyd's resignation was the mounting
exposure of mismanagement in the War Department. Scandals
had broken around him so rapidly in 1860 that by late December he was merely awaiting an opportunity to envelop his
departure in a cover of fog. First, there had been the Congres-

[17] Nevins, *Emergence of Lincoln*, II, 357–62; Nichols, *Disruption*, pp.
421–23.

sional inquiries into the public buildings and the explosions emanating from Captain Meigs. Then there had been a clash with Buchanan himself over payments to the Aqueduct brick contractors. Finally, December had brought revelations of misuse of the Indian Trust Fund in a complicated scheme through which Floyd was bolstering the shaky credit of the army's Western transportation contractors. Any President less diffident than Buchanan would have demanded Floyd's resignation immediately; Buchanan kept him on until Floyd found an excuse to leave of his own volition.[18]

Floyd's departure swung the balance of power in the cabinet to the side of the strong Northern, antisecession men whom Buchanan was bringing in as the Southerners departed. Already iron-willed Jeremiah Black had replaced the nearly senile Lewis Cass as Secretary of State, and a truculent Pennsylvania attorney named Edwin M. Stanton had succeeded Black as Attorney General. Now Joseph Holt moved up to become Secretary of War, and Holt's influence paralleled that of Stanton and Black. The Northern ascendancy promptly impelled Jacob Thompson to resign. Meanwhile Holt closeted himself with Winfield Scott, and both the Secretary and the general turned their eyes toward the Florida forts. It was because of their conference and of the newly inspirited policy of the cabinet that Captain Meigs saw a steamer approaching Fort Jefferson nine days after Florida passed her ordinance of secession.[19]

The *Joseph Whitney* carried from Boston five commissioned officers and sixty-two enlisted men to garrison Fort Jefferson; their commander, Brevet Major L. G. Arnold, assumed command of the fort. Meigs remained as chief engineer. Arnold

[18] 36:1 *Congressional Globe*, pt. 2, 2752–55; Nichols, *Disruption*, pp. 423–26; Nevins, *Emergence of Lincoln*, II, 372–74.

[19] Scott to Holt, Jan. 3, 1861, Scott Papers, L.C.; Nichols, *Disruption*, p. 433; Nevins, *Emergence of Lincoln*, II, 382; Elliott, *Winfield Scott*, p. 685.

brought with him only two field pieces, and Meigs advised
him that Fort Taylor contained more guns than its garrison
could well use; consequently the major sent Meigs with a
lieutenant of artillery to seek armaments at Key West. The
*Whitney* returned with six eight-inch columbiads, four field
pieces, and an ample supply of ammunition. By evening of
January 23 the guns were in place, one columbiad to each
face of the fort; and Captain Meigs was rejoicing over the
reinforcement as a great strategic coup at a turning point in
his country's history. "The best thing for us individually here
& for the Union at home," he wrote his father, "would be the
appearance off this Harbor of the ten thousand said to have
been offered by Louisiana to Florida to take this place."

A few days later a more considered judgment left him less
complacent; he urged that Fort Taylor be called on for still
more guns, since with only one columbiad to a front Jefferson
rested none too securely. A single shot hitting one of the guns
or its carriage, a single gun's bursting, would leave one sixth
of the circumference of the fort an unoccupied field of fire;
a hostile vessel could take position there and bombard the fort
unharmed. But there was no cause for despair, since the new
decisiveness of the administration continued in evidence. On
February 2 the sloop-of-war *Brooklyn* hove to off Fort Jefferson to land a few light howitzers before proceeding to Fort
Pickens with eighty-five men under Captain Israel Vogdes to
reinforce the artillery company already there. If Florida attempted to take the forts now, she would have to fight for
them.[20]

On February 13 Meigs's exile came to an abrupt end. The
mail steamer *Tortugas* landed bearing orders from the War

[20] Scott to Holt, Monday [Jan. 4, 1861], Scott to Holt, Memorandum,
Jan., 1861, Scott Papers, L.C. (copies in additions to Joseph Holt Papers,
L.C.); Meigs Let. B., 1860–1861, pp. 522–24.

Department to turn over the engineering duties at the fort to Lieutenant C. B. Reese, who had arrived from New Orleans the day before, and to return to Washington at once to resume charge of the Aqueduct. Two hours after he received the orders Meigs was sailing northward.[21]

On the evening of February 20 he was back in the capital, four months less two days after his departure. The next day he called with General Totten on Secretary Holt and Lieutenant General Scott; on the 22nd, Washington's Birthday, amidst much show of soldiers who were arriving in town to maintain order at the forthcoming inauguration of Abraham Lincoln, he walked with Louisa to Cabin John Bridge. He was home again, and his stand against Secretary Floyd had won public vindication.[22]

Everywhere Meigs found himself the object of outstretched hands and felicitations. Secretary Holt was particularly warm in his greetings, and he expressed heartily his appreciation of the energy Meigs had shown in strengthening Fort Jefferson.

Captain, we are delighted with the tone and spirit of your letters. We were deceived as to the condition of Fort Jefferson. The President had been led to suppose it entirely indefensible, a mere heap of rocks. We lost not a day when we learned the true state of the case, but we much feared that a small expedition would come before us and would cut you off.

Holt's advisers had learned something of the mettle of Captain Meigs: "But they told me that you would fight them with handspikes if you had nothing else."

Better than that, the Secretary welcomed Meigs by reassigning him to the Capitol as well as the Aqueduct. Captain Franklin received the headship of the Bureau of Construction of the Treasury Department, with control over the comple-

---

[21] Meigs Diary, Feb. 13, 1861.
[22] *Ibid.*, Feb. 20–22, 1861; Meigs Let. B., 1860–1861, p. 562.

tion of the Treasury Building and of new custom houses throughout the country. "Has it not been well done[?]" Meigs wrote. "It is like the movement of a tragedy of Euripedes in which justice after long delay is meted out with equal scales to all the persons in the drama." [23]

Meigs met Buchanan once more at a White House reception, and he could not resist casting a barb. "I have come back, Mr. President," he said, "to pay my respects and to thank you for justice *speedy as your knowledge of the truth*." Unhappily, he doubted that the President saw the point. Buchanan was not looking well:

His haggard face his cadaverous complexion his hollow eye his tottering gait tell the fearful tale of the ravages of the place, he so keenly sought so unfairly won & to which he proved so unequal, upon the physical frame & the mental organization. . . . Poor weak unhappy old man For him now no one who looks at him can feel any emotion more harsh than pity.[24]

What mattered to Captain Meigs was that he had found justice and vindication at last. Old Francis Preston Blair summed it up for the captain's friends: "They sent Meigs to gather a thistle, but thank God, he has plucked a laurel." [25] He had gained a reputation for integrity that would carry him far now that his personal battle was won, and he turned his attention to the greater battle for the nation.

A blustery wind swirled clouds of dust up Pennsylvania Avenue, and the crowds moving toward the Capitol, where the Senate still sat, lowered their heads and squinted their eyes. At the market stalls lining the avenue out-of-town visitors were looking for benches and tables soft enough to provide a resting place for the night. The blue uniforms of the regular

[23] Meigs Let. B., 1860–1861, pp. 573–76.
[24] *Ibid.*, pp. 576–79.
[25] *Ibid.*, p. 581.

army and the gay coats of the militia companies were much in evidence. Armed guards watched the temporary speakers' platform in front of the Capitol. It was the evening of March 3, 1861; next day, if Winfield Scott's soldiery could prevent Southern fire-eaters from carrying out their threats, or if the threats had been mere braggadocio, Abraham Lincoln would be inaugurated as the sixteenth President of the United States.

Meigs was a Douglas Democrat, not a Lincoln man. For this and deeper reasons he looked toward the future with little cheer. This evening he penned a note to his brother Charles in Indiana:

I see no escape [from war]. Should the new administration even fail to execute the laws prove false to its oaths & recreant to its trusts still other disputes would lead to border clashes. These to war & the bitter controversy would be settled by victory of the stronger & the defeat of the weaker.

Tomorrow Lincoln will be inaugurated. I have not yet seen him. I hope the prints do him injustice. He certainly does not seem to come much to the level of the great mission & I fear that a weak hand will command the ship & interfere with the strong & wise one which holds the helm of state [that is, with Seward's]. But in God is my trust He knows what is for our good & if he intends to take us throgh fiery trials I doubt not in the end freedom & man may gain.[26]

The next day Meigs stood in the pressing crowd that watched and listened when the tall man from Illinois rose to deliver his inaugural. The moment was electric with a sense of great events come to a focus. What sort of man would the new President prove to be? Was he as weak as Meigs and so many others feared?

That night the captain wrote another letter, this time to his brother John in Philadelphia:

We have a government at last. It was formed about one o'clock today when Abraham Lincoln from the steps of the Capitol an-

[26] *Ibid.*, pp. 583–84.

nounced that the Union of these states was & is perpetual & that
he was about to register an oath to preserve protect & defend the
constitution of the United States & to execute the laws.

It was a noble speech as delivered, delivered with a serious &
solemn emphasis befitting the occasion. No time was wasted in
generalities or platitudes but he grappled at once with his subject
& no one could doubt that he meant what he said. No point was
omitted no reference made to foreign entanglements, but the disease of the body politic was analysed, its character & its remedy
pointed out, & each sentence fell like a sledge hammer driving
in the nails which maintain states.

Kind & conciliatory it still left no loop hole for treason. . . .

Fort Sumter will be reinforced unless it has already been seized,
& this I do not believe possible. Pickens will be filled with troops
& our Forts on the reef of Florida are henceforth safe for the
Union.

War I fear will come but it will be conducted humanely tem-
perately & in such wise as to let this wild passion wear itself out.
If they bite they bite against a file. He will defend & protect the
public property, he will collect the duties & imposts, he will enforce the laws wherever he has the power & once more will freedom of speech & liberty of person be the rule of all our land, &
not the exception.

The impression is favorable . . . the people about me . . . applauded each sentence. Some . . . looked darkly & retired. Treason shrank out of sight & loyalty sat in the sun light. The country
is safe though there is yet tribulation . . . on it. . . .

I have had much talk in the last few days in the Senate chamber
with republican & other Senators. I feared until last night that
some weak shilly shally policy would prevail that we had a chief
with no character a buffoon. . . . When Trumbull who repre-
sents him, spoke though for himself alone that no govt could
give up Sumter without disgrace—it put into every patriotic heart
new strength & hope.[27]

Captain Meigs was determined that the Union must be preserved, and from the secession of South Carolina onward he

[27] *Ibid.*, pp. 586–89.

believed with increasing conviction that this end could be attained only by war. Abraham Lincoln was equally determined to save the Union, but he was not so sure that his determination necessarily implied war.

When Lincoln spoke in his inaugural of holding, occupying, and possessing the property and places belonging to the government, he was referring most obviously to Fort Sumter, in Charleston harbor, and to Fort Pickens, in the harbor of Pensacola. Forts Jefferson and Taylor on the Florida reef were too distant from the mainland to be of immediate importance. Meigs thought that holding Sumter and Pickens in itself meant war; the Southern Confederacy into which the seceded states had united had seized all the other Federal outposts on its soil, and logic demanded that it seize these as well. If Washington would hold them, believed Meigs, presently it must fight for them.[28]

Lincoln was not so sure. At Fort Pickens the Buchanan administration had acquiesced in a quasi-truce arranged by ex-Senator Stephen R. Mallory of Florida, with the Confederates agreeing not to attack so long as the Union did not relieve or reinforce. A not entirely dissimilar situation existed at Sumter; but there such a truce as existed was tacit rather than explicit, and South Carolina was quite likely to push the Confederacy into breaking it. Perhaps the quiet at Pickens and Sumter could be maintained into the indefinite future, so that Union sentiment in the South might have time to rally, or so that in some other way events might move toward a solution without recourse to bloodshed and arms.[29]

Unfortunately for Lincoln's hopes of peace, the Sumter situation had developed into an ugly dilemma about the very

[28] Meigs Let. B., 1860–1861, p. 589; *O.R.*, ser. 1, I, 368.
[29] Buchanan to Holt, Holt Papers, XXVI, 3547b–47c, L.C.; *O.R.*, ser. 1, I, 355–56; James G. Randall, *Lincoln the President* (4 vols., New York, 1945–1955), I, 317–21.

time of his inauguration. The Charleston authorities had been allowing Major Robert Anderson, commander of the artillery company which garrisoned Fort Sumter, to purchase meat in Charleston; at the close of February they denied him this source of supplies. This meant that unless Anderson received provisions from the North, he could hold the fort for only about six weeks. Thus the status quo could not continue beyond approximately the 15th of April. If Lincoln did not resolve to abandon Sumter by that time, he would have to provision it; and given the razor-sharp tempers of the Confederate authorities and especially of the South Carolinians, to send even a small relief expedition might provoke war. Buchanan had already attempted to send supplies and additional troops to Sumter; when his relief ship, the *Star of the West*, entered Charleston harbor on January 9, she had been turned back by South Carolina artillery.[30]

This raised the question whether to hold Fort Sumter really was necessary. The principal reason for wishing to maintain a foothold on Federal property in the South was psychological, in order to demonstrate that the Federal government not only refused to recognize in theory the right of secession, but that it also refused to abandon in practice its claims to property in the Southern states. Already most of the Federal forts in the seceded states had fallen into Confederate hands, so that by this time the important thing was simply not to abandon all the forts. At least one must be kept as a symbol. But need that one be Sumter? Fort Pickens was also in Federal hands, and the situation at Pensacola was far less explosive than at Charleston, where Fort Sumter flaunted the Stars and Stripes in the very center and principal Atlantic port of secessionism. Perhaps Lincoln should abandon Sumter and merely hold Pickens.

[30] Randall, *Lincoln the President*, I, 317–21; Nevins, *Emergence of Lincoln*, II, 461–62; Williams, *Lincoln Finds a General*, I, 35–37.

Lincoln had to consider also the attitude of the border states. So far, the Southern Confederacy included only seven members, with nothing north of South Carolina. Virginia's course was likely to prove decisive for the slave states not yet committed to secession, and in Virginia a state convention was debating the role of the state. The convention was not yet ready to vote secession, but if Lincoln raised an angry hand toward the Confederacy, he was likely to push Virginia into joining it. Especially was he likely to do so if he unwittingly set off an explosion in Charleston harbor.[31]

Lincoln probably went through all of March still uncertain whether he would abandon Fort Sumter or attempt to hold it, which meant sending a relief expedition. With Fort Pickens the situation was different; that place he was sure he would attempt to hold. On March 12 he ordered that Fort Pickens be reinforced.[32]

On February 2 Captain Meigs at Fort Jefferson had seen the sloop-of-war *Brooklyn* stop briefly in Tortugas harbor before continuing to Pensacola. On board were Captain Israel Vogdes and a company of the 1st Artillery bound for Fort Pickens. Already Pickens was the only one of the three Pensacola fortifications left in Federal hands. Lieutenant Adam J. Slemmer, who commanded the company stationed at Pensacola, considered Forts Barrancas and McRee, both of them on the mainland, untenable with his present strength, and on the day Florida seceded he moved his whole command to Fort Pickens, which lay on Santa Rosa Island in Pensacola harbor.

It was to reinforce Slemmer that Vogdes was proceeding when his path crossed that of Captain Meigs. But the local

[31] Randall, *Lincoln the President*, I, 319–28; John G. Nicolay and John Hay, *Abraham Lincoln: A History* (10 vols., New York, 1890), III, 375–95; Benjamin P. Thomas, *Abraham Lincoln* (New York, 1952), 251–52.

[32] Randall, *Lincoln the President*, I, 331.

understanding of Buchanan's Pickens truce plus a miscarriage
of orders after Lincoln took office prevented Vogdes from
landing. Toward the end of March, Lincoln was disturbed
to learn that Vogdes's reinforcement even now had not debarked on Santa Rosa Island.[33]

Time was running short. If Lincoln were to abandon Fort
Sumter, then he must hold Fort Pickens. If there existed a real
danger of losing Pickens, then he must make an effort to hold
Sumter. But at Sumter he must act soon. If Lincoln expected
to retain that place he must set in motion a relief expedition
which would reach it by April 15, the date when Sumter's
provisions would be exhausted. Therefore Lincoln had to possess a reasonable certainty that Fort Pickens was safe by the
first few days of April at the latest; otherwise he would have
to send relief ships toward Charleston harbor.

To complicate Lincoln's problem further, it now began to
appear questionable whether Captain Vogdes's company was
a large enough reinforcement to afford Pickens so much as
temporary security even if it did land. General Scott thought
not. What was worse, General Scott began to argue that in
the present state of the government's resources, Fort Pickens
could not be rendered secure at all; neither could Fort Sumter.
Scott estimated that it would require 20,000 troops to break
into Charleston harbor against the Confederate batteries surrounding the harbor and the fort, and there were only some
17,000 in the whole regular army. These troops simply had

[33] *O.R.*, ser. 1, I, 351–52, 355–56; Buchanan to Holt, Holt Papers, XXVI,
3547b–47c; Erasmus D. Keyes, *Fifty Years Observation of Men and
Events, Civil and Military* (New York, 1884), p. 379; Captain R. S.
Adams to Welles, April 1, 1861, Welles Papers, L.C.; *The War of the
Rebellion. A Compilation of the Official Records of the Union and
Confederate Navies* (26 vols., Washington, 1894–1922), ser. 1, IV, 109–
10; Meigs to Seward, April 1, 1861, Lincoln Papers, XXXIX, 8645–46,
L.C.; Meigs Journal, March 31, 1861, printed in *American Historical
Review*, XXVI (1920–1921), 299–303.

too much to do. From them it would be impossible to dredge
even the 1,200 men who were supposed to form the war garrison of Fort Pickens; the administration might as well ask
for 1,200 camels or elephants. General Totten, the chief engineer, agreed with General Scott. Lincoln was not ready to
throw up his hands in despair, but what else could he do? [84]

Secretary of State William Seward had a special interest in
succoring Fort Pickens. Like Lincoln he believed that by all
means one of the forts must be held, and unlike Lincoln he
had long since made up his mind that for political reasons it
could not be Sumter. He was inclined to agree that the military factors also made the Sumter situation an impossible one,
although he never claimed to be a military expert. Nevertheless, Seward was not willing to accept General Scott's de-
featism so far as Fort Pickens was concerned. He thought that
at least an attempt should be made to hold it, and since he
knew that he was not competent to challenge Scott on military
matters, he began to consider finding someone who might be.
This line of thought led directly to Seward's old friend, the
superintendent of the public works, Captain Meigs, who had
just returned from Florida. Seward suggested to Lincoln that
they have a talk with Meigs, and the President agreed.

This was Friday, March 20. Meigs returned home from a
trip to Great Falls to discover a request from the Secretary
of State that he come immediately to see him. He found Seward, and the Secretary announced that he wanted Meigs to
speak with the President. As the two men walked across the
lawn from the State Department to the White House, Seward
explained that the administration was in a corner on the question of the forts and that he thought the President should talk
with a soldier who could discuss military affairs from a pro-

[84] Randall, *Lincoln the President*, I, 332–33; Keyes, *Fifty Years*, p. 377;
Meigs Journal, April 16, 1861, copy in John G. Nicolay Papers, L.C.

fessional knowledge without injecting politics into the subject and who was capable of mounting a horse and taking the
field. They had heard General Scott and General Totten, but
no one would think of putting either of those old men on
horseback.

For the first time Captain Meigs was ushered into the presence of Abraham Lincoln. The President talked freely about
the forts, doubtless stressing his own determination to hold
one of them and the opinions of his senior military advisers
that it could not be done. Meigs said he believed enough men
could be found to volunteer to attempt to relieve Sumter, but
that persons of higher rank thought it should not be attempted,
that Sumter was not the place to begin the war. He did not
think he should quarrel with such considerations on the part
of his superiors. Lincoln then asked the direct question whether
Fort Pickens could be held. Meigs replied that it could be,
certainly, so long as the navy had done its duty and had not
lost the place already.

This was the sort of clear-cut answer that Abraham Lincoln
liked to hear, and he was generally willing to give anyone who
could speak softly but decisively an opportunity to act in that
way. He asked Meigs whether he could not go to Florida and
take command of Pickens, Taylor, and Jefferson. Meigs replied that he could not. He was only a captain, and he could
not command the majors who were already there.

At this point Seward broke in. "I can understand how that
is, Captain Meigs," he said; "you have got to be promoted."

Again Meigs replied that it could not be done; he was
merely a captain, and there was no vacancy just above him.

Nevertheless, Seward said to Lincoln, if the President wanted
this job done he should put it into Meigs's charge, and it would
be done. Captain Meigs could give an estimate of the means
required by four the next afternoon. Seward reminded the

President that the elder Pitt had reached far down into the officer list to find James Wolfe and send him to capture Quebec.

Lincoln did not allow himself to be rushed into a decision. The opinions of Scott and Totten were not to be ignored. He told Meigs he would consider the problem and let the captain know his decision in a day or two.[35]

When General Scott on March 28 had told Lincoln that the plights of both Pickens and Sumter were hopeless, Lincoln had replied that his administration must soon either do something about the forts or break up. Scott had better think of something to do, or Lincoln would find someone else who would. General Scott was the hero of Lundy's Lane and Chapultepec, and he was more than aware of his prerogatives as the personal embodiment of American prowess in arms. He was not accustomed to seeing his military remarks questioned by civilians. Wreathed in gold braid and indignation, he stalked homeward to prepare a written vindication of his views on the forts.[36]

March 31 was Easter Sunday, but the thoughts of the President, Seward, and General Scott were distinctly secular. In the morning Scott was still working on the memorandum for the enlightenment of Lincoln which he had begun the night before. At breakfast he discharged some of his thoughts upon his military secretary, Lieutenant Colonel Erasmus Keyes, and he encouraged Keyes to agree with him. The colonel knew what was expected, and he proceeded to dwell upon the difficulties of reinforcing Fort Pickens. He discussed the problems of landing heavy guns, gun carriages, and ammunition on the

[35] Meigs Journal, March 29, 1861, copy in Nicolay Papers, L.C.; *A.H.R.*, XXVI, 299–300.
[36] Keyes, *Fifty Years*, pp. 377–79.

sandy beaches of Santa Rosa Island and carrying them across
the sand to the fort; he said it would be futile to attempt a
weak-handed reinforcement.

When Keyes finished, Scott wheeled in his chair and pulled
from a pile of rolled-up maps and papers a document which
turned out to be a map of Pensacola harbor. "Take this map
to Mr. Seward," he said, "and repeat to him exactly what you
have said to me about the difficulty of reinforcing Fort
Pickens." Scott intended to squelch the primary advocate of
the Pickens expedition; one thing he failed to consider was
that his secretary had merely said that reinforcing Pickens
would be difficult. Keyes had not used the word impossible.

Colonel Keyes, brisk and officious in manner, marched to
Seward's house on F Street, entered, and found the little Secretary standing in the middle of the parlor, thinking. Seward
also had Fort Pickens on his mind that morning, and his
thoughts once again had fallen upon Captain Meigs. When
Keyes told him that he was sent by General Scott to explain
the difficulties of reinforcing Fort Pickens, Seward replied
that he did not care about the difficulties and asked Keyes
if he knew where to find Captain Meigs.

"I suppose he's at his house, sir," Keyes replied, not knowing
what to make of the question.

"Please find him and bring him here."

This was an odd turn of events. "I'll call and bring him on
my return from church," Keyes replied.

"Never mind church today," said Seward. "I wish to see him
and you together without delay."

Keyes entertained a brief thought of rebellion—after all, why
should the Secretary of State be ordering him about so sharply,
and on a mysterious errand at that—but he had cultivated the
habit of obedience, and he obeyed. He found Meigs about to
leave home for St. John's Church, and he diverted the captain

to Seward's. The Secretary of State told the two officers he wanted them to prepare estimates and practicable plans for relieving and holding Fort Pickens, and that they should do it by four that afternoon. They were to consult with General Scott and to appear at the White House, plans in hand, at four.[37]

Meigs and Keyes proceeded to the office of the Engineer Department, where Meigs quickly found maps and plans of Pensacola harbor and Fort Pickens. They spread these maps across several tables and set to work, studying and writing independently. They prepared lists of everything an almost empty fort would require, not only stipulating the number of troops of each of the various arms needed to prepare Fort Pickens for assault or siege, but drawing up tables of stores and provisions, calculating the weight and bulk of such items, and then estimating the tonnage of shipping needed to get them to Pensacola. When they finished they discovered they no longer had time to visit General Scott and still return to the White House by four. Accordingly, they went straight to the President's mansion.

They found Lincoln and Seward awaiting them, the President sprawled across his office furniture with one leg resting on a table, the other on a chair, his hands clasped behind his head. Seward asked the officers to report. Keyes hesitated, on the ground that he had not yet seen Scott. To Meigs this consideration of tact did not matter; he read his plan, and Keyes reluctantly followed him.

The two plans differed only in emphasis and detail. Meigs stressed the engineering problems, while Keyes, an artilleryman, discussed at length the problems of the guns. When the officers finished, Lincoln told them to see General Scott and put their ideas into execution immediately. They were to in-

[37] Keyes, *Fifty Years*, pp. 380–81; Meigs Journal, March 31, 1861, copy in Nicolay Papers, L.C.; *A.H.R.*, XXVI, 300.

form Scott that they acted under orders from the President, that Lincoln wanted Fort Pickens secured, and that Scott was not to fail them unless he could show Lincoln why refusing them something they asked was necessary. "I depend upon you gentlemen to push this thing through," were Lincoln's words as they left.

Meigs and Keyes went next to Scott's house. Scott demanded to know where Keyes had been all day, and when the colonel explained what had happened, it was obvious that Scott did not enjoy the way in which Seward and the President had short-circuited him. Nevertheless, the lieutenant general looked over the plans and approved them.[38]

The next morning Meigs and Keyes set to work in earnest in Scott's office. They selected Colonel Harvey Brown of the artillery to command the relief forces. Meigs would accompany him to Pensacola as chief engineer and would remain there until Fort Pickens was secure, when he would return to Washington and the public works. In New York Meigs and Keyes would charter a steamer, and Brown would sail as soon as possible with a company of artillery, two companies of infantry, and the Engineer Company of Sappers and Miners. The companies were to be filled to maximum standards. Colonel Keyes would send additional troops to follow in later vessels. The object and destination of the expedition were to be divulged to no one for whom the knowledge was not absolutely necessary. If the expedition were fired on, it was to defend itself. Colonel Brown was to establish his main depot and base of operations at Fort Jefferson. He was to be careful not to reduce too much the defenses of Jefferson and Taylor, since these fortresses were considered more important even than Pickens. But to hold Fort Pickens was his principal object; and to en-

[38] Meigs Journal, March 31, 1861, copy in Nicolay Papers, L.C.; *A.H.R.*, XXVI, 300–302; Keyes, *Fifty Years*, pp. 381–85.

sure that he would never lack for aid and cooperation, he received special orders from the President to display when necessary:

Executive Mansion, April 1, 1861.
All officers of the Army and Navy, to whom this order may be exhibited, will aid by every means in their power the expedition under the command of Col. Harvey Brown, supplying him with men and material and co-operating with him as he may desire.

A. Lincoln.[39]

Among those who would be expected to cooperate with Colonel Brown were the naval officers already stationed off Pensacola. But the plans of Meigs and Keyes called also for an especially powerful warship which would enter the harbor itself and take station there to intercept any Confederate expedition attempting to cross from the mainland to Santa Rosa Island. To this end Captain Meigs went again to the White House on Monday morning and with Seward's aid received an order assigning Lieutenant David Dixon Porter of the navy, a young, ambitious, and somewhat theatrical officer, to the Pickens expedition. To Porter's command the order transferred the steam frigate *Powhatan*, which lay in New York harbor undergoing repairs.[40]

Brown, Keyes, and Porter left Washington for New York on Tuesday. Meigs completed drawing up plans in Washington and followed his comrades on Wednesday, the 3rd, taking with him $10,000 advanced to the expedition by Seward from the secret service funds of the State Department. Meanwhile Keyes inspected vessels in New York harbor and chartered two of the

---

[39] *O.R.*, ser. 1, I, 367.
[40] Meigs Journal, April 1, 1861, copy in Nicolay Papers, L.C.; *A.H.R.*, XXVI, 301; David Dixon Porter, *Incidents and Anecdotes of the Civil War* (New York, 1885). Porter brings himself to the scene earlier than he appears in the other accounts, but the weight of Meigs's and Keyes's evidence is against him.

sturdiest and fastest he could find, the Collins steamer *Atlantic* and the Vanderbilt liner *Illinois*. He later added the steamer *Philadelphia*. Lieutenant Porter proceeded to the navy yard to try his hand at taking over the *Powhatan*, a task which proved delicate even with orders from the President, since so secretly was the expedition being planned that the Navy Department had not yet been informed of it and was not supposed to be.[41]

When Meigs arrived in New York he joined Keyes in supervising the loading of the *Atlantic*, which with no time to be lost was no small task. With difficulty the stevedores pushed, rolled, and hoisted into place the heavy ordnance gathered to strengthen the fire power of Fort Pickens; with difficulty a herd of horses was secured upon the forward deck. The horses were Meigs's idea, and they served a multiple purpose. For one thing, they helped to blind observers in New York to the destination of the expedition; no one expected that a load of horses would be going to a fort. Even Meigs's old engineering instructor at West Point, Dennis Mahan, was thrown off the scent by this move; yet it was because Meigs had remembered Mahan's teaching that the horses were going. Mahan had maintained that a mobile battery of light artillery was always essential to a fortified place. The horses would give mobility to the light guns of Santa Rosa Island; they would be available for picket duty, and they could help transport supplies from the ships to the fort.[42]

On Friday evening, April 5, the planners were jolted by the arrival of a dispatch from Secretary of the Navy Gideon Welles ordering the *Powhatan* to be detained in harbor. The mercurial Porter flew into a rage. He swore he would do nothing more for this vacillating government, he would go to California

[41] Meigs Journal, April 2–4, 1861, copy in Nicolay Papers, L.C.; *A.H.R.*, XXVI, 301; Keyes, *Fifty Years*, pp. 387–88; Porter, *Incidents*, pp. 16–20.
[42] Meigs Journal, April 4–5, 19, 1861, copy in Nicolay Papers, L.C.; *A.H.R.*, XXVI, 301.

to spend his time surveying. Meigs tried to quiet him and resolved to resist Welles's order; after all, he and Porter held their authority directly from the President. The next morning Meigs found Captain Samuel Mercer, the *Powhatan*'s regular commander whom Porter had relieved, trying to regain control of his ship. Meigs argued that no orders from a cabinet minister could countermand his own instructions from the President. The *Powhatan* was assigned to the Meigs-Porter-Keyes expedition by Lincoln himself, she was an essential part of the expedition, and no one had a right to take her, since Meigs was responsible to Lincoln alone and under instructions not to let even Secretary Welles know that the expedition was being prepared. An order from the Secretary of the Navy should have seemed sufficiently impressive to impel Meigs to consult with Lincoln or Seward to determine whether there had been a change of plan, but with his usual headstrongness, Meigs made no effort in that direction. He overbore Captain Mercer, and at noon Lieutenant Porter took the *Powhatan* down the harbor.[43]

Porter was not yet safe from interference. Word of the conflict in orders reached Welles in Washington on the night of the 6th. Welles hastened to Seward demanding to know what was afoot, and the two of them stormed into the White House about midnight to insist that Lincoln clear up the muddle.[44] What had occurred was a breakdown in administration. Lincoln had not yet secured a tight enough hold upon the reins of government to compel his cabinet to function as a team. Seward continued to regard himself as the "premier" and real head of the administration, and the result was that the Navy

[43] Meigs Journal, April 5–6, 1861, copy in Nicolay Papers, L.C.; *A.H.R.*, XXVI, 301–2; Porter, *Incidents*, pp. 20–21; Keyes, *Fifty Years*, p. 393; Nicolay and Hay, *Lincoln*, IV, 3–5.
[44] Gideon Welles, *Diary of Gideon Welles* (3 vols., Boston, 1911), I, 23–24.

and State Departments were pulling in different directions. What was worse, Lincoln had allowed Seward not only to meddle in army and navy matters outside his own proper sphere, but to assign military and naval officers, personnel, and supplies to a venture of his own choosing without so much as informing Secretary of War Simon Cameron or Navy Secretary Gideon Welles. The fact that Cameron was a crafty Pennsylvania politician who should never have received the War Department was no excuse for ignoring him now that he was there; and Welles was quite as capable of handling the navy as Seward.

When Meigs, Keyes, and Porter began preparing their expedition on April 1, as far as Washington knew Captain Vogdes's troops had not yet landed on Santa Rosa Island. On March 27 Major Zealous Tower of the Corps of Engineers wrote to Meigs from Pensacola harbor that Captain R. S. Adams, the naval officer in charge, would not permit a landing for fear of violating the local truce, and Meigs apparently received the letter on April 1 or 2; he passed the information on to Seward, and Seward conveyed it to Lincoln.[45]

Already the uncertainty of the Pickens situation had impelled Lincoln to order that an expedition to relieve Fort Sumter be prepared. If the President were not reasonably certain within a few days that Pickens could be held, he would have to order the Sumter expedition to sea. Like the Pickens expedition, the one intended for Fort Sumter was preparing in New York, this one under the supervision of the Assistant Secretary of the Navy, Gustavus V. Fox.

On April 5 Gideon Welles decided that the Sumter expedition would need the powerful guns of the *Powhatan* if it were to force its way into Charleston harbor, and for this

[45] Meigs to Seward, April 1, 1861 [?], Lincoln Papers, XXXIX, 8645–46, L.C.

reason he sent his telegram ordering the *Powhatan* to be held in New York. He did not know of Lieutenant Porter's orders to take charge of the *Powhatan;* he simply wanted to ensure that the *Powhatan* would be available. The only man who could have known of both expeditions was the President, and indeed Welles had read his orders concerning the *Powhatan* to Lincoln the day before he sent them. But the President had merely attached a perfunctory signature to Porter's orders a few days before, and now the name of the steam frigate failed to register with him; he did not discern the conflict in instructions.[46]

By the night of April 6, then, the *Powhatan* was moving down New York Bay on her way to Fort Pickens; and by the night of April 6, unhappily, the Sumter expedition had become more important than the Meigs-Keyes-Porter plan for the relief of Pickens. On April 6 Gideon Welles received a dispatch from Captain Adams at Pensacola explaining that that officer would allow no troops to go ashore at Fort Pickens until he received explicit orders from the Navy Department, since his last orders from the department, dating from the Buchanan administration, had forbidden a landing. New instructions, of course, should have gone to him long ago; certainly the circuit prompting their dispatch should have been completed when Meigs forwarded to Seward Major Tower's letter at the very beginning of the month. But it was another indication of the immaturity of the Lincoln administration at this point that no one had thought of them. Now Welles got off an immediate order telling Adams to forget about the Buchanan truce and put Captain Vogdes's company ashore; but it was too late to count on this order's reaching Adams by April 15. It was too late, in short, to ensure that Pickens would be safe by the time Sumter

[46] Welles, *Diary,* I, 21–25; Nicolay and Hay, *Lincoln,* IV, 5–6; Randall, *Lincoln the President,* I, 333–37.

would have to be either relieved or abandoned. Thus the sailing of the Sumter expedition became imperative, and Welles believed that the Sumter expedition must include the *Powhatan*.[47]

When Seward and Welles confronted him with their tales of woe on the night of the 6th, Lincoln immediately grasped the situation and recognized what had gone wrong—he had failed to recall his earlier order for the *Powhatan* when Welles read him the order of April 5. Seward argued that it was too late to correct the mistake, and that anyway to snatch the *Powhatan* from the Pickens expedition would ruin that gambit; Seward continued indifferent to the fate of Sumter. To Lincoln, however, the Sumter expedition appeared now to be a necessity, and if Welles thought it required the *Powhatan*, then the *Powhatan* it should have. He ordered Seward to telegraph New York at once to hold the *Powhatan*. Seward protested that it was rather late for a telegram to go through; Lincoln said do it.

Seward sent out to Lieutenant Porter a telegram which read: "Give up the *Pohatan* to Mercer." Whether he was being devious or merely careless when he signed the dispatch it would be interesting to know; he signed it "Seward." The *Powhatan* was well down the bay when the telegram reached the navy yard, but the commander of the yard hurried a fast tug after her. The tug caught the vessel, and Porter read the telegram. He refused to obey it. Here was simply another dispatch from a cabinet minister, this time not even from the Secretary of the Navy, and Porter carried orders signed by the President. He would proceed on his way.

He knew, of course, that the expedition of which he was a part had been largely Seward's project in the first place. One

---

[47] Welles to Captain R. S. Adams, Welles Papers, XLIV, 27409-10, L.C.; Welles, *Diary*, I, 24-26, 28-31; Nicolay and Hay, *Lincoln*, IV, 7-8; Randall, *Lincoln the President*, I, 337.

would have expected him, as one would have expected it of
Meigs earlier in the day, to take pause. But David Porter, like
M. C. Meigs, had become thoroughly enamored of the Pickens
expedition, and neither man was accustomed to finding himself
in error. That the *Powhatan* could have saved Fort Sumter for
the Union is a dubious proposition, but Lincoln would have
liked to give it a try, and Seward's meddling beyond the affairs
of his own department combined with the high-handed
methods of Meigs and Porter to thwart him.[48]

Captain Meigs himself set sail in the steamer *Atlantic* at
three in the morning on April 7, the same morning when
Seward and Welles quarreled at the White House. The ship
carried five companies of soldiers and seventy-three sailors.
Meigs's mood was one of confident satisfaction. He wrote in
his journal,

Well, Keyes and I have done our duty and set a ball in motion.
Porter, the officer whom the whole Navy by acclaim selected
from the profession, is on his way into the harbor of Pensacola
and into it he will go, God permitting, for man will not be able
to prevent him.[49]

The *Atlantic* struck a storm off Cape Hatteras, and for
twenty-four hours she lay head to wind, while her captain
swore that never but once had he seen so heavy a sea. The
horses lurched and kicked above her bow, and Meigs watched
them anxiously. But when the wind died and the sky cleared
only one was lost, and Meigs hurried to write to Secretary
Seward urging that the *Atlantic*'s sister ship, the *Baltic*, be
chartered from the Collins line before she fell into British or
Confederate hands—few ships so laden could have ridden

[48] Welles, *Diary*, I, 24–28; Porter, *Incidents*, pp. 21–23; Nicolay and
Hay, *Lincoln*, IV, 6; Randall, *Lincoln the President*, I, 337–39.
[49] Meigs Journal, April 7–8, 1861, copy in Nicolay Papers, L.C.; *A.H.R.*,
XXVI, 302; *O.R.*, ser. 1, I, 368.

through a Hatteras storm with a herd of horses aboard and suffered so little loss.

The ship was a hundred miles off her course when the storm ended, 138 miles east-southeast of Hatteras. On the morning of April 13 she put into the harbor of Key West, where the Stars and Stripes on the flagstaff of Fort Taylor frowned at the Stars and Bars which flew from the courthouse. Here Captain Meigs had civil business to transact. Judge Marvin of the United States District Court was loyal to the Union, but his clerk, marshal, and district attorney had resigned to leave him paralysed. Meigs brought commissions for new Federal officers, called the judge and the new officeholders together, and assured them that the United States intended to hold Key West, the largest town in Florida, and to support their authority. He left a proclamation for the declaration of martial law to be issued if necessary. His visit greatly strengthened the hand of the Union men; presently they proclaimed martial law, and secessionism at Key West was crushed.

At ten A.M. on the 14th Captain Meigs returned to Fort Jefferson. The *Atlantic* stayed there only long enough to pick up four light howitzers, some boxes of ammunition, and twenty Negro laborers; some of the blacks were said to be slaves belonging to ex-Senator Stephen Mallory, now Confederate Secretary of the Navy.[50]

Through the next two days the *Atlantic* ran before a fair wind for Pensacola; and on April 16, ten days from New York, she came in sight of the United States fleet anchored off the harbor. The *Powhatan* had not yet arrived. No battle, no disturbance had taken place, although Confederate General Braxton Bragg had been angered by what he considered the breaking of the truce when Vogdes's company landed. Meigs

[50] Meigs Journal, April 9–14, 1861, copy in Nicolay Papers, L.C.; *O.R.*, ser. 1, I, 368–70, 372–74; Nicolay and Hay, *Lincoln*, IV, 14–15.

and Brown took a boat in to the fleet and the fort to give instructions for carrying on the landing, and about midnight some 200 men marched into the fort. The next morning most of the rest of the troops disembarked, and Meigs spent the day overseeing the landing of the horses, which went overboard in canvas slings, were taken in tow by boats, and swam about three quarters of a mile to shore. The Confederates made no effort to interfere.[51]

Meigs was still unloading horses the next morning when the *Powhatan* steamed into sight and came churning down toward the harbor entrance, a British ensign snapping from her peak, ignoring the signals of the Federal fleet, and with the evident intention of trying by a ruse to delay Confederate fire long enough to enable her safely to run the shore batteries and enter the harbor. But after all the intrigue which had brought her to Pensacola, Colonel Brown now decided that he did not yet want her. None of the Federal warships had yet passed the harbor entrance, and Brown did not intend that any of them should until he had Fort Pickens in better condition for a fight, lest the entrance of the ships precipitate a Confederate bombardment. Accordingly, Brown hurried a dispatch to Captain Meigs urging him to try to stop the *Powhatan* short of the harbor.

Meigs knew David Porter well enough—he could spot a somewhat kindred spirit—to realize that talking the lieutenant out of any enterprise to which he had set his mind would be anything but easy, and Porter manifestly had set his mind on anchoring in the harbor off Santa Rosa Island. Meigs sped outward in a tug and when he reached the *Powhatan* pulled not alongside her but athwart her path. The *Powhatan* kept coming on, and Meigs stood in the bow of his tug waving

[51] Meigs Journal, April 15–17, 1861, copy in Nicolay Papers, L.C.; Nicolay and Hay, *Lincoln*, IV, 16.

Brown's order and shouting that he had an order not to run the batteries. Porter felt a momentary impulse to run him down, but he thought better of it. He quickly furled the white ensign and raised the Stars and Stripes in the hope that this action might provoke Bragg into firing and he might get his fight after all, but the shore batteries remained silent, and the ebullient lieutenant had to subside.

Porter ever afterward claimed that he could have blown the Confederate batteries into submission. Perhaps he was right; most of the Confederate gunners were raw, and in weight of metal Bragg's batteries were not so strong as the Federals supposed. But no one at Pensacola harbor knew that the United States and the Confederacy were at war. For all he could have known, by inviting a fight Porter might have wrecked the President's hopes for peace.[52]

On April 20 Captain Meigs was reading the New York papers brought by the *Illinois*, just arrived; their date was April 9. Suddenly he saw a flash of fire and a jet of smoke over the Pensacola Navy Yard on shore; a loud report sounded across the bay. Other shots followed from the navy yard, from Barrancas, and from Pensacola. Meigs jumped to his feet. He believed the ball had begun.

He was mistaken; the Confederates were either firing a salute or testing their guns.[53] But next day word reached Fort Pickens from the mainland that the real thing had taken place. On the morning of April 12 the ancient fire-eater Edmund Ruffin had pulled the lanyard of a gun in Charleston harbor, and the Confederate batteries had opened on Fort Sumter. For thirty hours they fired, while Major Anderson in the fort eked out his short supply of ammunition to reply, and the

[52] Meigs Journal, April 18, 1861, copy in Nicolay Papers, L.C.; Porter, *Incidents*, pp. 23–24.

[53] Meigs Journal, April 20, 1861, copy in Nicolay Papers, L.C.

Federal relief squadron watched helplessly from beyond the bar. Having done all he could for honor's sake, Major Anderson surrendered. And with rattle of drums and the booming of cannon in a last salute to the national flag, the garrison of Fort Sumter marched out of the fort and into a relief ship.

The strengthening of Fort Pickens was nearly complete. With the arrival of additional troops on the *Illinois*, the garrison mounted to 926 men. To these could be added if necessary 190 marines from the fleet, and perhaps two companies could be drawn safely from Key West. This would make a total of 1,282 men—the war garrison which Scott had said could never be gathered, and something to spare. Even without the companies from Key West there would be 1,116 soldiers and marines in Pensacola harbor. To this fighting force could be added the guns of some seven warships.[54]

Fort Pickens was in fact secure. It remained in Union hands throughout the war, and within not many months Pensacola itself again had to acknowledge the jurisdiction of Washington. If the Pickens expedition had been carried off at some cost to the Sumter expedition, this did not alter the fact that in itself the relief of Pickens was a success. The administrative and organizational skill which Meigs had developed in his years of supervising the complex details of the public works had been brought to a focus on the problem of succoring within a limited time a beleaguered fortress more than a thousand miles from its source of supplies. And, working hand in hand with Colonel Keyes, Meigs had accomplished the task with a remarkable precision and efficiency. The only flaw of any consequence in the planning involved the *Powhatan;* as it turned out, the need for that ship was questionable. Meigs plainly was a man whose administrative talents the Union might utilize in a higher place, particularly in some place where he could deal in problems of

[54] Meigs Journal, April 20, 1861, copy in Nicolay Papers, L.C.

logistics. His careful calculations of the supplies and transportation needed for the Pickens relief expedition demonstrated the first characteristics of a good quartermaster.

Meigs's task at Fort Pickens was finished, and at 10:30 in the morning of April 23 he stood on shipboard to return to the North. At Key West he encountered later news. Already he knew that Virginia had seceded; now he heard of Lincoln's call for 75,000 volunteers, of the enthusiastic response of the free states, of the intent to assemble the troops at Washington. His vessel next put in at Havana to take on coal, and here he learned of the Baltimore riot, the destruction of the railroad bridges between Washington and the North, and the difficulties facing the movement of Federal soldiers to the capital. His trip homeward now would be weighted by fears for Louisa and the children: "My family are in the midst of the . . . [dangers?] of war at Washington. God save them from its perils."

But on the homeward journey the weather held good, and the captain sped northward with fair skies and a smooth sea. He reached New York on April 30, and what he saw and the news he heard excited both anxiety and pride: anxiety for the Federal capital, still scarcely in communication with the free states, and pride in the rallying of the North.

Broadway looked like a peach orchard in full blossom all red and white with the Star Spangled banner which flew from every window and door the whole free States are in a tumult of enthusiasm caused by the attack on Sumpter, and the fact is recognized that slavery is doomed.[55]

On May 3 Captain Meigs was again in Washington. His family was safe, and he hastened at once to the Department of State to report to Seward. The Secretary took him to the White House, where he recounted his experiences to the

[55] Meigs Journal, April 23–May 1, 1861, copy in Nicolay Papers, L.C.

President and five of the cabinet members. "They showed great confidence in me," he told his journal, "and treated me with much consideration." When he went next to call on General Scott he received less consideration; the lieutenant general sent out word that he was busy. Scott had already dismissed Colonel Keyes as his military secretary. The old man did not approve of junior officers who consulted with Presidents and cabinets over his head.[56]

For the present, Meigs returned to the public works; but with the North hurrying to arms, no soldier was likely to remain there long.

The opening of a civil war [he had written at Fort Pickens] is not a thing lightly to be seen and though I saw my duty plainly in reinforcing this beleaguered fortress and rescuing my countrymen shut up there from the hands and power of rebels and traitors I could not think I saw the opening of the fire without regret. It must come soon however & God protect the right side.[57]

Soon M. C. Meigs must step again to the active defense of the flag to which he had dedicated his life; and he must do it in part to redeem the honor of his family, for his brother Henry would be serving in the army of rebellion.

[56] *Ibid.*, May 3–8, 1861.
[57] *Ibid.*, April 20, 1861.

# VII

# THE ARMY IS GATHERING

FOR SIX DAYS the capital moved in a trance, turning fearful eyes to the Virginia hills which now were hostile soil and to the roads from Maryland whence came rumors of riot and turmoil. Only a handful of regulars, a few militia companies from Pennsylvania, and the battered 6th Massachusetts defended the city from rebel forces which mushroomed in imagination with each passing day. The 6th Massachusetts had fought its way through a Baltimore mob to reach the capital, and no help had come since. The railroad bridges were out north of Baltimore, the line from Annapolis was torn up to Annapolis Junction, the telegraph lines had gone down, no mail arrived, no newspapers—nothing. "I don't believe there is any North," said the President to the men of the 6th. "The 7th Regiment is a myth. Rhode Island is not in our geography any longer. *You* are the only Northern realities."

And then at last it ended. Down the line from Annapolis jolted a train over hastily repaired rails. And when the expectant crowds met it at the depot, the 7th Regiment of New York Infantry came piling out of the cars, to go swinging in smart gray uniforms with pipe-clayed crossbelts down Pennsylvania Avenue to the White House. Behind them came others: the sweating 8th Massachusetts, which General Ben Butler had used to repair the Annapolis railroad; the business-like 1st Rhode Island in gray trousers and dark blue flannel shirts; the Massachusetts 5th; and then a great deluge of regiments and brigades from all across the North, to tramp the dusty avenues and light their campfires in the surrounding woods and fields.

When Captain Meigs returned from Fort Pickens some of the regiments were still encamped not in woods and fields but in the public buildings. The 1st Rhode Island was scattered among the display cases at the Patent Office; in the Capitol itself the 6th Massachusetts licked its wounds in the Senate chamber, the 8th slept under the paintings in the rotunda, and the 7th New York held mock debates in the Hall of Representatives.[1] Within a week the soldiers moved out, but to Meigs it seemed clear that the war must bring the public works virtually to a standstill.

When he curtailed operations on the Aqueduct, Cabin John Bridge was not yet complete in all its details, but the center supports had been removed and the weight of the arch rested on its own bearings. The iron and timber work of Rock Creek Bridge was finished, and the stonework Meigs allowed to proceed. Several tunnels called for additional effort, and the dam across the Potomac at Great Falls was incomplete. But only a few months' work remained to finish the whole project, and Meigs could take satisfaction in having completed everything save work which required only routine operations.[2]

Meigs believed that in wartime the Capitol project should be curtailed even more sharply than the Aqueduct. Both wings had long been in use, and only ornamental work remained—including, of course, the completion of the dome. For such frivolities Federal funds should not be expended when the Treasury was pressed to preserve the Union. Meigs surveyed

---

[1] Leech, *Reveille*, pp. 55–78.
[2] Annual Report, 1861, 37:2 Sen. Ex. Docs. II (serial 1118), pp. 84–89.

what he had accomplished, took credit for a lower death rate and better health among the legislators in recent sessions, and on May 15 ordered work on the Capitol suspended. In time Abraham Lincoln, whose imagination reached further than Meigs's, was to recognize that the incomplete dome seemed symbolic of the incomplete Union, and that a resumption of construction would testify to the confidence of the government that the Union would prevail. At Lincoln's urging, Congress authorized the work to proceed once more, and since Meigs's military duties precluded his giving attention to the Capitol, on April 16, 1862, Congress voted to transfer the work from the War Department back to the Interior Department, whence it had come in 1853. Meigs's removal to more urgent tasks brought a belated victory of sorts to Thomas U. Walter. He now carried on his functions as architect of the Capitol without interference from a superintending engineer.[3]

While Meigs tapered off the work on the public buildings to mere maintenance operations, he speculated as to what place he would find in the burgeoning wartime army. Soon he discovered himself wondering to what extent he was being driven by ambition rather than by the desire to serve, which his sensitive conscience cautioned him ought to be his principal motive during his country's crisis.

When he returned from Fort Pickens, men impressed by the success of the expedition he had helped to prepare began to promise him a distinguished future as the army expanded. Secretary of the Treasury Salmon P. Chase glared at him from beneath a looming forehead and assured him the cabinet would use him "largely" in the new army. Seward, for whom Meigs was becoming a sort of military secretary and oracle, announced that the cabinet would see him made a general. Mont-

[3] Annual Report, 1861, 37:2 Sen. Ex. Docs. II (serial 1118), pp. 77–83; *Doc. Hist.*, p. 808.

gomery Blair, Lincoln's Postmaster General and long an informal legal adviser to the captain, asked him if he would accept a major generalship. To all of them, Meigs wrote in his journal, he answered: "I prefer in time of peace, the place of Capt. of Engineers, to any other on earth. But I am always at the service of the U. S. in any place or position be they ordered." "Office," he added, "should seek the man not man the office." [4]

So wide a confidence did Seward feel in Captain Meigs's military judgment that he asked Meigs to draw up a memoir on the conduct of the war in general and the situation in Virginia in particular. Seward read Meigs's notes to Lincoln, who expressed pleasure at the captain's views. Meigs favored a cautious policy until the army was better trained, and this was what the President liked to hear in the month of May: Lincoln was trying to avoid being rushed into an offensive movement for which the new regiments were ludicrously unprepared. Lincoln passed the Meigs paper to Montgomery Blair, the Postmaster General, who was experiencing a radical phase and wanted action immediately. Blair did not relish the dish Meigs served, but happily he did not allow this circumstance to prejudice him against the captain, who for some time had enjoyed friendship with the Blair family. [5]

On Sunday, May 19, Meigs gratified a wish of the President by guiding Lincoln and Seward on a ride westward along the Aqueduct. This day Seward went so far as to show to Meigs the dispatch he had prepared for Charles Francis Adams in London to read to Lord John Russell on Britain's recognition of the belligerency of the Confederacy. If Seward cared for the advice of his military mentor even on this delicate diplomatic subject, he was favored with the opinion that it was a good strong note and would probably give the British pause. [6]

[4] Meigs Journal, May 6–8, 1861, copy in Nicolay Papers, L.C.
[5] *Ibid.*, May 10, 14–15, 1861.
[6] *Ibid.*, May 19, 1861.

Meigs's long military service had given him a peculiar consciousness of the power and prestige of the national government, and this circumstance seems to have heightened in him
that ebullient and even overweening pride and confidence in
American nationality which appears to have been so characteristic of Americans in the nineteenth century. Certainly
no pallid diffidence marked Meigs's thoughts on the possibility
that Britain might acknowledge Confederate privateers:

> We have accepted the British & French Russian &c declaration
> so long under negotiation that Privateering is abolished. Will Eng-
> land & France now acknowledge the privateers of the rebels. If
> they do the teeth of England in the mouth of the Thames within
> 12 mos will be brushed with the Stars & Stripes.
> This is the strongest government on earth. No fury of the
> French exceeded the strength of the deep calm strong determina-
> tion of the descendants of the Puritans to preserve the charter of
> their liberties in trust.[7]

After all the casual talk about a generalship, on May 10
Seward informed Meigs that he had got the cabinet to agree
to make him a colonel. For all the captain's assertions that he
desired only to serve, he could not have helped feeling his
hopes rise when men like Seward, Chase, and Montgomery
Blair talked to him of a high command; and now he experienced no little disappointment. Why, Frank Blair, Senior,
had even spoken of Meigs as a likely leader of the whole
advance into Virginia; more reliably, others had suggested
Meigs for the post of quartermaster general, vacated when
Joseph E. Johnston joined the Confederacy. And there were
reasons beyond those of ambition for the captain's chagrin;
he believed, and rightly so, that it was not as a colonel of infantry, which was what Seward now contemplated, that the
country could best use his talents. Ambition, a reluctance to

[7] Meigs Let. B., 1861, pp. 71–72.

be governed by ambition, and a genuine desire to give the
nation his highest possible service all mingled in Meigs's
comments in his journal:

Younger men than myself have been put into high positions by
both sides and McClellan who graduated some ten years later
though a Major Genl of Ohio militia is now in command of the
West. Genls Beauregard and Bragg, the latter of my class, the
former younger at West Point are both Generals by Davis' appointment. Had I gone to Davis I could have taken almost any
rank. To be made a Col of a marching regiment is to give up my
profession in which I may be useful, to become a Col. a position
which can be filled by hundreds better than by me. No room
for brains and some fighting fellow is enough, while if I retain
my position as Capt of engineers I should probably be chief engineer of any forward movement and would be of some use to
the country and a better chance of distinction. I think I must not
accept it. Blair is disgusted, says that Seward has brought me into
antagonism with Cameron and that the President again today
brought up the appointment of Mr Aspinwall for Q M Genl,
and [Seward was] unwise, though honest enough to quote me
[and thus] made Cameron angry. They had better make me Q. M.
Gen'l than to keep up the present already rotten system. [Cameron
was giving his political friends a field day as army contractors,
and it looked as though another Floyd sat in the War Department,
with infinitely vaster opportunities to do harm.] I do not think
I can stand this. I fear that I am growing ambitious. I thought I
desired only to be useful, but I feel the break down too much.
I read to Blair my letter to Seward upon giving my family some
compensation for my work upon the Capitol, Post Office etc &
he says the letter is a good one but that being brought up at an
improper time by Mr Seward, it has injured my military prospects. Played hob with them, he says. Well I did right.[8]

A few days later Meigs saw Seward again and told him he
did not desire the colonelcy. It would be a step forward in
rank and pay, but Meigs said he could be more useful as chief

[8] Meigs Journal, May 10, 1861, copy in Nicolay Papers, L.C.

engineer of an expedition, at his present rank, than as the colonel of a marching regiment. Soon afterward Blair called at Meigs's home on H Street and discussed the possibility of the post of quartermaster general. Blair encouraged Meigs to accept the place if it were offered, and Meigs rather inclined to like the idea. A few days later Blair told him that the cabinet had discussed his colonelcy and that he, Blair, had consented to it only as a step to Meigs's becoming a general officer and quartermaster general. Blair believed that there Meigs would have a highly important command of great usefulness, and one for which his abilities and experience made him well fitted.[9]

Blair was right. Probably no other officer in the army had so large an experience as Meigs in dealing with private business-men and supervising contracts for large quantities of material. The captain's direction of the public works had given him administrative experience of a sort that would be invaluable to him at the head of the Quartermaster's Department. He was accustomed to responsibility and he did not fear to make decisions. He was energetic and self-reliant; if anything he possessed an excess of those qualities. He had handled over eight million dollars of the public funds during his years in Washington and had accounted for every cent. No one of any knowledge and judgment questioned his honesty; and a man of firm and unyielding honesty, not afraid to cross swords even with the Secretary of War, was sorely needed. The Cameron regime was purchasing huge amounts of military equipment through agents as curiously chosen as Alexander Cummings, long editor of the Philadelphia *Bulletin* in Simon Cameron's bailiwick and now editor of the New York *World*, but a man without experience or qualifications as a quartermaster officer, to whom Cameron had given direction of army purchasing activities in New York City.[10]

[9] *Ibid.*, May 15, 18, 1861.
[10] 37:2 House Rep. 2 (serial 1142, 1143), p. 55.

Blair believed that the cabinet had agreed that Meigs was the man for quartermaster general. But Simon Cameron, the Secretary of War, doubtless remembered the unhappy experiences of John B. Floyd, and he began to back water. He told Blair he did not recall that the cabinet had come to a genuine understanding, and he postponed signing Meigs's commission. Lincoln pushed Cameron in Meigs's favor, and Seward of course continued to support his friend. But to Cameron, signing that commission probably smacked of thrusting his own head into a noose. The Secretary of War knew full well that certain of the operations of his department were— well, perhaps somewhat irregular; and he knew that Captain Meigs could play the devil with such a situation. Blair charged that Cameron was breaking faith. Cameron suggested that the cabinet examine the qualifications of Nathaniel P. Banks, the influential Massachusetts Republican who was in Washington seeking the place. Meigs began to exercise his talent for feeling abused.[11]

On the 1st of June Meigs and Cameron had a long conversation. The Secretary was pleasant enough, but he told Meigs frankly that he feared the captain's temper. "I gave him assurances," Meigs reported blithely, while Cameron must have wondered at the value of such assurances from the turbulent captain. On the evening of June 7 Cameron invited Meigs to visit him to talk over the Quartermaster's Department again; but when Meigs arrived, the War Secretary talked little about that and much about everything else. Meigs finally had to tell him he must go home and let the Secretary go to bed, and Cameron said he would talk with him again next day. "Is this the way to do work?" Meigs asked his diary.[12]

The following day Meigs saw Seward in order to tell him

[11] Meigs Journal, May 27, 1861, copy in Nicolay Papers, L.C.
[12] *Ibid.*, June 1, 5–6, 1861.

that he was tiring of the run-around. If he were to be a colonel of infantry he ought to be recruiting his regiment. Seward assured him he would not be cheated, that he would surely be quartermaster general. Meigs would find that too many cooks spoil the broth; the trouble, said Seward, was that there were too many politicians in the cabinet, so that when they met, talk and not quick action was the result. At this point, Seward was summoned to the White House, and he left Meigs with the cheerful assurance that God would have lost this country long ago through the stupid blunders, vacillation, and delays of its government had not He intended to save it; but Meigs could depend on it, the President was a loyal and resolute man, and he would see to it that Meigs became quartermaster general. The interview was not without its balm, but it was nevertheless not quite satisfactory. And for once Meigs recorded in his journal a sour word on Seward: "It is curious that, no matter at what time I go to the Secretary, by chance or by appointment, at his house or office, I always find this editor with him or waiting to see him." Meaning, of course, Thurlow Weed.

That same day word leaked out that the quartermaster general was to be not Meigs but Cameron's crony Alexander Cummings. Most of the newspapers were indignant at the idea, and Meigs surmised that Cameron had been putting out a feeler. Next day Cameron called at Meigs's house and left word he would like to see him at nine in the evening. Meigs went, and Cameron told him the way to his appointment was clear at last. Apparently the Secretary had conceded defeat. He wished only to keep it quiet a few days, he said, in order to have time to mollify ranking officers of the Quartermaster's Department who thought they deserved the place.[13]

[13] *Ibid.*, June 8, 1861.

On June 13 the clashing gears of the Federal bureaucracy at last fell into position to settle Meig's status.

I received today the appointment of Brig. Gen. and Q. M. Genl in the Army of the U. S., to rank from the 10″ of this month. This is an important position, and I hope that God will give me strength and wisdom for my duties, so that I may discharge them with credit to myself and profit to my country. I enter at once upon the duties of the office.[14]

As Meigs began to acquaint himself with his new problems, the camps encircling Washington continued to grow. New regiments arrived to parade down the avenue, and the army which was gathering was nothing if not colorful: Ellsworth's Zouaves in their trim blue jackets and ballooning red trousers, the Highlanders of the 79th New York in their kilted dress uniforms, Colonel Michael Corcoran's 69th New York with a golden harp emblazoned upon its emerald flag, the Garibaldi Guards with their *bersaglieri* hats and the red blouses which they copied from Italy's One Thousand, and which Garibaldi in turn had copied from William Marcy Tweed's New York fire companies.

Whether this agglomeration of men actually deserved the name of an army was something else again. It was approaching a strength of 30,000, but no regular officer, not even Scott in his march to Mexico, had ever commanded a force of comparable size. Nor was anyone prepared by training or experience to cope with the logistical problems of the army. Meigs's preparation for the post of quartermaster general was probably the best in the army, but it was not what it should have been. There was no general staff; there were no staff schools; there was scarce any American military literature worthy of the name, and certainly none on the problems of

[14] *Ibid.*, June 13, 1861.

supply. That Scott and Secretary of War William L. Marcy and General Jesup had managed to send an expedition to Veracruz and then to Mexico City without having everybody in it starve and go naked had been a modern miracle. But since the Mexican War the regular army had numbered 17,000 men at most, scattered generally by companies, and if supplying the troops had involved traversing immense distances, nevertheless it had not been a problem of overwhelming complexity. Now the officer corps of the regular army was being swamped; it could look for little help from the ignorant volunteer officers. It could only muddle through with spot improvisations, for no one had ever bothered even to contemplate what would happen if the army should one day experience wartime expansion. The wonder is that utter chaos did not cripple hopelessly the mobilization of the North at the very outset.

Somehow the War Department and the Quartermaster's Department within it had managed to gather subsistence and shelter and a certain amount of wagon transportation for the troops encamped around the capital even with the unprepared and, if it need be said, unqualified Simon Cameron at the head of the War Office and nobody holding the full authority of quartermaster general. Somehow they managed to scrounge from the army's depots uniforms for those few regiments which needed them, although fortunately this problem was taken care of mostly by the states and the militia companies themselves. The whole process was accompanied by extravagance on a grand scale, and Cameron's operations were to provide tasty morsels for Congressional investigators in the months to come. But the important thing was that it was done, and Meigs assumed office to find at least that the volunteers were clothed, sheltered, and eating.

All the same there was an almost overwhelming amount of work to be done, first, in checking what had been accomplished

already and what supplies were still needed; second, in dealing
in particular with the problem of providing horses and wagons
for transportation so that the army might move forward; third,
in establishing an ordered contract system so that supplies
would flow smoothly; fourth, in finding quartermaster officers
who bore at least a semblance of qualifications for their tasks;
and fifth, in organizing the Quartermaster's Department so that
the quartermaster general might keep his hands on the reins of
command in Washington, know what was transpiring at depots
and in the field, and feel a certain confidence that when he
issued a directive, what he ordered would be done without
undue delay and distortion. General Meigs promptly became
almost a stranger to his family, sometimes spending nights as
well as days at his office.

Meigs soon concluded that Secretary Cameron was an utter
babe-in-the-woods so far as administering an army was concerned. The energetic Meigs was not long in counseling him
and in taking action on problems beyond the immediate scope
of the Quartermaster's Department. On June 21 Meigs wrote
to Cameron a report on the procurement of small arms,
properly a concern of the Ordnance Bureau. He advised that all
factories in the United States capable of manufacturing rifle
muskets of the United States pattern should immediately be set
to work to the limit of their capacity. Cameron was shifting
and procrastinating, and in the end the army was likely to have
to depend too heavily upon weapons from the arsenals of
Europe, some of them satisfactory arms, others museum pieces.
On the 22nd Meigs wrote the Secretary that he should set about
procuring 300 wrought-iron field guns, 200 of them to be
rifled. The same day he addressed himself to the manufacturers
of rifled projectiles, calling upon them to decide which type of
projectile should be adopted for the service from among those
already known; time, he said, was more important than getting

the best, the second best doubtless being good enough for practical purposes.

On the 25th he spoke to Cameron. The Secretary told him he had ordered the 300 guns which Meigs had recommended, and Meigs urged him to follow up this step by procuring at once carriages, caissons, ammunition wagons, battery wagons, and harness for the guns. The Ordnance Department, said Meigs, certainly had some supply of these things in store, but to equip the new guns and to replace those items which would be broken, lost, or destroyed in service, a full supply for all the new guns would not prove too many to procure. Since the government arsenals were already taxed to capacity, Meigs suggested that some of the idle railroad car shops be set to work on artillery carriages. They had the needed machinery and workmen skilled in this sort of task, and they should long since have been given an opportunity to aid the war effort. The North possessed superior industrial strength, but it must learn to utilize that strength.[15]

Overshadowing all other business in these late days of June was the question of a forward movement into Virginia. Lincoln's call of April 14 for 75,000 volunteers had stipulated a term of only three months' service; and now the North was clamoring that the volunteers be used to end the war before their term expired. Meigs's old friend and sponsor Jefferson Davis was President of the Southern Confederacy, and since Virginia's secession his capital was in Richmond, so that now from the Northern press there came the famous cry of "On to Richmond!" The rebellion must be crushed before the summer

[15] *Ibid.*, June 21–22, 1861; Quartermaster General's Report Book, V, 435–36. On the mobilization problems of the Union army in general, see Marvin A. Kreidberg and Merton G. Henry, *History of Military Mobilization in the United States Army, 1775–1945* (Washington, 1955), pp. 83–129, 139–40.

was out, but of the difficulties confronting the officers of the
army few Northern civilians had any conception, and still less
did they care. The soldiers were at Washington, and the guns
were there. They must advance, and Richmond must fall.

While the troops assembled at the Federal capital General
Scott had been more concerned about the safety of Washington
than any offensive movement of his own. On May 24 the
vanguard of the Union army had crossed the Potomac, but the
principal purpose of the operation was merely to secure the
heights of Arlington, which commanded Washington from
the south shore of the river.[16] Meigs had been a reflective
spectator of the first forward movement of the war:

> At night about 12 o'clock a column of two or three regts.
> passed our corner, down 14″ Street with no music, every bayonet
> glancing brightly in the moonbeams. I watched them from the
> window with sadness to think that they were going to suffer for
> the ambition and villainy of these . . . [?] politicians of the
> South. How much has Davis to answer for? How much Cobb,
> Toombs and the rest of these men?
>
> Among them all is no patriot, unless Davis may be one, and
> he is led away by his mad ambition to do that which I am sure
> his conscience rejects.
>
> . . . This is the end of Buchanan's Kansas policy.[17]

About the middle of June the Federal forces began cautiously
feeling their way forward. On June 25 Meigs was summoned to
a council of war. The pressure for an advance in strength could
not be contained much longer. The Union high command must
decide whether an advance was practicable and, if so, where
and when it should take place. Meigs found the President, the
cabinet, General Scott, and General Joseph Mansfield present.
Because General John A. Dix was expected and did not appear,
the group adjourned after hearing a report by General Scott

[16] Williams, *Lincoln Finds a General*, I, 66.
[17] Meigs Journal, May 23, 1861, copy in Nicolay Papers, L.C.

on the current situation of the Federal forces and their rivals.

In the Washington area on both sides of the river the Federals had about 50,000 troops; up the river at the entrance to the Shenandoah Valley were some 10,000 to 16,000 men under Major General Robert Patterson, a veteran of 1812 well regarded by Scott but aging rapidly. Thus the Federals had perhaps 66,000 troops available. At Manassas Junction, Fairfax, Centreville, and the surrounding area Confederate General Pierre G. T. Beauregard, the dapper Creole who had bombarded Sumter, had about 24,000 infantry and 2,000 cavalry. A Confederate force of fewer than 10,000 watched Patterson in the lower Shenandoah. Scott asserted that the Federal troops were better armed, equipped, and paid than the secessionists. The Confederates, he said, were out of money, their troops had no pay, their men received little food and were badly clothed, but they excelled the Federals in experience in the use of arms. The Confederates were less amenable than the Federals to discipline.

On the whole Scott was inclined to believe that his soldiers were better than their opponents, but most of them were utterly raw. And Scott was a professional who did not like to depend upon raw troops. They were too much liable to panic. Given time, said Scott, the Federal soldiers could be turned into heroes. They were individually brave, but as soldiers they needed that confidence in the courage and steadiness of their comrades which they would gain only with experience.

General Scott turned to the subject of an advance. He asked Meigs how many men he would want to drive Beauregard from Manassas. The quartermaster general replied that since the enemy had 26,000, he would ask for about 30,000 and a full supply of artillery. Scott asked how many batteries he would consider a full supply. Meigs answered that he would want about ninety pieces, or three to each thousand men. This was an intelligent estimate, but Scott considered it excessive. Meigs argued that although two to the thousand was the common figure, with raw troops it would be well to have more rather than less. Scott said he thought fifty pieces manned by well-drilled crews would suffice. Mansfield would not venture an opinion; he desired more time to think it over.[18]

A second council of war met on the 29th. This time Major General Irvin McDowell was among the members; Scott had designated him to command the advance. General Scott led off by describing the positions which the troops were occupying around Washington, which Meigs with reason believed bore little relation to any definite purpose. The general-in-chief then called on McDowell to read his ideas for an advance so that the group might discuss them. Although Meigs did not consider the presentation which followed a very able one, McDowell offered a well-reasoned document. Its principal flaw probably was its failure to assign enough men to the forthcoming advance against the Confederate lines at Manassas. While Meigs had said he would have moved forward with 30,000 men, McDowell stipulated an additional 10,000 in reserve. But since he calculated rightly that the enemy might be reinforced to about 35,000, he was allowing a none too large balance to offset the greater difficulties of the offense. Perhaps he was concerned about transportation for a larger force; this was Meig's responsibility, and transportation so far had not been especially abundant, whether or not the new quartermaster general was doing all he could to hurry on wagons and horses and mules.

At this point General Scott reiterated his long-standing reluctance to commit the raw troops around Washington to an offensive. He urged instead his "anaconda policy": to strangle the South with a naval blockade while remaining for the time

[18] *Ibid.*, June 25, 1861.

being inactive on land. But the council overruled him, and discussion returned to the offensive in Virginia.[19]

I was called upon [wrote Meigs] for my opinion and said that I did not think we would ever end the war without beating the rebels; that they had come near us. We were, according to Gen. Scott's information given to us at the Council of the 25″, stronger than they, better prepared, our troops better contented, better clothed, better fed, better paid, better armed. That here we had the most violent . . . of the rebels near us; it was better to whip them here than to go far into an unhealthy country to fight them, and to fight them far from our supplies, to spend our money among enemies instead of our friends. To make the fight in Virginia was cheaper and better as the case now stood. Let them come here to be beaten.[20]

This was almost as clear a statement as could have been made on behalf of the Union strategy which concentrated upon Richmond and, more important, upon the enemy army in front of Richmond. This Confederate force would have to be beaten if the war were to end; and it was most convenient to beat it where it was.

The council decided to undertake a movement as soon as the army could be put in readiness and the necessary transportation assembled. Scott asked Meigs when he could have the transportation ready. The quartermaster general replied with an optimism which the sequel failed to warrant. He told the council to fix the time of the movement, and he would have the wagons and horses on hand when they were wanted. The date set was Monday, July 8; McDowell was to move down the Orange and Alexandria Railroad toward Manassas with

[19] *Ibid.*, June 29, 1861; Williams, *Lincoln Finds a General*, I, 75–76; T. Harry Williams, *Lincoln and His Generals* (New York, 1952), pp. 20–21.
[20] Meigs Journal, June 29, 1861, copy in Nicolay Papers, L.C.

30,000 men, his object the defeat and destruction of Beauregard.[21]

By July 6 Meigs realized that he had spoken rashly. He had ordered about 6,000 horses and mules for the forward movement, but it was clear that they would not reach Washington in time to permit an advance on the 8th. They arrived as rapidly as the single-track railway from Baltimore could bring them, but the Washington depot was blocked with loaded cars. Thus what was to be a recurrent problem of the war made its first important appearance: the jamming of rail lines and a shortage of supplies at the front not because of a genuine scarcity but because the railroad cars stood too long without being unloaded.[22] In time Meigs became acutely aware of the problem and recognized long before a number of field commanders the necessity of detailing enough men to unload cars promptly; some of the field commanders never seemed to recognize it. This does not excuse Meigs's failure now; if a jamming of loaded cars was the primary cause of delay, then vigorous steps should have been taken to break the bottleneck at once. With the terms of the three-months' men soon to expire, every day counted, and the want of adequate transportation cost McDowell no less than eight valuable days.

On the 7th an additional transport problem confronted Meigs. Patterson in the Shenandoah was complaining that his force was too small for his mission—a betrayal of excessive timidity—and Scott decided that he had better send reinforcements. About 9,000 troops left Washington for the Shenandoah by railway via Harrisburg to Hagerstown, and Meigs was called on for wagon transportation from Hagerstown. He could not supply it out of the stocks at Washington; he needed every-

---

[21] *Ibid.*
[22] *Ibid.*, July 5–6, 1861.

thing there for McDowell. Accordingly, he could do nothing more than telegraph Pittsburgh, Philadelphia, and Harrisburg to send wagons to meet the soldiers at Hagerstown, while he ordered that money be sent to the quartermaster at Hagerstown for the purchase of animals in the neighborhood. These efforts brought gratifying results, but Patterson's force, like McDowell's, continued to be handicapped by an over-all shortage of transport.

Not until Tuesday, July 16, did McDowell's 30,000 march southward. Watching them, Meigs prayed for their success and regretted his confinement to a desk job. He wished he could be in the field, leading on horseback one of the advancing columns of the Union.[23]

Scattered and vague reports flowed back to Washington of the cautious, halting march of McDowell's army toward Centreville. Federal cavalry was small in numbers, but it was not entirely lacking. Yet McDowell marched his cavalry in the midst of his column with his 2nd Division instead of sending it forward to reconnoiter. Partly for this reason his infantrymen were wearied by frequent halts while the advance searched out possible ambushes, and the frustrations of a continually interrupted march began to set the soldiers to straggling.

On the night of the 18th McDowell's troops encamped around Centreville. That day the left wing had experienced an unexpected collision with the enemy at Blackburn's Ford on Bull Run, and the effect was to upset McDowell's plans for turning Beauregard's right. Accordingly the Federal commander paused at Centreville to think, and when subsequent events demonstrated that the delay was costly, he blamed the quartermasters for failing to get two ration trains to him that morning. It was true enough that the supply service failed to

[23] *Ibid.*, July 7, 16, 1861; Williams, *Lincoln Finds a General*, I, 80–85.

fulfill a promise. But one ration train which did arrive included enough food to maintain the army for two days, and McDowell's faultfinding with the quartermasters amounted merely to an attempt to evade responsibility for a failure that was his.[24]

On Saturday, July 20, word reached Washington that General Joseph E. Johnston, Meigs's predecessor as quartermaster general, who now commanded the Confederate troops in the Shenandoah, had slipped away from Patterson to join Beauregard in front of Manassas. Johnston was said to have raised Beauregard's strength to 60,000. The first report was true, although not all of Johnston's Army of the Shenandoah had yet arrived along Bull Run. Johnston had blinded old Patterson neatly and had then put his troops on the cars to move by railroad from near Thoroughfare Gap to Manassas Junction. The second report was not true; Johnston's entire force numbered only about 11,000, and he would increase Beauregard's strength to 36,000 at most. Unfortunately, this was still enough to afford the Confederates a substantial numerical advantage over McDowell, whose 30,000 were dwindling with the discharge of several regiments as their terms expired. Meigs believed the 60,000 figure, and his mind was not on natural science when Bache, Henry, and the rest of his club met at his home that night.[25]

Having wasted enough time in generally futile scouting to ensure that most of Johnston's men would be with Beauregard in time for the impending battle, McDowell determined to shoot his bolt on Sunday, the 21st. His initial aim was to turn the enemy's position along Bull Run. Since he had decided

[24] Williams, *Lincoln Finds a General*, I, 77–80, 88–90; *B. & L.*, I, 167–93.
[25] Williams, *Lincoln Finds a General*, I, 78–90; Douglas Southall Freeman, *Lee's Lieutenants* (New York, 1945), I, 42–43; Meigs Journal, July 20, 1861, copy in Nicolay Papers, L.C.

when he heard of the fight at Blackburn's Ford that a move around Beauregard's right could not succeed, he had searched instead for a means of turning the enemy's left. His plan called for a feint toward the stone bridge which carried the main turnpike across Bull Run straight into the Confederate left flank; meanwhile his principal column would cross Bull Run by a ford farther upstream and roll up the enemy army from the flank. It was an intelligent plan, but McDowell got it off to a bad start by compelling his green troops to make a night march along narrow roads to reach the jump-off point.[26]

In Washington General Meigs anticipated when he went to bed on Saturday night that Sunday would bring the battle, and he ordered his horse and carriage to be ready at six in the morning so that he could ride out to Bull Run and see the show. He overslept, and the morning was well advanced by the time he had breakfasted and was crossing the Long Bridge. Just beyond Alexandria he met files of awkward, canvas-topped ambulances carrying wounded soldiers, casualties of Blackburn's Ford. Beyond them he was disgusted to encounter a regiment marching home; it was the 4th Pennsylvania, whose time had expired. Leaving the army when it was needed most, it straggled along the road for miles.

At two or three in the afternoon Meigs clattered into Centreville, where a crowd of officers, soldiers, Congressmen, and assorted sightseers stood scattered across the top of a high, round hill looking over the valley of Bull Run. Already for some miles he had heard the thump-thump of heavy gunfire from out of the valley. Reaching the hilltop, he could see three large clouds of smoke rising from the slopes beyond the creek. The spectators told him that the battle seemed to have passed southward during the early afternoon, an indication that events were moving well for the Union; but disturbing rumors

[26] Williams, *Lincoln Finds a General,* I, 90–91.

of a check also reached the hill at Centreville. Meigs rode on down the slope toward Bull Run to the point where McDowell's flanking movement had turned off the pike in the morning. Here he left his carriage and directed his servant to return to Centreville and await him there, unless a rout occurred, in which case the servant was to return at once to Washington. Meigs then mounted the little bay horse which another servant had led for him and continued toward Bull Run, until in a patch of woods he found a cluster of Union troops.

This was part of Robert Schenck's brigade of Daniel Tyler's division, the men who had made the feint in the morning. Meigs remained with them and, using his glass, attempted to make out what was happening on the hill across Bull Run— the plateau that would become famous as the Henry House Hill. He stood under a prominent tree, and Confederate shells whistled overhead. He discovered that his first exposure to hostile fire was not particularly exciting; he felt much as though someone were throwing paving stones at him. But his exposure did him little good, since all that he could see on the hill opposite was a line of skirmishers deployed on the slope; everything else was wrapped in smoke. Around him General Schenck, one of the political brigadiers, was demonstrating his inability to form his men into line of battle. When Colonel Alexander McCook of the 1st Ohio appeared, Meigs advised him to assume command and get the brigade into line. McCook presumably set about accomplishing what he could.

Before the colonel could have worked much of an improvement, the situation across the creek suddenly clarified itself, and in an ominous way. A large force of the enemy emerged from the smoke and advanced in good order down the turnpike toward the bridge in front of Meigs. No sooner had this threat appeared than McCook's skirmishers began to stream into the woods from the left, saying that the enemy was upon them and driving them. Then there came a rattling volley of musketry from the east—the last straw, for it meant that somehow the enemy had forced his way to the rear of Schenck's brigade.

An engineer officer from McDowell's staff rode up to Meigs and invited him to follow into the woods lest he end the day a prisoner. Meigs did so, moving northward in search of a hole in the enemy's encirclement. When they came upon a party of Ellsworth's Fire Zouaves they joined them. The woods now were full of the stigmas of retreat: guns, cartridge boxes, flasks, all thrown away in haste. Meigs had to ride carefully so that his bay would not step on a musket and lame itself. Eventually he reached the turnpike again; here were the guns of two sections of Battery E, 2nd Artillery, with only three of their eight wheels intact. Otherwise this part of the road was deserted; apparently a charge had swept along it.

Riding eastward on the turnpike, Meigs eventually caught up with a mixed crowd of fugitives doggedly or excitedly making their way toward Washington. At Centreville he found Colonel Dixon Miles, who was supposed to be commanding the rear guard but who at the moment was drunk. To the southeast he could still hear Union artillery attempting some sort of stand. He tried to rally some of the retreating troops as they passed through Centreville, but he had no authority over them and no assistance, and the effort was futile.

The retreat continued. Meigs did all he could to be useful, which was not much, and after dark he rode homeward. He reached Washington about three in the morning and stopped at the White House to tell the President what he had witnessed. Other visitors were bustling in and out, but Meigs had a fairly long talk with Lincoln, who had later news by telegraph than the quartermaster could give him. The President was deeply moved by the defeat, but he had not panicked.

He was looking, first, to the safety of Washington, and then to plans for trying again.[27]

When General Meigs reflected upon the battle in the quiet of his home, he inclined to think that the Union had not done so badly after all. For he believed that Beauregard's force had numbered at least 60,000, perhaps 90,000, and he regarded the failure of the Confederates to follow up their victory as evidence that they had been roughly handled—which indeed they were. Still, there was no blinking the fact that the first great battle had gone wrong, and that the North must do much better if the Union were to survive. "It was a bad defeat; the papers of the day give full accounts of it—and here I leave it. Our army is much demoralized, and we must form a new one." A defeat, yes—but no more than that. Already General Meigs, like the President and most of the people of the North, was thinking of the new army that would follow.[28]

[27] Meigs Journal, July 21–22, 1861, copy in Nicolay Papers, L.C.; Quartermaster General's Letter Book 56, pp. 122–25; Williams, *Lincoln Finds a General,* I, 90–99.

[28] Meigs Journal, July 22, 1861, copy in Nicolay Papers, L.C.

# VIII

# THE TRIALS OF MOBILIZATION

OUT OF the West came the young Napoleon who would rally the survivors of Bull Run and crowd his camps with the new volunteers and forge the army that he would lead to victory. Resplendent he came in coat of blue and trimmings of gold and sash of crimson, mounted on a dark brown charger, his right hand reaching into his coat in the reminiscent gesture—Major General George B. McClellan, thirty-four years old, commander of the Army of the Potomac, and soon to be general-in-chief of the Armies of the United States.

General Meigs welcomed McClellan's coming, but he knew that the event promised a burgeoning army with painful trials for a Quartermaster's Department not yet truly readjusted from peace to war. He must have wondered how the department would fare in the days ahead. He seems to have felt no other misgivings, no doubts about McClellan's merits; indeed, scarcely anyone seems to have doubted. The press cheered McClellan, Washington cheered, the soldiers cheered. The young general smiled expansively amidst the adulation and clutched the more tightly a triumph that was almost too good to be true. Too good to be true—and therefore to be handled cautiously, and not to be exposed to unnecessary risks. These mighty blue files of the Army of the Potomac were the cornerstone of his power and glory, and McClellan must see that no harm came to them.[1]

While McClellan labored to retrieve the defeat of Bull Run, and Meigs busied himself aiding him, the quartermaster general could not devote his attention to McClellan's needs alone. New Federal armies were gathering all along the Confederate borders for campaigns which now seemed likely to be most formidable, and particularly along the rivers of the West thousands of men gathered for assaults on the western barriers of Jefferson Davis's empire. Meigs's contacts with the western armies were not so close and his supervision of their supply was more generalized than in the East, but while he thought about McClellan his mind had to turn also to the West. Particularly he had to consider the supply problems of Major General John Charles Fremont's large department, with headquarters in St. Louis.

Still, the North looked especially to McClellan as the leader who would redeem the errors of McDowell and point the way to final victory. McClellan was the leader, but the problem now was to secure him an army. If we were to believe McClellan's own account, he came to Washington to find "regiments cowering on the banks of the Potomac." [2] He saw what was to be done, he waved his hand, and an army appeared. In truth there was more to it than that. McClellan found more than a disorganized and demoralized rabble when he reached the capital; he found the beginnings of a powerful fighting force. Lincoln had called Congress into special session commencing on the 4th of July, and Congress promptly had validated the emergency calls for troops which the President had issued in its absence. Lincoln announced that already

[1] Williams, *Lincoln Finds a General*, I, 104–5; Bruce Catton, *Mr. Lincoln's Army* (Garden City, N. Y., 1951), pp. 60–62. See also George B. McClellan, *McClellan's Own Story* (New York, 1887).
[2] Quoted by Williams, *Lincoln Finds a General*, I, 113.

310,000 men were under arms, 80,000 of whom would soon be mustered out. Congress voted him a volunteer army of half a million men, to be enlisted for three years. When the defeat of Bull Run stunned the North with the knowledge that this would be a war in earnest, the hundreds of thousands began to flow in.

Already the administration was considering how it would care for them. A commission of prominent doctors and scientists had been appointed by the President to cooperate with the Medical Bureau of the army to maintain the health and efficiency of the soldiers. Thomas A. Scott of the Pennsylvania Railroad had taken his place at Cameron's side in the War Department, in part to further the fortunes of his own Pennsylvania and Cameron's Northern Central at the expense of rival lines, but in part also to cooperate with the railroad managers of the North so that the volunteers could move to Washington and the rendezvous points in the West swiftly and efficiently. The chief signal officer presented recommendations on the use in wartime of that new instrument of rapid communication, the telegraph. General Meigs and the chief of the Ordnance Bureau had ordered hundreds of new cannon. The arsenals were at work to capacity, and at Meigs's urging Seward had the officials of the State Department combing the arsenals of Europe. Meigs and his officers of the Quartermaster's Department were grappling with the problems of supply.[3]

Probably the first in priority among the problems of supply which rested upon Meigs as quartermaster general was that of uniforming the new troops who came to join McClellan's and the other growing armies. Before the war the Quartermaster's

[3] *Ibid.,* I, 113–18; A. Howard Meneely, *The War Department, 1861* (New York, 1928), pp. 199–201; Meigs Journal, July 29, 1861, copy in Nicolay Papers, L.C.

Department had supplied the army with uniforms from a single depot, the Schuylkill Arsenal in Philadelphia. Here material purchased from private suppliers had been made up into uniforms and shoes. With the coming of the war, the organization of the depot was on a scale hopelessly inadequate to meet the new demands. Upon Lincoln's first call for volunteers the stocks on hand disappeared almost immediately. The Quartermaster's Department promptly contracted with private clothing manufacturers for the supply of army goods, but the manufacturers as well as the arsenal were unable to turn out uniforms rapidly enough for the hundreds of thousands who were taking the oath of allegiance. The Quartermaster's Department lacked a sufficient number of experienced officers to supervise both the making of contracts and the expansion of the government's own manufacturing facilities. Thus civilians had to be appointed, and many of them proved unqualified; here Simon Cameron's weak and politically conscious hand did some of its greatest harm. Presently standard uniform cloth, blankets, and undergarments were in grave shortage.[4]

The President's calls for volunteers went out not directly to the people but were channeled through the state governments. This was primarily because the administrative machinery of the Federal government could not cope with the task of mustering thousands of men into service. Now the inadequate administrative machinery of the Federal Quartermaster's Department compelled the government at Washington to drop upon the states the task of clothing and equipping many of the troops as well. Actually, the militia organizations had already entered Federal service carrying state equipment. And the customary nineteenth-century habit of thinking in terms of state rather than Federal activity had led the gov-

[4] *O.R.*, ser. 3, II, 802; ser. 3, V, 224.

ernors to take upon themselves large responsibilities in the problems of supplying the troops of their states, whether those troops were organized state militia or new volunteers. Yet more than a traditionalist adherence to states' rights was involved here. The Federal government was not falling down on the job merely because its officials were blind to the forces of centralizing nationalism. There was simply nothing else to be done. Competition among the states and between the states and the Federal government in bidding for contracts might and did lead to a squandering of public funds, but Federal administrative facilities would not permit the Washington government to assume the entire task.[5]

Purchasing authorities, both Federal and state, presently found themselves moving in a cesspool of noisome dealings. In the matter of clothing, the needs of the volunteer regiments were so urgent and the supply at hand so limited that state agents and the Federal Quartermaster's Department lay almost wholly at the mercy of any contractors in sight. And if the power of the contractors was not quite so great when it came to horses, wagons, lumber, and other items, nevertheless the opportunities for exploitation of the public need remained plentiful. Again, the absence of any previous planning worthy of the name for an emergency such as this, plus the scarcity of experienced quartermasters to serve as inspectors and purchasing officers, meant that corrupt persons might readily obtain appointment to responsible positions and then proceed to deal hand in glove with venal contractors.

Corruption in army purchasing at the outset of the war is a frequently told tale. Nobody questions that a goodly number of people were lining their pockets by dubious means, and

[5] Shannon, *Organization*, I, 53–54; Meneely, *War Department*, p. 115; Bell Irvin Wiley, *The Life of Billy Yank* (Indianapolis, 1951), pp. 21–22; Cyril B. Upham, "Arms and Equipment for the Iowa Troops in the Civil War," *Iowa Journal of History and Politics*, XVI (1918), 27–51.

that some of them were officers of General Meigs's Quarter-master's Department. Testimony on the subject covers more than 2,000 pages of a Congressional report, and there is no need to cover the ground again here. A few examples will suffice.[6]

At the beginning of September an Illinois brigadier named Ulysses S. Grant established his headquarters at the strategic town of Cairo, at the southern tip of Illinois, where the Ohio flows into the Mississippi. The quartermaster here was one Captain R. B. Hatch, and Grant was not long in the place before he began to receive indications that peculiar things were happening in his quartermaster's office. Apparently Hatch had adopted the pleasant custom of purchasing lumber for the government at one price and having the bill made out for it at another and higher figure. The difference he sometimes may have shared with the contractors, while some of it found its way into his own pocket.

Grant began to sniff out this interesting information and had an aide-de-camp gather testimony highly embarrassing to Captain Hatch. Citizens began to complain of Hatch's covet-ousness to General Meigs. Grant looked into Hatch's records and found some of them mysteriously missing; a further in-vestigation dredged them from the bottom of the Ohio River. With this, Grant clapped Hatch under arrest. He referred his evidence to Meigs's office in Washington, and Meigs passed it on for action by the judge advocate general. That official pre-pared a charge and sent it to Grant with the request that he convene a court-martial. Grant replied that he was not ready to do so; his officers were turning up still more information about Captain Hatch, and if he waited a little longer there would doubtless be additional charges to prefer. For example,

[6] 37:2 House Rep. 2 (serial 1142, 1143); Shannon, *Organization*, espe-cially I, 46–48, 53–55, 99–103; Meneely, *War Department*, pp. 258–77.

the gunboat service on the Western waters demanded that Hatch make large purchases of coal, and his relations with the dealers resembled those with the lumber dealers. Furthermore, he apparently developed a lucrative business in selling to the government at regular prices horses and mules which had been captured from the enemy by the government itself —that is, by its soldiers.[7]

Major D. H. Rucker, an energtic, hard-swearing individual, commanded the Quartemaster's Department depot at Washington, the main depot for the supply of McClellan's Army of the Potomac. In late September Rucker reported to General Meigs that he had just discharged all inspectors of horses at that depot; they were accused upon good evidence of taking bribes for passing horses of inferior quality. Meigs had feared something of the kind and had requested General George Stoneman of McClellan's cavalry and General William F. Barry of the artillery to lend him qualified inspection officers; he had none of his own. The request had not been met, and Rucker's findings were the result.[8]

At the end of the year a Mr. Keams was dismissed from the important post of inspector of the Schuylkill Arsenal, the army's principal clothing depot. After his departure large quantities of the goods he had accepted were reexamined and had to be condemned.[9]

In August three prominent citizens of Chicago called upon General Meigs as representatives of the Union Defense Committee of that city. They informed him that General Fremont at St. Louis had given their committee certain authority to

[7] Meigs to Major J. F. Lee, Lincoln Papers, LXVI, 14358–59, L.C.; complaint of loyal citizens of Cairo to Meigs, Feb. 11, 1862, evidence on Quartermaster's Department at Cairo, Feb. 12, 1862, Edwin M. Stanton Papers, III, L.C.; Q.M.G. Let. B. 58, p. 532; 37:2 House Rep. 2 (serial 1142, 1143), pp. li–lii, 10–29.
[8] Q.M.G. Let. B. 56, pp. 453–54.
[9] Q.M.G. Decision Book 2, p. 117.

assist in the outfitting of new regiments. In the course of exercising this authority they had happened upon information concerning the purchase of horses at Chicago which they thought General Meigs might like to know, namely, that horses were being purchased by quartermaster's agents in Chicago at from $75 to $80 and then charged to the government at $105 to $110. Furthermore, Messrs. Sawyer, Wallace, and Mix, who were advertising for the purchase of 1,000 army horses, were considered by the committee to be neither reliable nor loyal to the Union; and the same was true of a Mr. Howard Priestley who was connected with the supply of horses to the government. The three gentlemen urged General Meigs to have his agents consult with the Union Defense Committee both as to the character and standing of prospective contractors and the current prices of merchandise and supplies. Meigs instructed his quartermaster at Chicago to do so. This was an arrangement possibly subject to abuse by the members of the committee, but under the circumstances it was probably a wise thing to do.[10]

More and more it appeared that stories of misconduct or outright peculation by quartermaster officers tended to center with singular frequency in General Fremont's Western Department. Fremont's chief quartermaster was a Major Justus M. McKinstry, who had graduated from West Point one year after Meigs but with whom Meigs had never been closely associated. McKinstry's chief assistant was Captain P. T. Tumley. McKinstry, Tumley, and the other quartermasters of the Western Department, those at St. Louis being for the most part particular cronies of General Fremont, displayed a somewhat questionable proclivity toward taking advantage of that section of the law on public contracts which allowed contracts to be made without public advertisement and competi-

[10] Q.M.G. Let. B. 56, pp. 324–25.

tive bidding in cases of pressing emergency. General Meigs
chided McKinstry on this point as early as his second day in
the post of quartermaster general, June 14, 1861.

Meigs granted that emergencies sometimes existed which
made public advertising and competitive bidding impossible,
and that in wartime it might also be improper on some occasions to give public notice lest the quartermaster betray intended operations in the field. But the quartermaster general
believed that as the usual thing and for nearly all large purchases or contracts some public notice was both possible and
advantageous. The notice, he said, afforded opportunity for
competition, satisfied the public that business was being conducted fairly, and developed resources and supplies which
quartermasters would not otherwise know. Therefore he instructed McKinstry that whenever it was practicable to give
even a day or two of public notice, he should do so. McKinstry was also to comply with the regulations to transmit to
Meigs's office in every case both the original bids and the
contracts.[11]

This prompt order from Washington McKinstry largely
ignored, and the quartermaster general continued to cast a
jaundiced eye on vouchers from St. Louis which testified that
the quartermasters there continually paid prices which Meigs
considered too high. Fremont and McKinstry, annoyed by
General Meigs's carping at their expenditures, began to complain that the quartermaster general was withholding funds
which they needed if they were to equip their troops adequately and carry on the operations expected of them. This
is the story Fremont told his friend Francis P. Blair, Junior,
the son of Meigs's friend and President Jackson's old adviser
of the same name, the brother of the Postmaster General, and
in his own right a Missouri Congressman. Young Frank Blair

[11] Q.M.G. Let. B. 55, p. 438.

wrote of it to his brother, and Montgomery Blair showed the letter to Meigs. Meigs in turn wrote to the Missouri Blair denying that he had held back any funds required by Fremont or McKinstry. Again he emphasized that he would prefer to have supplies purchased only after public announcement. He stated that public notice did not require postponing the opening of bids for a month or a week or even two days:

If forage, wagons, horses are wanted the law, the necessity are fully met by putting a notice in the paper and purchasing as fast as offers come in, the next day or the same day, take the then lowest bidder or the then most advantageous offer. The next day after you will have a still better offer take that for a portion of your supplies, and so on until you have all you need. By this system I have brought down the prices of horses from $128. to $120. of wagons from $141. to $108. since I came here, and have got abundant supplies.

Meigs did not fully approve of the methods of the Quartermaster's Department in St. Louis; but he had met promptly all requisitions from that place, and he had instructed his officers to spare no effort and no means in their power in aiding Fremont's operations.

I take it for granted that Gen. Fremont leaves estimates of prices of supplies to his Quarter Master and when I find as Quarter Master General that the prices are *probably* too high, it is my duty . . . to say so.

At the same time, I understand that there may be reasons of time, of quality, which induce a General to order a purchase at a higher rate, and while I communicate to the Quarter Master information as to the ruling prices of horses . . . I called upon the Treasury to send *all the money he asked for*.[12]

This was true. On July 27 Meigs had learned through a telegram from Fremont to Montgomery Blair—again Fremont had been operating through his friends the Blairs rather than

[12] Q.M.G. Let. B. 56, pp. 297–99.

through the customary channels—that the public service in Missouri urgently demanded three times the amount of Major McKinstry's last requisition. Meigs immediately had requested Secretary Cameron to ask the Secretary of the Treasury to make the necessary remittance.[13]

General Fremont could not fairly complain that the office of the quartermaster general failed to support him.

All the requisitions for Missouri have been promptly passed thru this office—the delay, if any has occurred is at the Treasury Depart: which has allowed the Department to fall in debt in Cincinnati and Philadelphia each about a million of dollars for clothing & camp equipage.[14]

By the time Meigs wrote his letter to Frank Blair affirming his cooperation with Fremont but criticizing by implication at least Fremont's purchasing methods, Congressman Blair must have begun to feel his own doubts about Fremont. The Pathfinder had surrounded himself with a coterie of sycophants of dubious character, and charges not only of extravagance but of graft as well began to fall upon the purchasing agents. The general kept his headquarters in an opulent mansion rented by the government at $6,000 a year, and there maintained a sort of republican court into which it was difficult to penetrate in order to conduct any business with him. What was worse, Fremont failed to confound his critics by winning military success. General Nathaniel Lyon had taken out a force to clear Missouri of organized secessionists and had met death and defeat at Wilson Creek; Fremont was blamed for failure to give him adequate support. For these and other reasons Frank Blair and Fremont began to draw apart, and by the beginning of September they had quarreled. Fremont thus added a tactical error to his other sins. He owed his

13 Q.M.G. Rep. B. 5, p. 449.
14 Q.M.G. Let. B. 56, pp. 297–99.

position in the first place largely to the friendship of the Blairs, and now having broken with one of them he was sure to have the whole clan against him.[15]

The general chose this inopportune moment to irritate the President. On August 30 Fremont issued a proclamation stating that he found it necessary to assume the administrative powers of the state of Missouri and declaring confiscated the property of all persons who supported the enemy; the slaves of secessionist owners in Missouri henceforth were to be free men. Lincoln had been playing adroitly the delicate game of holding for the Union Missouri and the other border slave states which had not seceded, and Fremont's presumptuous proclamation threatened to undo all his efforts at one stroke. The President promptly requested Fremont to modify his proclamation in accordance with existing law. He wrote a kind letter which assured the general there was no intent to censure him. In reply Fremont refused to withdraw his order unless openly commanded to do so. He sent his wife and brains, Jessie Benton Fremont, eastward to cross swords with Lincoln in an angry interview in which she not only reiterated the refusal to withdraw the offending proclamation but threatened that her husband might renounce allegiance to the United States and set up his own suzerainty in the Mississippi Valley.[16]

Meanwhile Fremont's proclamation and his quarrel with Frank Blair had combined to send Montgomery Blair and General Meigs to St. Louis for an on-the-spot report. Luckily

[15] Randall, *Lincoln the President*, II, 15–21; Williams, *Lincoln Finds a General*, III, 30–33, 61–62; Allan Nevins, *Fremont, the West's Greatest Adventurer* (2 vols., New York, 1928), II, 575–82; William Ernest Smith, *The Francis Preston Blair Family in Politics* (2 vols., New York, 1933), II, 53–75.

[16] Randall, *Lincoln the President*, II, 16–21; Williams, *Lincoln Finds a General*, III, 59–61; Nevins, *Fremont*, II, 561–74, 584–90; Smith, *Blair Family*, II, 75–77.

for Blair and Meigs their train passed Jessie Fremont's in transit, and they were spared an interview with that female terror. They reached St. Louis at midnight of September 12 and remained until the 18th. Meigs was interested especially in the activities of Fremont's quartermasters, and what he found did not please him. McKinstry, who was now sporting the single star of a brigadier general, was a rapid talker whose glibness struck Meigs as rooted in a fear that his statements would not bear examination. Meigs had to admit that Mc-Kinstry had shown energy and resourcefulness in securing clothing, but his contracts were in confusion and seemed to be extravagant. Similarly, McKinstry had been able to purchase better horses than Meigs himself had gathered in Washington, but again the prices were too high. The quartermasters were buying tents of bad patterns at prices fixed not by supply and demand but by General Fremont. Fremont had built more gunboats—at this stage an operation of the Quartermaster's Department—than had been ordered.

If the quartermasters in the command were not what they should have been, neither was Fremont himself. Meigs and Blair found him installed in great style in the fine house rented by the government, surrounded by sentinels and bodyguards. His intimates were broken-down politicians and desperate men whom Meigs considered fit instruments for revolution, crime, and plunder. Regular officers told Meigs they regarded Fremont not only as incompetent but as a man looking less to the country than to the presidency; they considered him to be utterly without principle. While rebel bands killed and ravaged through Missouri, Fremont discouraged the formation of new regiments for defense. When Missourians sought to see him to complain, his guards turned them away. There were rumors that Fremont planned what Jessie implied to the President: to set up for himself an independent empire. "I do not think he is fit for his place," was Meigs's final conclusion; "he is prodigal of money; unscrupulous, surrounded by villains, inacceptable to the people and ambitious; should he see the opportunity he would not hesitate to play Aaron Burr." [17]

On their return to Washington, Meigs and Blair reported to Lincoln and the cabinet, and Meigs spoke his mind about Fremont plainly. The Fremont regime in St. Louis was beginning to topple, and the first victim was General McKinstry. Suspicion of McKinstry had been crowding so close that Fremont decided to ditch him as an impediment even before Meigs's trip to the West. When Meigs returned to his office he found a telegram from Fremont asking him to name a suitable officer to take McKinstry's place, and the quartermaster general sent to St. Louis an experienced quartermaster, Major Robert Allen.[18]

Meanwhile Meigs called on General McKinstry and Captain Tumley to make a full report on all contracts for horses and wagons made under their direction since July 1, to include a statement whether the contracts had been negotiated with due public notice and if not, why not. The two quartermasters were also to transmit an abstract of all payments for horses, wagons, fortifications, gunboats, steamboats purchased or chartered, and rafts constructed, giving the accounts involved, the names and dates of payments, and referring to the contracts under which the purchases were made. In short, Meigs intended an exhaustive review of all that Fremont's quartermasters had done.[19] When he received the information he requested, a cursory examination showed that the Quar-

[17] Meigs Journal, Sept. 10–18, 1861, copy in Nicolay Papers, L.C.; Randall, *Lincoln the President*, II, 20–21; Nevins, *Fremont*, II, 582–84; Smith, *Blair Family*, II, 75.
[18] Q.M.G. Let. B. 56, p. 445.
[19] *Ibid.*, pp. 430–31.

termaster's Department had been paying accounts which belonged properly to the Engineer and Ordnance Departments,
and that other expenditures exceeded the amounts appropriated by Congress. To establish other irregularities would demand a more detailed examination. Meanwhile Meigs admon-
ished Major Allen to bestir himself to set things aright:

> Leave no margin for profit in jobbing contracts. Let speculators
> wait. I have within a few days for example a letter from the
> Union Defence Committee of Chicago naming a person to supply
> 1000 horses quite as good as the Government has been getting in
> Chicago and offering these horses at ninety-five dollars each.
> Why then should the large prices in St. Louis be paid. It is
> reported that horse contracts are sold by speculators in St. Louis.
> The papers so publish and loudly declare this, that the officers
> of the Quarter Masters Department cannot ignore the accusation.
> Whenever a bill bears the aspect of jobbing, speculation or il-
> legality set it aside as one of those to be deferred. . . .
> Of course you understand your duty in case the commanding
> General assumes the responsibility of ordering an account to be
> paid. He is the responsible head in his Department and must judge
> in extreme cases. . . . But he should be made aware with all re-
> spect and loyalty of the legal and other obligations, so that he can
> act with knowledge and be protected against errors arising from
> inexperience in the Regulations.[20]

By the time Meigs addressed this advice and injunction to
Major Allen, Fremont's days as commander in the West were
almost over. After the visit of Meigs and Montgomery Blair
to St. Louis, Fremont's quarrel with Frank Blair intensified
to the point where the general threw the Congressman into
prison for attacking him in letters to the President and a member of the cabinet.

The imprisonment clinched the enmity of the Blairs. And
although Fremont had rid himself of McKinstry, he did nothing effective to clear up the suspicions which shrouded the

[20] *Ibid.*, 492–93.

activities of his agents. Nor did he win any military renown. On the contrary, he reported the surrender to the enemy of an outpost at Lexington numbering 2,800 men. When Fremont took the field, Washington sent Brigadier General Lorenzo Thomas, the adjutant general, to undertake another investigation of the whole Missouri scene, and the upshot was an order of October 24 dismissing Fremont from his command.[21]

Two official committees, one representing the executive, one the legislature, presently brought to public notice the methods of Fremont's quartermasters. Lincoln appointed Joseph Holt, the forceful Secretary of War of the last months of Buchanan's administration, David Davis, and Hugh Campbell a Commission on the Debts of the Western Department, with power to investigate fully the accounts of Fremont's agents, to pay such of them as had been contracted legitimately, but to refuse payment of accounts contracted in violation of law. General Meigs instructed Major Allen that in the meantime he should pay no claims that had originated prior to October 14 and none arising out of General McKinstry's contracts whether originated before or after that date.

Now Secretary Cameron instructed Meigs to have Major Allen make a clean sweep of all of McKinstry's agents; too many of those who had blackened the reputation of the old regime in St. Louis were still functioning under the new. Such men must go.[22]

Meanwhile, the House of Representatives had established in July a special committee on army contracts under the chairmanship of Charles H. Van Wyck of New York. It was this committee whose report fills over 2,000 pages in the Congres-

[21] Randall, *Lincoln the President*, II, 20–23; Williams, *Lincoln Finds a General*, III, 63–65; Nevins, *Fremont*, II, 600–615.
[22] Q.M.G. Let. B. 57, pp. 335, 439, 482–83.

sional documents. The group continued its hearings from July 1, 1861 until April, 1862, and it deliberated until the following July before it presented its report. Its field was fraud and corruption in the procurement of army supplies in general, but in particular it turned its attention to the Fremont regime in St. Louis.[23]

Meigs had thought on his visit to that city that Fremont was paying exorbitant prices to a special friend for building fortifications around the city; investigation showed that this friend received for his work $190,000, an amount probably three times what the cost should have been, and this in spite of the gentleman's having no knowledge of military engineering. Fremont contracted with another friend—like the first, he was a Californian—to build thirty-eight mortar boats at $8,250 each; an experienced builder estimated the proper cost at a maximum of $4,927.[24]

The Holt-Davis-Campbell Commission learned of, and the Van Wyck Committee confirmed, the activities during Fremont's tenure of the St. Louis firm of Child, Pratt and Fox and of a Detroit firm of which a Mr. Brady was a partner. Both these organizations acted as middlemen between Fremont's quartermasters and private suppliers, merely transferring or ordering goods from other parties and taking profits which the Presidential commission thought sometimes ran as high as one hundred percent. For example, an agent of the firm of Code, Hopper and Gratz offered to General McKinstry some thousands of newly covered canteens, at thirty-six and one-half cents each. General McKinstry instead of accepting the offer directly referred the agent to Mr. Brady. The latter personage then bought the canteens at thirty-six or

[23] 37:2 House Rep. 2 (serial 1142, 1143); Shannon, *Organization*, I, 58; Meneely, *War Department*, pp. 258–60.
[24] Cited in Randall, *Lincoln the President*, II, 20.

thirty-six and one-half cents and proceeded to deliver them to General McKinstry at forty-four cents. This was at a time when a requisition upon General Meigs's agents at New York or Philadelphia could have produced 10,000 canteens within a few days at the lower contract prices prevailing in those cities.[25]

Rather than conduct competitive bidding and award contracts upon the results, the agents of the Quartermaster's Department at St. Louis customarily purchased upon a "requisition," an example of which was reproduced by the Van Wyck Committee:

Headquarters Quartermaster's Department
St. Louis, September 2, 1861.
Messrs. Livingston, Bell & Co. will furnish quartermaster's department with—

5,000 pairs cavalry boots, 5,000 suits infantry uniforms, 5,000 canteens, 10,000 infantry hats, 10,000 army shoes, 10,000 army overcoats, 5,000 knapsacks, 10,000 pairs socks, 10,000 undershirts, (army pattern).

All to be made of the best army material and conform to army regulations and requirements; the cost of manufacture, material, and transportation to be furnished to this department, upon which the quartermaster will allow a fair mercantile profit to the contractors, Messrs. L., B. & Co.

J. McKinstry,
Major and Quartermaster.[26]

Upon such vaguely worded requisitions, the Van Wyck Committee discovered, the firm of Child, Pratt and Fox furnished from time to time army supplies to a value of over $800,000; apparently the price of not a single article was determined beforehand. Accordingly, the committee were interested to learn what Child, Pratt and Fox might consider "a fair mercantile profit." They questioned on this point the

[25] Q.M.G. Let. B. 57, pp. 482–83, 490–91.
[26] 37:2 House Rep. 2 (serial 1142, 1143), p. 54.

bookkeeper of the firm, and on a representative sale of blankets
he informed them that the profit would be about forty percent.[27]

All this made sensational and appalling reading, and it still
does. But it is possible to infer too much from such a thing
as the Van Wyck Committee report. In the first place, in the
time-honored manner of Congressional committees, the Van
Wyck Committee had a nose for the sensational and were not
always judicious in their evaluation of testimony. Sometimes
their report was misleading. The committee placed great stress
upon an incident of October, 1861, at which time, the testimony indicated, 1,000 horses were ordered by the quartermaster general to be shipped from Pittsburgh to Springfield,
Illinois, by railroad. The committee believed that the horses
were almost wholly unfit for service; of one lot of 252 of
them, the committee reported, 225 were rejected upon inspection by a Western quartermaster. If this were true, and it may
well have been, then the inspectors of horses at the points
where the animals were first purchased were seriously at fault.
General Meigs realized that such things occurred, and he was
constantly trying to obtain more reliable inspection officers.

But the committee went on to make more of these 1,000
horses than mere faulty inspection. To the Congressmen the
most shocking aspect of the case was the buying of the horses
in Pennsylvania for use in the West. "No good or valid reason," said the committee, "can be assigned for purchasing
horses in Pennsylvania to be sent, at vast expense, to Illinois.
Better and cheaper horses could have been purchased in Illinois, and the cost of transportation saved." The committee
considered the whole transaction "most extraordinary and disgraceful." [28]

[27] *Ibid.*
[28] *Ibid.*, pp. lvi–lvii.

It was less extraordinary when viewed in the light of General Meigs's explanation. At the time of the incident, said Meigs, the supply of horses moving to the Army of the Potomac was threatening to become excessive; horses ordered for an artillery force were arriving before the guns. Rather than feed idle horses at Washington, Meigs directed the quartermaster at Pittsburgh to stop all horses being forwarded to the capital through that place and to send them West, in order to meet the needs of the armies there. Accordingly, several hundred horses were halted at Pittsburgh and at points farther west. Most of them certainly came originally not from Pennsylvania but from Ohio, Indiana, and Illinois. The action of the quartermaster general was neither most extraordinary nor disgraceful, but a sensible method of dealing with an unusual situation.[29]

Nevertheless, most of the findings of the committee cannot be challenged. Misconduct and corruption existed among the agents of the Quartermaster's Department. But many of the really grave instances of corruption came from a single place: the Fremont-McKinstry headquarters in St. Louis. And it was rare in any event to find misconduct on the part of a regular army quartermaster. The difficulties sprang largely from the need in an emergency to rely upon agents whose qualifications could not be examined adequately, and whose appointment was controlled not by General Meigs but by local officers and state officials. This was the final verdict of the Van Wyck Committee itself:

While the investigations of the committee have impressed them with the conviction that, with a few exceptions, the quartermasters and commissaries in the regular employment of the government as members of the old regular army, are gentlemen of ample and equal capacity and fidelity, and in the midst of our misfor-

[29] Q.M.G. Rep. B. 6, pp. 33–34.

tunes have been ever jealous for the public welfare, the occasional and irresponsible agents employed by the departments to purchase supplies have, either through want of experience or integrity, sacrificed the public interests.[30]

Paying high prices did not guarantee Meigs's quartermasters and other Federal agents satisfaction in their purchases. All too often in the early months of the war uniforms turned out to have been fashioned from a cheap imitation of regulation army cloth. When worn, such garments were likely to disintegrate; a Wisconsin regiment which received an issue of bright blue uniforms had to be supplied with overalls ten days later so that it might appear with decency on the streets.[31]

Obviously, much of this sort of thing was due to profiteering, but much of it was due also to sheer scarcity of standard cloths. To fill pressing needs General Meigs was willing to purchase almost any cloth on the market. Some civilian garments that his agents bought were not even redyed in the uniform color of the army. Much of the material was of inferior quality, and Meigs recognized this fact.

But the troops were clothed and rescued from severe suffering [he wrote], and those who saw sentinels walking post in the capital of the United States in freezing weather in their drawers, without trousers or overcoats, will not blame the department for its efforts to clothe them, even in materials not quite so durable as army blue kersey.[32]

Meigs urged that in order to meet the emergency uniforms be purchased abroad, but the response was a noisy protest from the "Buy American" lobby of the day. In August, 1861, the quartermaster general arranged through the American legation in Paris to purchase from the contractors to the French

[30] 37:2 House Rep. 2 (serial 1142, 1143), pp. 54–55.
[31] Shannon, *Organization*, I, 95.
[32] *O.R.*, ser. 3, II, 802–3.

army a complete set of clothing and camp equipage for 10,000 men, including in addition to uniforms such items as knapsacks, blankets, tents, cartridge boxes, and medicine chests. The material proved to be of excellent quality, and its cost differed little from that of American goods. It served to equip ten regiments, some of them operating in Missouri, some around Washington.[33]

Even small purchases abroad doubtless would have sufficed to arouse the ire of a certain class of patriots, but the ensuing uproar was all the greater after some newspapers blew up overseas purchases of $800,000 to $25,000,000 or even $60,-000,000. The Board of Trade of the city of Boston responded by dispatching to Washington an emissary who bore a letter filled with impassioned threats and pleadings. The Boston businessmen foresaw the ruin of government finances through the drain of specie abroad, a business panic, unemployment, and general distress, all because the army had bought some supplies in Europe. Nor, if their importunities were ignored, would the banks and businesses of the country feel obliged to do aught but let the government stew in its own juice:

The banks [the Boston letter said] have taken a grave responsibility, and acted in the most patriotic manner, based upon their entire confidence both in the ability of the Government and its disposition to do all that can be done to make the burden of this dreadful war for the maintenance of our glorious Union bear as lightly as it is possible . . . upon the industrial classes as well as upon the great interests of the country. But if the enormous amounts which they place at the disposal of the Government are to be used in drawing their lifeblood from them, they would be obliged to abandon the system which has thus far worked so admirably.

The woolen mills of the United States, continued the letter, stood fully capable of supplying every need of the army; to

[33] *O.R.*, ser. 3, I, 393, 683; ser. 3, II, 804.

buy abroad would lead to a glutting of the market, and in consequence, "Self-preservation . . . would warn them to stop operations, throw their hands out of employment, and innocently on their part—nay, of necessity—spread dismay, distress, and ruin among the people." [34]

Whatever the merits of this argument, had its major premise been true—and such merits would be difficult to find—the Boston Board of Trade had wandered far off base. At the moment nothing was more unlikely than a glut in the clothing market. General Meigs avowed that should the Board of Trade be correct in its opinion, and the domestic factories prove able to supply regulation cloth in sufficient quantity before cloth could be imported from Europe, he would be glad to purchase the material at any reasonable price; but there existed no evidence that this was the case. "Could 150,000 suits of clothing, overcoats, coats, and pantaloons be placed to-day in depot," he wrote, "it would scarce supply the calls now before me." [35]

Despite Meigs's cogent defense of his purchases in France, no similar order ever was placed again. Early in 1862 a new Secretary of War imposed a definite suspension upon contracting abroad. An exception was made in the case of foreign blankets, which General Meigs continued to purchase throughout the war because the domestic manufacturers simply proved incapable of furnishing an adequate supply. In late 1864 Senator Henry Wilson of Massachusetts questioned Meigs about these purchases, and the quartermaster general assured him: "They are not purchased in competition with the domestic blankets for I consider it the duty of this Department to procure all that it can get at any reasonable price from domestic manufacturers." The question was one of necessity. There was

[34] *O.R.*, ser. 3, I, 583–86.
[35] *O.R.*, ser. 3, I, 583, 608–9.

no danger that the blankets might leak into the civilian market and compete with the American product there: "These are, if imported, expressly for the U. S. and under orders from authorized officers, delivered to the U. S. in bond, and are admitted duty free." The blankets were an exception to the rule; by this time they had long since been the only article of military equipage which American manufacturers did not offer in sufficient supply.[36]

Whether the American mills which croaked so loudly when the government purchased abroad did not themselves import foreign materials is another story.

While shortage of materials was probably the major cause of the clothing problem of the first months of the war, faulty distribution was another. Uniforms might lie uselessly in quartermaster's depots while troops marched in rags.[37] Again, considering the inadequacy of Quartermaster's Department personnel, both civilian and military, in numbers and experience alike, it is difficult to imagine how the distribution system could have been anythng but faulty. After the war was a year old Meigs was still complaining to his superiors in the War Department of aides insufficient in numbers and in preparation.[38]

It is not pleasant to contemplate corruption and graft interfering with the supply of the urgent needs of American soldiers, nor even less to envision a soldier's uniform disintegrating on his back under the first storm. The Lincoln administration has been castigated severely for allowing these things to take place. A part of the criticism has been just; the country would surely have profited from an early removal of Secretary of War Simon Cameron and some of his henchmen.

[36] Q.M.G. Let. B. 82, p. 21.
[37] Shannon, *Organization*, I, 88–90.
[38] *O.R.*, ser. 3, II, 789.

On the other hand, Americans who in two world wars have witnessed the difficulties of rapid expansion of the armed forces, even when mobilization had been more or less carefully planned—Americans who can remember, for example, the wooden guns and mock tanks of the Louisiana maneuvers of 1941—should be able to sympathize with a government that increased its army from 17,000 to nearly 500,000 in four months, with the aid of no mobilization plan whatever.

When Beauregard fired on Fort Sumter, it will be remembered, the regular army of the United States carried on its rolls 17,113 officers and men. Just less than three months later the President reported to Congress that the army numbered about 310,000. On August 3, after one month more, the War Department announced that it had under arms 485,640 three-year men. In four months, then, the strength of the army had increased twenty-seven times. During World War I, in contrast, in the comparable period between April and August, 1917, the army did not quite triple itself. There was no genuinely comparable period in World War II, since the Selective Service Act of 1940 initiated the expansion of the army over a year before the outbreak of hostilities. But it is instructive to note that it was considered an important achievement to raise the army from an authorized strength of 375,000 in June of 1940 to an actual strength of about 1,500,000 a year later, something over a fourfold increase in the space of one year.

Thus the army grew far less rapidly in either of the world wars of the twentieth century than in the Civil War. It is true that by 1917 and certainly by 1940 the problems of maintaining and training a soldier had become far more complex than they were in 1861. Yet in 1861 the troops had to eat and be clothed and given shelter and arms, albeit simpler arms, just as in 1917 and 1940. And in 1861 there existed none of the planning machinery to prepare for the task of mobilization, the lack of which in 1917 or 1940 would have appeared unthinkable.[39]

Under these conditions it is not surprising that the mobilization of 1861 was accompanied by blunders, snags, inefficiency, and a looseness of control that opened the way to jobbery. What is surprising is that by the late summer of 1861 the United States possessed an army of half a million, rationally organized and probably as well or better supplied and equipped as any army in history. Even the most hostile critics of the Lincoln government concede that the spectacle of soldiers parading the streets in flour sacks characterized only the early months of the war. Thereafter the quality of clothing became generally acceptable. And while there were occasional shortages of this and other items of supply, such shortages usually reflected the attrition of hard campaigning. If extravagance continued—and Meigs would have been the first to admit that it did and to regret it—nevertheless extravagance was better than scarcity. Far worse indictments of army supply services are on record than that which General McDowell expressed in December, 1861, before the Congressional Committee on the Conduct of the War:

There never was an army in the world that began to be supplied as well as ours is. I believe a French army of half the size of ours could be supplied with what we waste. The amount of the waste is fearful. I am ashamed of the amount of scolding I have to do on the subject of waste of bread. I have seen loaves of bread thrown away that had not even been broken open. Our men will not use it if it is a little stale. I have begged them not to draw it, if they cannot eat it. They get large pay, and when the sutlers come around with their pies, tarts, and cakes, the men stuff them-

[39] Williams, *Lincoln Finds a General*, I, 115–16, 118, 120–21; Dwight D. Eisenhower, *Crusade in Europe* (Garden City, N. Y., 1948), pp. 2–4; Kent Roberts Greenfield *et al.*, *United States Army in World War II: The Organization of Ground Combat Troops* (Washington, 1947), esp. pp. 1–155.

selves with those things and waste the rations drawn from the government. It is a waste that comes out of the country at large. But I believe we ought to supply twice the force we do with what it costs us to supply this force.[40]

McClellan's Army of the Potomac was fed, clothed, and equipped. Through the months of early autumn its officers drilled it to proficiency in the parade-ground evolutions of the day, and November brought a flood of dazzling reviews. Tightly packed masses of men in blue marched on Arlington Heights, accouterments gleaming under the pale sun of Indian summer, a fine spectacle for the capital. But the capital and the North began to murmur restlessly, and some began to express doubts about the Young Napoleon. Here was the army, terrible with banners. But when would it do something? When would it march to meet the rebels?

As the year approached its end, McClellan had commanded the Army of the Potomac for about five months, the Armies of the United States for nearly two. He had drilled the troops around Washington endlessly, and to all appearances they had become a competent fighting machine—at least as competent as they could be before they were tested in battle. Yet to drill and to fight affairs of outposts was all that the army accomplished. Not even the President himself could discover anything of McClellan's plans for the future, if such existed. The Radicals, much of the press, and a strong tide of public opinion were pushing for action; and politically Lincoln found the pressure difficult to bear. He felt he should at least be able to learn from McClellan something of his intentions, so that he could put off the impatient with some definite word of action impending. Instead he received from the general only a dose of insolence.

On top of all this, at the end of the year McClellan took

[40] 37:3, *Report of the Committee on the Conduct of the War,* I, 139.

sick, and his chief of staff (and father-in-law) with him. Since not a single healthy person knew now what the general's plans might be, nobody could do anything. Lincoln nearly despaired. The announcement from McClellan's headquarters said the general suffered only from a cold, but rumor had it that the ailment was typhoid fever, which could have meant a McClellan sick for weeks or even about to die. On January 10 the distraught President stopped at General Meigs's office. "General, what shall I do?" he asked Meigs. "The people are impatient; Chase has no money and he tells me he can raise no more; the General of the Army has typhoid fever. The bottom is out of the tub. What shall we do?" [41]

Already in Scott's day Meigs had complained that the general-in-chief ought to have a staff of officers high enough in rank to advise and sustain him and prevent the whole burden of command from weighing upon one man's shoulders.[42] McClellan had failed to alter Scott's system, and to this it had come. With the general-in-chief sick in bed, the army was headless. Such a situation was insupportable. If the general-in-chief would not create an adequate staff, then the President must improvise a substitute in a council of principal officers. This is what Meigs invited Lincoln to do. If the Confederates in Virginia were as strong as they were reported to be (they were not), then they might attack any day. Lincoln should at least consult with the principal officers, and perhaps he might select the responsible commander for an emergency.[43]

Lincoln accepted the advice. That evening he called into conference two of McClellan's division commanders, Major

[41] M. C. Meigs, "The Relations of President Lincoln and Secretary Stanton to the Military Commanders in the Civil War," *A.H.R.*, XXVI, 292; Randall, *Lincoln the President*, II, 74–75; Williams, *Lincoln Finds a General*, I, 122–36.

[42] Meigs Let. B., 1861, p. 87.

[43] Meigs, "Relations," *A.H.R.*, XXVI, 292.

General Irvin McDowell and Brigadier General William B. Franklin, the latter having been Captain Franklin of the Capitol Extension. The President reiterated to McDowell and Franklin that if something were not done soon, "the bottom would be out of the whole affair." He asked their opinion on the possibility of beginning promptly active operations with the Army of the Potomac. The generals agreed that a movement ought to begin, but they differed on the kind of movement. McDowell preferred an advance down the Virginia railroads, Franklin a journey by water to the York River to operate thence against Richmond. The President asked the generals to attempt to reconcile their differences during the next day and to meet with him again in the evening.[44]

When the group convened again at the White House, some of the cabinet were also present. McDowell read a paper which he said represented both his views and Franklin's. Franklin now agreed with him that because of the difficulties of transportation, if operations were going to commence immediately the idea of the water route had better be abandoned. It was obvious, however, that Franklin was reluctant to accept the land route, and Montgomery Blair pressed for the water route. Accordingly the President made no decision; instead he proposed that General Meigs be consulted on the feasibility of providing transportation for a movement to the York. The council would meet again at three P.M. the next day, Sunday, January 12; General Meigs would attend.[45]

McDowell and Franklin called on Meigs in the morning, and the three soldiers together thrashed out what they should say

[44] Irvin McDowell in William Swinton, *Campaigns of the Army of the Potomac* (New York, 1866), pp. 79–82; also printed in Henry J. Raymond, *The Life and Public Services of Abraham Lincoln* (New York, 1865), pp. 772–77.
[45] McDowell in Swinton. *Campaigns,* pp. 82–83; David Donald, ed., *Inside Lincoln's Cabinet: The Civil War Diaries of Salmon P. Chase* (New York, 1954), pp. 59–60.

at the council that afternoon. Meigs agreed with McDowell that the enemy should be fought in his present position, at Manassas. The quartermaster general believed that to assemble water transportation even for 30,000 men, let alone the bulk of the Army of the Potomac, would require four to six weeks. He restated this view when the generals met with Lincoln, Seward, Chase, and Blair at the White House. Lincoln, however, announced that the morning had brought out McClellan, looking well. Since the council had been called because of McClellan's illness, now that the general-in-chief was up and about the President preferred to postpone further discussion until the next day, when McClellan would be able to attend. Perhaps in this way the councils suggested by Meigs performed their most valuable service: to impel McClellan to get out of bed.[46]

When McClellan appeared the next day he may have been looking well, but his attitude was sour. He considered the councils a plot by McDowell to stab him in the back, and he virtually said so. When Blair asked him directly what he intended to do with his army, he did not answer. There followed an awkward silence. Meigs, who was sitting next to McClellan, spoke softly in an effort to bring the general-in-chief to say something. McClellan objected that if he moved he would face an enemy who outnumbered him. Meigs replied that nevertheless he must at least show he had something in mind, for the President expected it.

"If I tell him my plans," McClellan half sneered, "they will be in the New York *Herald* tomorrow morning. He can't keep a secret. He will tell them to Tad." This was nonsense.

"That is a pity," said Meigs, "but he is the President—the

[46] Meigs, "Relations," *A.H.R.*, XXVI, 292; Meigs Diary, Jan. 12, 1862; McDowell in Swinton, *Campaigns*, pp. 83–84; Donald, ed., *Inside Lincoln's Cabinet*, pp. 60–62.

Commander-in-Chief; he has a right to know; it is not respect-
ful to sit mute when he so clearly requires you to speak. He
is superior to all."

McClellan at length decided he had better say something,
but he chose to divert the council from the Army of the Potomac by promising an advance in Kentucky. Further than
that, he said he was unwilling to elaborate his plans; he believed that the fewer the people who knew about military
movements the better—which is a sensible policy within limits.
Lincoln then asked whether McClellan had in mind any particular time for advancing; he would not ask the time, but if
McClellan had established a date in his own mind, Lincoln
would be satisfied for the present with that. McClellan said
he had. Recognizing the futility of attempting to pry any
further information from the petulant general-in-chief, Lincoln adjourned the meeting.[47]

So the bottom was still out of the tub. Meigs's suggestion
for a council of war had accomplished little. It brought no
reform in the organization of the high command, and for
months to come McClellan would continue to skirmish with
Lincoln and the War Department rather than with the enemy.

This truly was a time of troubles. The *Trent* affair threatened to erupt in war with England, and Simon Cameron's
impudence and incompetence were driving Lincoln toward a
new Secretary of War. On top of everything else, Meigs
looked at his account books and found the appropriations for
his department exhausted while debts rose like flood waters.
In the emergency session of the summer before, Congress
had voted funds for the support and equipment of an army
of 300,000 and promptly had gone on to authorize army increases that totaled far above 300,000. By January more than

[47] Meigs, "Relations," *A.H.R.*, XXVI, 292–93; Meigs Diary, Jan. 13,
1862; McDowell in Swinton, *Campaigns*, pp. 84–85; *McClellan's Own
Story*, pp. 155–59.

twice that number were in service, and financial chaos seemed about to result. The quartermaster general continued to find supplies by prevailing upon contractors and manufacturers to sell to him on credit. But he feared the end of this policy would be to impose such a strain upon his suppliers' credit that they would break down and leave him unable to furnish the army even with such things as forage for its immediate needs.[48]

Here was democracy foundering, a great nation seemingly unable to save itself because the captain would not grasp the helm and the crew could only bicker among themselves.

Congress had returned to Washington in December, but its interests ran more to recriminations over the disasters of Bull Run and Ball's Bluff than to giving the administration constructive help. Not until January was well advanced did Congress bail out Meigs's department with a new appropriation, freeing the quartermaster general at least from the fear that his operations would halt for lack of money.[49]

He still had as much trouble as he could handle. A persistent cause of irregularities and confusion in supply was the slipshod administration of the War Department in the hands of Simon Cameron. "Cameron means well but is weak and infirm of purpose," was Meigs's verdict on the Secretary, and it pretty well hit the mark.[50] In Republican politics Cameron was doubtless a Machiavellian spoilsman. But his trouble in the War Department seems to have been at least as much a matter simply of finding himself in a job he was not big enough to fill, and like John B. Floyd before him turning for aid to his friends, who generally lacked qualifications for the responsibilities granted to them, and who sometimes were dishonest.

[48] *O.R.*, ser. 3, I, 866–68.
[49] *Ibid.*
[50] Meigs Journal, July 29, 1861, copy in Nicolay Papers, L.C.

As a personal and political friend Cameron named Alexander Cummings as purchasing officer in New York, injecting into the city an irresponsible agent at a time when New York contained officers of the Quartermaster's and Commissary Departments who were familiar both with the needs of the army and the markets of the city, neither of which qualifications Cummings possessed.[51]

The beginning of January was perhaps the darkest hour alike for the quartermaster general and the Union cause, but with the new year there gradually dawned light. The councils of war at the White House served at least to rouse McClellan from his sickbed. Congress moved to appropriate new funds for the Quartermaster's Department. And Lincoln lost patience with Simon Cameron. He packed that somewhat devious gentleman off to St. Petersburg as minister to Russia, and in Cameron's place he named Edwin M. Stanton Secretary of War. The transfer occurred because the President had come to recognize that Cameron, saddled on him partly as a result of a bargain at the Chicago convention of 1860, could not measure up to his post, and to a lesser extent because Cameron had inserted in his annual report for 1861 a statement urging the employment of slaves as soldiers, a gesture similar to Fremont's proclamation of August 30 and like it calculated to estrange moderate Unionists from the administration. Lincoln named Stanton in Cameron's place because he was a War Democrat and a man of energy and ability.[52]

Stanton has come down to us at worst as an unctuous double-dealer and at best an enigma. He professed the utmost regard for the President, but at the same time he held hands behind Lincoln's back with the Congressional Radicals who were the President's most dangerous enemies. He played a

[51] 37:2 House Rep. 2 (serial 1142, 1143), p. 55.
[52] Randall, *Lincoln the President*, II, 54–62.

kindred devious game with his friend General McClellan. His political and personal animosities may have affected his treatment of generals and thus the conduct of the war.[53] But if Lincoln was seeking from Stanton vigor and energy in the War Department, these he got in full measure. The irregular purchasing agents disappeared. Instead of the indecisive queries of Simon Cameron, General Meigs began to receive from the Secretary of War crisp, incisive directives to do this or do that. And at the outset of his administration Stanton sought to effect a thorough survey of misconduct in the Quartermaster's Department. Upon receipt of the evidence against corrupt or careless inspecting at the Schuylkill Arsenal, Stanton had Meigs issue the following circular:

> February 19, 1862
> All the officers of the Quarter Masters Department are instructed to make special reports to the Quarter Master General upon every case of which they have knowledge in which—
> 1st  Fraud has been practised upon the Government by contractors by means of a different, or inferior article from that contracted for
> 2nd  Where Inspectors have neglected their duty
> In order that suits may be brought against both fraudulent contractors and negligent Inspectors.
>> By order of the Secretary of War,
>> M. C. Meigs, Quarter Master General [54]

For Meigs the advent of Stanton was by far the most important event of January. The Secretary and the quartermaster general were soon to share confidence in each other, and they learned to work in ready cooperation. Stanton might bark at Meigs in occasional impatience, and his restless watchfulness over the affairs of his department kept the Secretary dispatch-

[53] T. Harry Williams, *Lincoln and the Radicals* (Madison, Wisconsin, 1941), especially pp. 90–93, 125–26.
[54] Q.M.G. Let. B. 58, p. 243.

ing instructions to the quartermaster general. But in the larger details of administration Stanton was willing to trust Meigs, for Meigs produced results. And the quartermaster general knew now that there stood behind him a determined figure ready to support to the limit any needful request.

The coming of Stanton marks, in fact, a turning point in the wartime history of the Quartermaster General's Office; it ended for Meigs the most critical period of the war. By now the initial expansion of the army was complete. Wholly untested persons needed no longer to be appointed to highly responsible positions, and those who still held on might gradually be weeded out. The worst of the corrupt and incompetent among the quartermaster agents were already discovered and eliminated; most of the rest speedily followed. The ejection of the small remainder would depend primarily upon the gradual refinement of Meigs's administrative techniques and insight.

True, inferior goods and equipment continued from time to time to reach the Union army. Contractors continued, more than occasionally, to enjoy rewards that were probably exorbitant. Occasional instances of misconduct continued to mar the record of quartermaster officers.[55] But such instances became increasingly exceptional. Scandals at the outset of the war sprang from the fantastic expansion of the army accompanied by a need to purchase supplies through inexperienced and often unqualified agents in a seller's market. When these extreme conditions ceased, the honest men who headed the War Department and the Quartermaster's Department were able to bring fraud and peculation largely to an end. Considering the breakdown of public morality which was to become apparent after the war, this was no mean achievement.

[55] See, for example, the cases of Samuel Wilson, horse and grain dealer from Pennsylvania, and James Belger, quartermaster at Baltimore, Q.M.G. Let. B. 60, p. 332, and Q.M.G. Let. B. 67, pp. 40–41.

# IX

# THE QUARTERMASTER GENERAL

THE COMING of Edwin Stanton to the War Department was a turning point, but it could not bring to the Union forces perfection in army command. Too many difficulties of the Civil War command system, and of the Quartermaster General's Office in particular, were rooted in traditional methods of administration to yield to the personal abilities of a Stanton or a Meigs. Changes in method as well as in men were required, but the changes in method did not often take place. Throughout the Civil War, the command system of the army rested upon that chaos of independent bureau chiefs which would not disappear until Elihu Root founded the modern United States Army during the presidency of Theodore Roosevelt.

Under the Constitution the President was Commander-in-Chief of the army, and while he might delegate specific tasks he could not delegate the final responsibility of leadership. Ultimately the command of the army was his. As his deputy the Secretary of War exercised direct control of the military arm; the Secretary of War was the functioning commander of the army. It is true that there usually existed the post of general-in-chief, occupied at the outset of the war by Winfield Scott and now by George McClellan. But this highest of professional posts was an anomaly. No statute defined the relations of the general-in-chief with the Secretary of War, and one reason why no statute existed is that any legal definition would have had to reflect the reality of the situation, which was that in point of law the responsibilities and powers of the general-in-chief were minimal. If the general-in-chief became the true head of the army, he usurped the place of the Secretary of War and violated the constitutional principle of civilian control of the military. If, on the other hand, the Secretary of War as the President's deputy genuinely commanded the army—and constitutionally such was his duty—then the general-in-chief became superfluous.

What was needed, and what Elihu Root was to accomplish, was to abolish the office of general-in-chief and to substitute as the principal professional office the place of chief of staff to the Secretary of War, recognizing that authority was the Secretary's. What took place, meanwhile, was constant bickering between the civilian Secretary and the professional general-in-chief. Friction had reached something of a climax when Jefferson Davis was Secretary of War, leading General Scott to transfer his headquarters from Washington to New York, where he basked in lordly but somewhat impotent isolation rather than endure constant reminders that it was the Secretary who really was running the show. Presently McClellan's shortcomings were to lead even to a temporary suspension of the post of general-in-chief.[1]

Among the most severe limitations upon the power of the general-in-chief was the existence of the independent bureau chiefs. These were the heads of the seven bureaus into which army administration was divided: the adjutant general, the

---

[1] For the nineteenth-century command system, see especially John M. Schofield, *Forty-six Years in the Army* (New York, 1897), pp. 468–83; William H. Carter, "Creation of the American General Staff," 68:1 Sen. Doc. 119 (serial 8254); Elliott, *Winfield Scott*, pp. 425–28, 648–57; Lewis, *Sherman*, pp. 601–23.

commissary general, the surgeon general, the paymaster general, the chief engineer, the chief of ordnance, and, of course, the quartermaster general. General Meigs and his fellow bureau chiefs were not responsible to the general-in-chief of the army; General McClellan and his successors, Henry W. Halleck and Grant, did not command them. They reported directly to the Secretary of War. When the Secretary of War happened to be a weak man, such as Simon Cameron, the independent bureau chiefs were the real rulers of the army, each probably moving in his own way. It goes without saying that such a system was not particularly efficient. When the Secretary of War happened to be a strong personality, such as Edwin M. Stanton, then a certain coordination of the work of the bureau chiefs could be effected by the Secretary. Again, however, efficiency was not prominent; for with a strong Secretary the system put more authority into the hands of one man than a single human being could well exercise. Stanton had to have fingers in too many pies. It was asking too much that he familiarize himself with the detailed work of the seven bureaus.

Under Simon Cameron, then, General Meigs found himself the chief of his own empire. Under Edwin M. Stanton he felt the authority of the Secretary of War, and Stanton put his own impress upon the whole War Department. But even under Stanton the Secretary's oversight of the quartermaster general was somewhat erratic, for Stanton bore too many duties to permit his exercise of a sustained supervision over General Meigs. The sharp orders from the Secretary to Meigs were frequent, but they could not flow constantly.

Under these circumstances a principal shortcoming of the army organization was the lack of machinery to coordinate the work of the quartermaster general with the over-all plans and demands of the service. Particularly there existed no agency for systematic formulation of supply needs in accordance with systematic plans of the size and mission of the army. Beyond that, there was nothing resembling an office of industrial mobilization to ensure that the national economy would be able to satisfy the requirements of supply officers such as General Meigs. No one gave thought to directing the conversion of industry from peacetime to war production, to government aid in the development of industrial facilities, or to ensuring the government a preferential supply of strategic materials. If any officer possessed authority to perform these tasks, it was the Secretary of War; but again, the Secretary had too many other things to do.

Supply problems were not even centralized in the hands of the quartermaster general, for Meigs was not the only supply officer among the seven bureau chiefs. Thus General Meigs had to coordinate his own work with that of several of his colleagues, although the War Department possessed a minimum of machinery to assist such coordination. The procurement and issuance of arms and ammunition, provisions, and medical and hospital stores did not belong to the Quartermaster's Department; these duties were functions of the Ordnance, Subsistence, and Medical Departments. On the other hand, the Quartermaster's Department did transport ordnance, subsistence, and medical stores, carrying them from depots to camps, on the march, and to the front.[2]

More positively, what were the duties of Meigs's department? The 1861 edition of the *Revised Regulations* of the army spelled them out specifically:

1064. This department provides the quarters and transportation of the army; storage and transportation for all army supplies; army clothing; camp and garrison equipage; cavalry and artillery horses; fuel; forage; straw; material for bedding, and stationery.

1065. The incidental expenses of the army paid through the

[2] *O.R.*, ser. 3, V, 213.

Quartermaster's Department include per diem to extra-duty men; postage on public service; the expenses of courts-martial, of the pursuit and apprehension of deserters, of the burials of officers and soldiers, of hired escorts, of expresses, interpreters, spies, and guides, of veterinary surgeons and medicines for horses, and of supplying posts with water; and generally the proper and authorized expenses for the movements and operations of an army not expressly assigned to any other department.[3]

Thus the duties were formidable. General Meigs himself stated simply, "The great duty of this department is to provide for and supply the wants of the army."[4] The statement is broadly accurate; but again it must be emphasized that Meigs did not concern himself with securing arms, food, and medicines.

If heavy responsibility rested upon the shoulders of General Meigs, his power as quartermaster general was not always commensurate with his responsibility. The office of the Civil War quartermaster general was not the office of a master planner, taking within his purview the logistical needs of all the armies, securing materials to meet those needs, and distributing them to the fields of battle. Such attributes were not entirely lacking in Meigs's position, but by and large the procedures of the Quartermaster's Department were decentralized procedures, with the result that Meigs's tasks were largely advisory and supervisory, sometimes even clerical.

Throughout the war it was primarily the chief quartermasters of the principal supply depots and the territorial military departments who made the contracts and purchases for needed supplies. They supervised the inspection, storage, and safekeeping of the supplies; and they provided for transportation from the principal quartermaster depots in the

[3] *Revised Regulations for the Army of the United States, 1861* (Philadelphia, 1861), p. 159.
[4] *O.R.*, ser. 3, II, 789.

North to advanced depots established near the theaters of combat. From the advanced depots supplies moved down through the hierarchy of army, corps, division, and brigade until they reached the lieutenant who acted as regimental quartermaster. This officer retained charge over the impedimenta of his regiment which continued to be quartermaster's property, such as the wagons, harness, and the animals of the regimental train and the tents and equipage of the regiment. He received in bulk and issued to the proper regimental officers the clothing, forage, fuel, and so on furnished by the Quartermaster's Department for the use of the regiment. A brigade quartermaster performed similar duties on the next higher level, transferring to the appropriate persons the property which passed though his hands and bearing responsibility for the brigade train, its material, and its animals. The same was true of division, corps, and army quartermasters, with the chief quartermaster of an army being primarily responsible for ordering, storing, and delivering the supplies necessary to keep the army an effective fighting unit.[5]

In a number of ways the system was both more cumbersome and more liable to delays and tie-ups than the supply arrangements of World War II. In the 1940's army and army corps disappeared almost entirely from the chain of supply, becoming for the most part tactical organizations only. The division supply officers knew the requirements of their units, and they drew directly from the theater depots; supplies did not pass through superfluous hands at army and corps. Below the division the brigade, of course, had been eliminated; and as far as possible the division stores were drawn on directly by battalions, by-passing even the regiment.[6]

The central role of army and department quartermasters in

[5] O.R., ser. 3, IV, 894–96; ser. 3, V, 220–21.
[6] Greenfield, et al., Ground Combat Troops, pp. 364–65.

the Civil War system deserves reemphasis. Many types of supplies for the troops within one of the geographical military departments were secured through advertisement by the chief quartermaster of the department. The commanding general of the department upon receiving the proposals of prospective suppliers held authority for making the award. Thus final decision and responsibility for quartermaster's supplies in a department lay not with Meigs nor even with Meigs's officers but with the line commander. Meigs examined the contracts of such commanders, and if he discovered any important errors he was able to notify the Secretary of War and receive rectifying orders. Similarly, direct authority over the supply of an army in the field rested with the line commander of the army, acting through the army quartermaster.[7]

After the First Bull Run campaign, Meigs only rarely assumed personal charge over the supplies of a field army. The principal exception was the Gettysburg campaign, when the Army of the Potomac had to be assisted in rapid shifts of its supply lines. An illustration of the limits of Meigs's role appeared in his inability to control contracting in Fremont's department in 1861, even when he was well aware of irregularities. In his letter to young Frank Blair, Meigs stressed the point that quartermaster officers assigned to department and field commanders were responsible in the first instance to those officers rather than to the quartermaster general in Washington.

Tell General Fremont [Meigs wrote] that no man more than myself desires to sustain him, no one is more ready to take a responsibility to assist him, and that he has in my opinion already the power which you say ought to be conferred upon him by the

[7] Meigs explained this aspect of the organization of his department most clearly in his postwar reports. See *Report of the Quartermaster General, 1868*, pp. 6–7; *1873*, p. 12; *1874*, p. 10; *1876*, p. 12; *1877*, pp. 6–7; *1878*, pp. 11–12; *1879*, p. 7; *1880*, pp. 7–9; *1881*, pp. 8–9; *1882*, pp. 14–15.

President. Whatever a General commanding *orders,* the subordinates of his staff [such as his quartermaster] are by regulations compelled to do if possible.

If Gen. Fremont orders Capt Tumley *to pay $1000* for an axe, Capt. Tumley will be supported by this Department in obeying, the propriety of such a payment however will be between Gen. Fremont and the Gov^t.

The General is charged with *saving the country.* The Country will be very careful to approve his measures and will judge his mistakes if any, very tenderly, if successful. Success crowns the work and let him spare no responsibility, no effort to secure it, and above all let him not take in ill part what is done with a sincere desire to assist him and let him not estrange friends by too hastily finding fault with their counsels.[8]

For certain types of army supplies, such as uniforms, it was generally not feasible for the regional quartermaster officers to do their own contracting. Here Meigs's important duties began to emerge. It was up to Meigs to ensure the maintenance of stocks in the general depots of the Quartermaster's Department. The depot quartermasters did most of the direct contracting, but they did so in accordance with estimates of needs prepared by the quartermaster general. The army and department quartermasters then drew upon the general depots, so that it was up to Meigs to anticipate the clothing requirements of the United States Army as a whole and to fill them. Similarly Meigs had to assemble adequate reserves of horses. He had to provide the armies with tents, and he had to construct barracks and hospitals when such were needed. He had to assemble ships for ocean transport and steamers for the rivers, he assisted in securing railroad transportation, and he collected wagons for the use of the armies beyond the railheads. When clothing or horses or the like were in short supply in one region, Meigs could order stock transfers from the depots of another region.

[8] Q.M.G. Let. B. 56, pp. 297–99.

His office was a coordinating center for the activities of quartermasters from the Rio Grande to the Chesapeake.

Probably the largest single bloc of Meigs's time went into financial duties. Usually with inadequate knowledge, Meigs had to submit to Congress annually an estimate of departmental expenses for the coming fiscal year. More than that, he had to maintain honesty in the supply system through a careful auditing of the accounts of all quartermasters. The quartermasters submitted their returns of property and accounts for disbursement to Meigs's office in Washington, where Meigs's assistants conducted an initial examination. When the assistants had approved the accounts, requisitions for remittances of money went to General Meigs himself. His perusal of such requisitions enabled Meigs to keep an accurate check upon purchasing operations, not only to disapprove improper purchases but also to call to account officers guilty of extravagance. Upon receiving Meigs's endorsement the requisitions went to the Secretary of War; after that personage approved them they moved to the Treasury Department to be filled.

Meanwhile six inspectors, holding after 1864 the rank of colonel and acting under the immediate supervision of General Meigs, busied themselves visiting armies, depots, and military posts throughout the country, scrutinizing the performance of the officers of the department and noting any abuses.[9]

Upon the reports of the inspectors, the reports and communications of the principal quartermasters at depots and in the field, and the knowledge gained from his own periodic tours of inspection both behind the lines in the North and with the armies in the combat zones, General Meigs based his decisions and directives. How many horses an army should have, how long its trains should be, such questions were less his business

[9] O.R., ser. 3, IV, 894–96; ser. 3, V, 220–21.

than that of the army and department commanders and
quartermasters, though he often offered expert counsel. Yet if
it was not for Meigs to decide what quantity of supplies a
field army needed, it was for him to ensure that whenever an
army called upon a depot for a reasonable quantity of supplies,
or sometimes even for a proposterous quantity, that call would
not go unanswered. Meigs had characterized the role of the
quartermaster general, with perhaps some but not excessive
exaggeration, before he held the office:

It is . . . the second place not in military rank but in actual real
influence over the war, in the army. A major general commands a
corps d armee on a single line. The Lt General commands the
whole army. The Q. M. Genl. supplies the means of moving that
army, & his command extends from the Atlantic to the Pacific
the Lakes to the Gulf.[10]

To assist him in his tasks at his department headquarters,
Meigs possessed a staff which was inadequate at the beginning
and continued to be so through most of the war. When he
came to his office in June, 1861, he found there thirteen clerks,
a staff accustomed to the tasks of a bureau expending four to
five million dollars a year. Even Meigs's somewhat conservative
estimates predicted for the coming fiscal year an expenditure
of seventy-five million dollars. Congress failed to appreciate the
discrepancy. It voted no important increases in Meigs's office
force, and the quartermaster general had to make do with the
employment of temporary clerks, on his own initiative. His
resources did not permit him to hire nearly enough of them.[11]

Even had the number of his civilian and military assistants
been greater, Meigs would have suffered from the sketchiness
of the departmental organization, a flaw which hindered any

[10] Meigs Let. B., 1861, p. 86.
[11] Q.M.G. Rep. B. 5, p. 446; Q.M.G. Dec. B. 2, pp. 134, 207; *O.R.*,
ser. 3, I, 682.

efforts to delegate authority and which sent the most obscure minutiae converging upon his desk. Compounding the difficulty was Meigs's own apparent inability at first to recognize the value of delegating many of his tasks. From the beginning his reports to the Secretary of War bewailed the inadequacy of his staff, but they did not yet point to the need for a thorough reorganization. The great desideratum was a change in the law which would enable Meigs to effect in his office a formal division of labor; meanwhile he might have spared himself the reading and answering of at least the obviously trivial among the communications addressed to him.

As it was, hundreds of dispatches and memoranda might pass over his desk in a day, and scores of dispatches might leave the office over his signature. More suitable for the intervention of a subordinate were issues like the following:

Jany 3rd 1862

Colonel,

Mrs. Wentworth Childs has a little property near Tenally town, upon which the Anderson Zouaves are encamped. She states that her timber and fencing are being destroyed, and that she is convinced that the true cause is some irregularity in the supply of wood by the Q. Master. That the men do not get their full allowance.

Upon her father Mrs Murdocks land [*sic*], a part of the same tract, Col. de Trobiands regt. is encamped and from similar causes she thinks they are committing numberless depredations.

Please investigate this, and apply the remedy.

M. C. Meigs,
Quarter Master General

Col. Rucker
Q Master
Washington City[12]

The wonder, given Meigs's temperament, was that he kept his patience. So numerous were the visitors interrupting his

[12] Q.M.G. Let. B. 56, p. 149.

tasks that he had to ask that the headquarters of his department in Winder's Building be closed after three P.M. to all but officers of the United States, in order to "give the Department two hours or an hour and a half in which they could do something besides answer applicants for contracts." "I think it important to the public service," wrote Meigs to the chief clerk of the War Department. "There is no time now, in which I can take up a subject and give it deliberate thought. While writing a page, twenty people interrupt me." [13]

Sometimes he could not help but be curt to visitors:

August 2, 1861

Dear Sir:

I do not remember to what you allude when you say in your note of yesterday that my manner was not courteous though you have no doubt that my intention was to be so.

Certainly I have never intended anything but courtesy to you. In the hurry of business with twenty persons seeking to stop me on my way to obey a call from the Secretary, I am sometimes obliged to pass suddenly, and not to hear calls, but I have never been intentionally rude to any man. The bids you refer to will be examined and considered. . . .

M. C. Meigs,<br>Quarter Master General

Hon. J. K. Moorhead
House of Representatives[14]

With Congressmen and prospective or disgruntled contractors came also place seekers. Sometimes these gentlemen might importune with the backing of one of Meigs's relatives:

Dear Sir:

The letter of M. E. Wilsen, forwarded by you, in which he requests that his brother may be appointed Quarter Master of the 95″ Regiment of Pennsylvania Volunteers, has been received.

[13] *Ibid.*, p. 168.
[14] *Ibid.*, p. 149.

It would afford the Quarter Master General pleasure to be able to make this appointment, but the law provides the mode of appointing Regimental Quarter Masters, who, like other officers of Volunteers, are appointed by the State authorities.

M. C. Meigs
Quarter Master General

Dr. J. F. Meigs
Philadelphia[15]

On one occasion General Meigs felt obliged to chide even President Lincoln for pushing upon him a recommendation for an appointment. Lincoln appealed to Meigs on behalf of a Mr. J. L. S. Ladd of St. Louis, who desired the post of Inspector of Army Supplies for the Eastern District of New York. Meigs had to reply that in the first place no such office existed. Furthermore:

I submit that it is only by leaving the selection, employment and dismissal of agents for whom he is responsible, to the Quarter Master himself, that proper control over them and over the quality of the supplies can be maintained.

I never interfere between the Quartermaster and those whom he thus hires, and I trust that the President will not permit the recommendations of any person's friends to induce him to interfere.

It would be unjust to the officer who is responsible for the conduct of these inspectors. If an unworthy man is employed, upon proof of his unworthiness the Quarter Master would be directed to discharge him. Beyond this I do not think he should be interfered with.[16]

While he struggled with a mass of paperwork, Meigs's chief concern remained the welfare of the troops in the field. Even after most items of supply became available in approximately adequate quantity, a great difficulty continued to be the finding

[15] Q.M.G. Let. B. 61, p. 587.
[16] Meigs to Lincoln, Dec. 21, 1861, Lincoln Papers, LXIII, 13515–16, L.C.

of men who could administer their distribution and assure the meeting of supplies with troops.

It is difficult to find a remedy [Meigs wrote]. All the demands are urgent. The Quarter Masters are inexperienced. They find a box of overcoats passing a Regiment perishing for want of them, and Balaklava and Red tape serve as an excuse for taking the responsibility of seizing what is on its way to Regiments in still greater distress.[17]

Occasionally, commanders simply could not be satisfied, and requests could not be met: "General Rosecrans' orders for clothing appear to be excessive, and he has just telegraphed to me for four experienced Quarter Masters. He might as well ask for four new moons." [18]

Meigs labored constantly for greater honesty and greater efficiency in all the activities of his department. In late 1862 he was still complaining to the Secretary of War and to Congress of the insufficiency of his office staff in Washington. What his complaints now signified was not so much that his department still lacked the ability to see that supplies and equipage reached the troops who needed them, but that the staff was not large enough to provide that thorough examination of financial accounts which the public interest required. Delay in the audit of accounts paved the way for improvidence and possible corruption, and these things Meigs wished to root out. Therefore he described to the Secretary of War in November, 1862, the flood of accounts that poured ceaselessly into his office for examination.

Every large unit of the army from brigade through division through army corps through field army, as well as every depot of supply, had its quartermaster officer, a person charged with

[17] Q.M.G. Let. B. 57, p. 111.
[18] *Ibid.*, p. 112.

the expenditure of considerable sums and responsible for transmitting to Meigs's office in Washington a monthly statement of his operations. At the moment the number of such officers was nearly 300, which meant for the Washington office the examination of 3,600 accounts per year. More than that, every company commander in the army was responsible for the clothing received by him for issue to his command and was required to file quarterly reports on the subject. This, Meigs pointed out, meant that should the strength of the army rise to a million men—which eventually it did—with the number of companies totaling not less than 10,000, there would be 40,000 clothing returns received and examined in his office per year.

The labor actually entailed in reviewing all these reports was even greater than appeared on the surface. The general inexperience of the officers of the army led to an expenditure of much time simply in corresponding with officers who failed to make their returns or whose returns were somehow incorrect. Prompt and careful attention to all accounts Meigs rightly believed to be of primary importance; beyond the actual procurement and distribution of supplies, he said, the second duty of his office was "by proper examination of the reports, returns, and accounts of its officers to enforce a strict economy in the disbursements of public money, and a strict accountability for the public property in charge of its officers." [19]

Not only was Meigs's staff small, but its rate of turnover was distressingly high. Efficient clerks tended to be drawn out of the office by the lure of better positions elsewhere. Congress had neglected to provide sufficient incentives in promotion and pay for the small staff that did exist.[20] The quarters occupied by the department in the capital were of no help; they were

[19] O.R., ser. 3, II, 789.
[20] O.R., ser. 3, III, 1122.

inadequate. Winder's Building, the structure originally used, Meigs found to be of simple and cheap construction and fire-proof; but in 1862 the department moved some of its activities to other buildings. This step relieved pressure, but the new quarters continued to be cramped, and valuable time was lost in communicating between scattered branches. Within another year the department vacated Winder's Building entirely, mov-ing into so-called temporary quarters—they were to be used for several years—in the red brick, twin-towered building of the Corcoran Art Gallery on the northeast corner of Seven-teenth Street and Pennsylvania Avenue. Here the department found accommodation after a fashion for all of its central staff and its files, but the place still left much to be desired. Its principal advantage was proximity to the headquarters of the army in Winder's Building and to the War Department on the White House grounds.[21]

Not only an inadequate clerical force and cramped quarters but also inexperienced or even incompetent quartermaster officers with the troops in the field and at the depots of supply continued to add to the weight of the cross Meigs had to bear. Like the rest of the Civil War army, the Quartermaster's Department frequently received as officers persons whose principal qualification was their ability to endear themselves to the politicos in their state capital. Apparently their political patrons habitually overlooked the most rudimentary con-sideration of their capacity to fill the offices to which they were appointed. As the war moved into 1863 the pages of reports still complained of quartermaster officers who failed to take their responsibilities seriously, who were almost totally unacquainted with their duties, and who possessed no visible qualification for their posts. A report to the Secretary of War had to point out an elementary fact, namely, that

[21] *O.R.*, 3, II, 792; ser. 3, III, 1123; ser. 3, IV, 878.

None but good accountants and persons who have been engaged in business of a mercantile character, or who have had experience as regimental quartermasters and proved their fitness for the office, should be appointed assistant quartermasters.[22]

With the quartermaster officers in the field even more than with the civilian clerks in Washington sluggish promotion was an obstacle to securing and retaining persons of ability. Rank in the Quartermaster's Department bore little relation to the responsibilities of an office. At one time, for example, a depot quartermaster at Washington had over 9,000 men and 1,000 teams of work animals under his direction; he transacted business amounting to several million dollars a year. Few brigadier generals of infantry carried so great a responsibility. On his shoulder straps he wore the twin bars of a captain.[23]

His experience was not unusual. A captaincy was the common rank of all but the most prominent quartermasters, an arrangement, wrote Meigs, "by which we have hundreds of Quartermasters ranking alike as Captains, with no more organization than you have in a flock of sheep or goats." [24] Meanwhile high casualty lists among commissioned officers of the line and constant increases in the size of the army enabled line officers to soar upward through the ranks with marked rapidity. Quartermasters began to transfer to other branches of the service. A man would no sooner become familiar with the work of the department than he would be likely to leave it. Even certain staff departments seemed to be favored over the Quartermaster's Department, for while Meigs's men remained mostly captains, the equivalent officers in the Adjutant General's Department advanced to the grade of major.[25]

[22] O.R., ser. 3, III, 1121.
[23] O.R., ser. 3, II, 805; Q.M.G. Let. B. 75, p. 398.
[24] Q.M.G. Let. B. 75, p. 409.
[25] Q.M.G. Let. B. 66, p. 269.

In 1862 General Meigs returned to lobbying activity in Congress. His aim this time was to push through a bill which would raise the rank of certain quartermasters and in this way bestow upon such officers the authority essential for rational organization of the Quartermaster's Department and do justice to some of the most capable officers in the department. He believed that many such had foregone opportunities for promotion through transfer to other branches because their services were too valuable to be dispensed with by the Quartermaster's Department. A bill passed the House on July 9, but the Senate failed to take action.[26]

Meigs's persistency had not deserted him; early in 1863 he tried again. He transmitted to Henry Wilson, chairman of the Senate Military Affairs Committee, a modification of his 1862 bill. In place of the mob of captains with a scattering of higher officers that made up the Quartermaster's Department, Meigs proposed a hierarchy consisting of one major general—the quartermaster general—two brigadiers, four colonels, eight lieutenant colonels, twenty-four majors, and forty-eight captains. Only with such a gradation of rank, he argued, could the department create a suitable chain of responsibility. In order to fill vacancies in the establishment he recommended the transfer to the permanent corps of a number of able and experienced volunteers. He regretted the necessity of suggesting that the quartermaster general be a major general, since the proposal seemed to cast doubt upon his own disinterestedness, but he believed this to be the only way of affording the quartermaster general rank commensurate with his responsibilities while yet giving proper rank and recognition to his subordinates.[27]

[26] *Ibid.*, pp. 268–70.
[27] Q.M.G. Let. B. 75, pp. 407–9.

Meigs was too busy in 1863 to devote much time to pressing Congress on behalf of the bill. He could do little more than wait and hope, knowing that only with intelligent reorganization could he establish fully effective control over his own department. Again Congress disappointed him.

In the spring of 1864, while the rival Union and Confederate armies grappled below the Rapidan and along the Atlanta railroad, Meigs somehow found time to return to the charge. Discouraged quartermasters were still transferring from the service, and confusion still plagued the department command system, because the rank of quartermaster officers did not accord with their duties. Again Meigs urged that Congress authorize a neat hierarchy of quartermasters below the quartermaster general.

In support of his recommendations Meigs busied himself gathering as impressive a body of witnesses as possible. Among them he appealed to the politically potent Major General Benjamin F. Butler to second his plan. He secured an endorsement from the new lieutenant general, Ulysses S. Grant, who reiterated all Meigs's arguments and backed them with the weight of a military reputation unrivaled since Washington's. Grant reaffirmed that under the existing system good quartermaster officers were resigning from the department in disappointment. "Much," he said, "depends upon keeping up the efficiency of the corps, whose labors are heavier, and whose rewards have been lighter, than those of their comrades in other Departments." [28]

To his suggestions for revising the hierarchy of quartermasters Meigs added this year a plan for enhancing the efficiency of his office at Washington. His experience by now had taught him the values of a division of labor, and he had

[28] *Ibid.*, pp. 236–38, 360, 407–9.

organized his staff informally so as to effect such a division. One section would supervise the supply of horses, another the clothing supply, another the procurement and maintenance of ocean-going vessels, and so on. What he desired now was to give this scheme the sanction and authority of legislation, which would enable him to exploit it still more fully.

He would divide the Quartermaster General's Office into nine divisions, corresponding to the principal categories into which the work of the department more or less naturally fell. The First Division would be charged with providing animals for the armies. The Second would administer clothing and equipage; the Third, ocean and lake transportation; the Fourth, rail and river transportation; the Fifth, forage and fuel; the Sixth, barracks and hospitals; the Seventh, wagon transportation; the Eighth, inspection; and the Ninth, finance. The logic of the arrangement was obvious. If at the head of each department Meigs could place a qualified officer of suitable rank, at least a colonel, then the plan would relieve the quartermaster general of his excessive administrative burden.[29]

In view of his failure to secure reorganization in the two previous years, Meigs was not especially optimistic. "Our legislators," he remarked, "do not seem to understand the value of organization. They do not go so far as to make an army consist of Privates alone, but they seem to object to any gradation of ranks." He glumly observed that the scheme would have a better chance of passage if it were a bill for regulating contracts instead of a reorganization plan. But there were too many laws for regulating contracts already, and a new arrangement in the Quartermaster's Department would do far more to ensure an efficient and honest supply service. "Let any member propose a new provision of law stated to be intended to restrain contractors or officers," Meigs wrote, "and it goes

[29] *Ibid.*, pp. 407–9.

through with little examination." The effect was to make it all the more difficult for a new quartermaster to learn the legal requirements of a valid contract, and the nation was too busy with the war to spend much time pursuing defaulting contractors anyway. "The officers time must be directed to procuring in some other way the supplies which a defaulting contractor has failed to deliver." [30]

Despite Meigs's pessimism, his reorganization plan at last broke out of committee and onto the floor in both houses. It became law on July 4. By the end of 1864 Meigs was able to report that the results he had anticipated were already beginning to appear, and that already the stricter supervision and inspection embodied in the new law had enabled him to rid the service of a number of dishonest or incompetent agents.[31] By the same time he enjoyed at last the efficiency of a clerical force adequate in size. In 1863 the Quartermaster General's Office had mustered 213 civilian clerks and employees, more than twice as many as the whole War Department employed in 1859, but still not enough to meet the new demands. By 1865, however, the number was 591, and Meigs was seeing the departmental reports and accounts examined in time to redress most errors.[32]

The reorganization of the Quartermaster's Department in 1864 was the most important administrative achievement of Meigs's tenure as quartermaster general. Thanks to Meigs's penchant for orderly procedure, to his wartime experience, and to his persistent campaign with a sluggish Congress, the Quartermaster's Department at last won for itself an establishment geared to the requirements of the war it was fighting.

Proper administration of the Quartermaster's Department

[30] *Ibid.*
[31] *O.R.*, ser. 3, IV, 883–84.
[32] Q.M.G. Let. B. 1876A, p. 434; *O.R.*, ser. 3, I, 682; ser. 3, II, 789; ser. 3, III, 1122; ser. 3, IV, 877; ser. 3, V, 324–39.

was only the first step toward efficient supply of the troops. To the methods of Meigs and his department in procurement and distribution of supplies this study now returns, taking up the narrative with the installation of Edwin Stanton in the War Department.

# X

# SUPPLIES FOR THE ARMY

SECRETARY STANTON inaugurated a new and better era in the War Department, but ambiguity enfolded the man like a cloak. A reluctance to be straightforward showed itself promptly after his accession in his anomalous arrangements for governance of the United States Military Railroads. In theory these lines operated under General Meigs, but the quartermaster general could never be sure just where lay the boundaries of his authority.

The railroad network of the North, far superior to that of the Confederacy, was essential to the work of the Quartermaster's Department and to the successful supplying of the Union army. No one with Meigs's regard for modern technology could overlook the importance of the railroads, and from the beginning Meigs used them eagerly. But from the beginning, exploitation of the railroads brought problems as well as speed and convenience.

Before Meigs assumed the office of quartermaster general, while Major Sibley was still acting in the post, Simon Cameron had appointed as his assistant for railroads Thomas A. Scott of the Pennsylvania Railroad. Scott prepared a general list of railroad rates and sent it to the Quartermaster's Department; the ostensible purpose was to guide quartermasters in fixing compensation to the railroad companies for carrying troops and supplies. Scott and Sibley later claimed that the list was intended to be one of maximum rates, but the phrasing of the directive suggested that Scott at least regarded it as a list of normal rates, and as such it was used, particularly in Fremont's department. With the coming of Meigs the status of the list did not change. Meigs like Scott and Sibley treated it as an authority rather than merely a guide, even though he, like his colleagues, was later to claim that the rates listed were simply maximums.

Hence, when the Van Wyck Committee investigated government contracts it discovered that the Quartermaster's Department had abandoned issuing invitations for competitive bidding on railroad transportation; that the department was paying for such transportation in accordance with the list of rates submitted by Tom Scott, himself a railroad executive; and that especially in Fremont's command the military business was going to railroads which ingratiated themselves with the quartermasters, perhaps through a bit of bribery.[1]

General Meigs had slipped. The railroads were fattening themselves on the public need, and the quartermaster general was among the few people who might have curbed them. As it was, the remedy had to be sought by Congress. On January 31, 1862, President Lincoln signed into law the Railroad Act, which empowered the government to take possession of any railroad lines in the United States if the public safety required it. Henceforth, reasoned reforming Congressmen, if the railroads should prove reluctant to content themselves with equitable rates, then the roads would find themselves in government hands.

---

[1] Q.M.G. Let. B. 56, pp. 210–11; Thomas Weber, *The Northern Railroads in the Civil War* (New York, 1952), pp. 102–6, 127–30; George Edgar Turner, *Victory Rode the Rails* (Indianapolis, 1953), pp. 110–15, 155, 246–47; Samuel Richey Kamm, "The Civil War Career of Thomas A. Scott" (unpublished Ph.D. thesis, University of Pennsylvania, 1940), pp. 67–71, 74–79.

The threat of seizure acted as a spur, impelling the railroads to take action which stayed the hand of the government. At the request of Secretary Stanton representatives of the Northern railroads met in Washington, and now they were able to agree upon a reasonable schedule of rates for military transportation. The Quartermaster's Department did not return to competitive bidding, and the charge for carriage of troops remained as before, two cents per man per mile. But the rates for military freight fell considerably, to a point far lower than those charged to private business, and this was the main question involved. The new schedule continued in effect throughout the war, except that the wartime revenue laws allowed the railroads to add to their rates the amount of the taxes imposed on them.

Occasionally some of the roads made application for special permission to set higher rates. In the case of the vital and overworked Louisville and Nashville Railroad, Meigs agreed, with probable justification, provided that the road would pay the cost of rebuilding its Nashville bridge across the Cumberland River.[2]

A different situation confronted the Federal government and its supply service when Union armies pushed into the South. There the Railroad Act of 1862 brought captured lines into the system of the United States Military Railroads, operated under a military director and superintendent who was supposed to be subject to the orders of the quartermaster general. On February 11, 1862, Lincoln appointed to the place Daniel C. McCallum, formerly superintendent of the Erie Railroad. Meigs's department began to pay the bills of the Military Railroads, but Meigs soon discovered that McCallum was virtually independent of him.

[2] Weber, *Northern Railroads*, pp. 129–30; Turner, *Victory Rode the Rails*, pp. 246–49, 286–94.

This result followed from Stanton's fondness for keeping his fingers in as many War Department pies as possible and from McCallum's preference for a role more assertive than that of a mere subordinate to General Meigs. Stanton encouraged McCallum to transmit reports and correspondence directly to the War Department, and McCallum was happy to comply. Sometimes Stanton forwarded his instructions to McCallum through Meigs, sometimes he gave orders directly.

Confusion of this situation was heightened when in April Stanton gave Herman Haupt authority over the railroads captured in northeastern Virginia, an authority which should have fallen within the scope of McCallum's command but which Haupt exercised independently of McCallum. Still worse, Haupt soon found a third railroader, Daniel Stone, operating within his territory independently of him and McCallum alike. Haupt insisted that his authority in Virginia be reconfirmed, and it was, but his own relation to McCallum remained for a time anomalous.[3]

The results were better than the system of command. Herman Haupt was a railroading genius, and in Virginia in 1862 he devised techniques of railroad rebuilding and military railroad operation which McCallum later applied in a vaster theater of war with immense success. Meanwhile McCallum's independence of Meigs probably did no harm to the Union cause. Meigs continued to supervise the utilization of the privately owned Northern railroads for military transport. And it was the quartermasters who, with the army commanders, decided what McCallum's railroads were to carry. The actual operation of the military railroads remained in the hands of a professional railroad executive, where it belonged.

[3] Q.M.G. Let. B. 1880D, pp. 2060–61; Turner, *Victory Rode the Rails*, pp. 150, 155–58; *O.R.*, ser. 3, V. 295–99.

Congress had voted a new appropriation for the Quartermaster's Department as 1862 began, and some sort of order was emerging in the army's dealings with the railroads. A new and more vigorous Secretary governed the War Department. But such things alone could not tempt victory to the Union banners. In the end only success in the field could count toward that result. Happily, the new year brought also the first genuine Union success in the field, and Meigs was among its architects.

The rivers of the South might be made allies of the Union cause. They ran deep into the Confederacy, and if the North could fill them with warships, it would be able to pierce Jefferson Davis's grand defensive line. The Mississippi in particular offered an avenue of conquest into the South; in Union hands, furthermore, the river would sever Louisiana, Arkansas, and Texas from the Confederate East. Farsighted Union leaders such as Lincoln and Winfield Scott recognized the importance of the Southern rivers at the outset. So also did Meigs; on his first day in the office of quartermaster general, in June, 1861, he summoned to Washington from Cincinnati his brother-in-law Commander John Rodgers in order to consult with him on gunboat construction.

Rodgers was already building gunboats under orders issued through General Scott shortly before Meigs's appointment to high command. Meigs now insisted upon a change in the original plans. Of the sixteen vessels contemplated, he demanded that one or two at the very least be ironclads. He was among those who perceived that modern technology was about to make wooden-walled warships well-nigh useless. He won his point, and eventually iron plates appeared upon the sides of nearly all the gunboats; only so clad could the boats stand up against Confederate batteries and enemy vessels on the rivers.

Meigs insisted also that the gunboats be hurried to completion without delay. He saw in them a possibly decisive weapon, and he would not risk the Confederacy's winning control of the rivers before the Union gunboats could appear. On June 17 he wrote, "I have promised Gen Scott that if money will make them these gunboats shall be ready at Cairo on the 20 Sept." [4]

In August, John Rodgers relinquished supervision of gunboat construction to Captain Andrew Foote. It was Foote who led the gunboats to their first success and the first great victories of the North in the war. The Confederate defenses in Tennessee depended upon control of the Cumberland and Tennessee Rivers, and if the Union could win those streams, the Confederate forces would have to fall back into Mississippi and Alabama. To defend the streams the Confederates erected two fortifications near the crossing of the Tennessee-Kentucky line, Fort Henry on the Tennessee and Fort Donelson on the Cumberland. About noon on February 6, 1862, four ironclad gunboats followed by three wooden ones, all under command of Captain Foote, steamed up the Tennessee to engage the guns of Fort Henry.

Foote hammered Fort Henry into submission, splitting wide open the Confederate line in Tennessee. Then he turned to cooperate with troops under Brigadier General Ulysses Grant for the capture of Fort Donelson. Here the gunboats were not so successful; they had to meet a plunging fire from the fort, and the deciding action had to be won by the infantry. But the rebuff of the gunboats at Fort Donelson could not destroy their value. Once the obstacle of the fort disappeared, they were able to range swiftly upriver and assist in the rapid seizure of Nashville. By the end of February much of

[4] *O.R.*, ser. 3, II, 792; Q.M.G. Let. B. 55, pp. 432, 445; Meigs Let. B., 1861, pp. 93–96.

Tennessee besides its capital was in Federal hands, and the pattern had been set for a cooperation of gunboats and soldiers on the Western waters which eventually would tear the Confederate West to shreds.

The gunboats of Fort Henry and Fort Donelson were vessels of General Meigs's Quartermaster's Department. The department had contracted for their building, and they were to remain its property until midway in the war, when they finally passed to the navy. Meanwhile their guns and ammunition were supplied partly by the navy, partly by the Ordnance Department of the army. Their crews included both army and navy personnel, while their commanders, of course, were naval officers.[5]

The triumph of Foote's gunboats delighted General Meigs, for with their appeal to his mechanical leanings the gunboats ranked among his favorite projects. When he heard the news of Henry and Donelson, he sent to Foote quick praise:

Whenever you need authority or advice, write, and your dispatch will have prompt attention. At other times stick as you have done to the work of crushing out this Rebellion. I wish we had the same single mindedness and energy in some other places.[6]

For the swiftness of success in the West merely underlined McClellan's timid caution in the East.

Not until the middle of March, 1862, did McClellan begin to move. He adhered to his resolve to advance upon Richmond by the Peninsula of the York and the James rather than strike directly southward by land. To guide Meigs's quartermaster officers in assembling the necessary ocean transport for

[5] *O.R.*, ser. 3, II, 792–94. On the war on the Western rivers see H. Allen Gosnell, *Guns on the Western Waters: The Story of the River Gunboats in the Civil War* (Baton Rouge, 1949).

[6] Q.M.G. Let. B. 58, p. 420.

McClellan's movement, Secretary Stanton named as Assistant Secretary of War John Tucker, an experienced shipbuilding executive. Despite his acute sense of prerogative, Meigs co-operated graciously with Tucker. His increased responsibilities seem to have prompted an unwonted readiness to acknowledge that in the shipping business he was a novice. Transports gathered at the docks of Alexandria with remarkable dispatch.

The movement to the Peninsula became a definite project toward the end of February. From that time until March 17, when McClellan's embarkation got under way, more than four hundred vessels arrived at Alexandria and points nearby; only choleric George McClellan could claim that the assembly had been slow.[7]

Within twelve days after March 17 the bulk of the Army of the Potomac rested on the Virginia Peninsula. The United States Army had never attempted a shifting of troops comparable to this. Scott's army bound for Veracruz in 1846 had traveled a much longer distance, but the army had been tiny in comparison with McClellan's. Rarely, in fact, had anything approaching McClellan's maneuver been tackled anywhere; by the beginning of April 100,000 men had taken ship. As McClellan's chief quartermaster wrote: "The magnitude of the movement can scarcely be understood except by those who participated in it. Each division took with it its own transportation as far as it was practicable, and the remainder, together with the supply trains, were pushed forward as rapidly as possible."[8] The whole expedition was organized by men who were essentially amateurs at this sort of thing, and the whole operation came off without an important hitch.

Once the troops were aboard ship Meigs's duty was to shovel supplies southward to them, hoping that the quarter-

[7] *O.R.*, ser. 1, XI, pt. 1, 158.
[8] *Ibid.*

masters on the spot could carry the stuff to its destination. Beyond exerting a vague and distant management, he could do little more. Helpful advice and a watchful eye he could offer, but quartermaster operations in the field were the task of McClellan and the chief quartermaster of his army, Colonel Stewart Van Vliet. Van Vliet performed skillfully, utilizing his ocean transport to establish a series of temporary bases along the shore of the York River and thus hopping up the Peninsula behind the advance of the army. When the tide of battle turned against the Union, Van Vliet responded alertly to McClellan's call for a withdrawal from the York to the James.

When Meigs and his officers assembled the fleet for the Peninsular campaign, they leased the vessels under short-term charters. They did not anticipate a prolonged need for large-scale ocean shipping in government service. When Confederate General R. E. Lee repulsed McClellan in the Seven Days Battles, however, there was no immediate withdrawal from the Peninsula. Instead, much of the Army of the Potomac remained at Harrison's Landing on the James River until well into August. To supply these troops demanded the retention of more than half the transports first assembled and a heavy outlay of government funds in rentals. Furthermore, to McClellan's shipping needs Meigs had to add those of expeditions such as T. W. Sherman's to Hilton Head and Ambrose Burnside's to New Berne. It became apparent not only that the Quartermaster's Department was in the shipping business in a big way, but that it was likely to stay there for a long time to come.[9]

This meant that Meigs had to find some method of cutting down the expenses of maintaining the fleet. The department had acquired most of its rented vessels in haste. The heavy

[9] *O.R.*, ser. 3, II, 796.

demand had raised charter rates abruptly, and since Meigs and his agents had failed to anticipate that the need for the vessels would be prolonged, they had been willing to pay extravagant prices in the thought that the expense soon would end. Outfitting the ships for military duty, insuring them, and compensating for damage done them by troops had further lifted costs. When it turned out that most of the charters would have to be renewed, Meigs recognized that the rates being paid were often exorbitant, but now he could do little about it. He still had no time for haggling over prices, since the demand for vessels remained urgent, and urgency left no opportunity to invite open competition through the submission of bids. More than that, so few of the nation's seaworthy vessels were not needed by the government that there could have been little opportunity for competition anyway. The shipowners had Meigs over a barrel, and in an age of business buccaneering, they did not hesitate to take advantage of it.[10]

Beyond all this, in the chartering of vessels as in everything else many of Meigs's agents were utterly unprepared by experience. The result was not only that rates were high, but that in return the government might get only flimsy old crocks, dangerous to move from harbor. By the end of 1862 the problem had captured the attention of the inevitable Congressional investigating committee, this time under the chairmanship of the upright Senator James W. Grimes of Iowa.

Among other things, the committee found that Union troops under General Nathaniel P. Banks had traveled to New Orleans in vessels so dangerous that their safe arrival appeared almost miraculous and so unsanitary that infection and disease should have been epidemic. The Banks affair made sensational reading, and the findings led to a recommendation by the committee in February, 1863, that henceforth vessels

[10] *O.R.,* ser. 3, II, 796–97; ser. 3, IV, 889–90.

be chartered only by commissioned military agents, not by civilian employees of the Quartermaster's Department. Meigs complained that this was asking him to make bricks without straw. When he requested an increase in the authorized strength of his office, Congress responded grudgingly; then the legislators expected him to ensure honesty by using military officers whom he did not command. He admitted that "A civilian assistant employed temporarily is exposed to great temptation without the restraints attached to a permanent commission." He preferred to use military officers; the problem was to find them.[11]

It was a situation in which the ability and good intentions of the quartermaster general did not suffice; he needed help. Congress rose to the occasion. A law based upon the findings of the Grimes Committee provided for detailing naval officers to the inspection and appraisal of vessels offered for charter or sale to the Quartermaster's Department. Not only were ships chartered subsequently at rates more nearly corresponding to their true value (if still high), but several pending claims against the government were settled at considerably reduced rates. In some cases the inspectors discovered that the amount paid for a vessel had already far exceeded the value of the ship and its services. In this event the Quartermaster's Department now acted to take possession of the vessel, leaving the claimants to seek from Congress the redress of legitimate grievances. Henceforth, also, General Meigs introduced into all charters a clause giving the United States the right to purchase the vessels at any time during their charter service by paying a reasonable percentage upon the original evaluation and upon the cost of maintaining the vessel. Thus if the charter rates proved excessive, the Quartermaster's Depart-

---

[11] Q.M.G. Let. B. 66, pp. 126–28, 244–54, 292; Q.M.G. Let. B. 67, pp. 20–23, 40–41, 46, 82–83.

ment simply bought the vessel in question. By the end of 1864 Meigs was the proprietor of a fleet aggregating 206,973 tons, 48,279 tons of which represented vessels owned outright by the Quartermaster's Department.[12]

Rarely did coastal operations against the ports of the Confederacy slacken, and in order to sustain such operations, Meigs continued to hold most of the seagoing steamers of the nation throughout the war. Practically every steam vessel constructed in wartime immediately joined the quartermaster fleet. Among the new ships were powerful propeller-driven steamers of 900 to 1,100 tons burden, of a type developed during the conflict, swift and sturdy for their time, burning twelve to sixteen tons of coal per day, and capable of eight to ten knots. Large sailing vessels also served, relics of a day that was passing even during the war, while the British merchant marine exploited the preoccupation of the Americans to forge into a decisive lead in maritime commerce with ships of iron and steam.

Sometimes the Quartermaster's Department itself went into the shipbuilding business, both on the ocean and on the inland rivers. At Philadelphia it constructed several light-draft steam ferry transports, the forerunners of modern landing craft. Each of them could carry a battery of artillery with its horses, a train of wagons, or a regiment of infantry. They could cross any river or estuary on the Eastern coast and in good weather make short sea voyages, but they were of light enough draft so that, unlike all the other ocean transports, they could run inshore and land without the use of wharves or docks.

Early in 1863 Meigs suggested to Colonel S. B. Holabird, the chief quartermaster at New Orleans, that he use some of

[12] *O.R.*, ser. 3, IV, 889–90; ser. 3, V, 287–93.

the city's many unemployed to construct steamboats. The Mississippi was still closed between Vicksburg and Port Hudson, and it was difficult to send light-draft boats suitable for river use around to New Orleans by sea. Meigs canceled the suggestion when Grant captured Vicksburg to open the river, but the idea demonstrated the resourcefulness of the quartermaster general. Late in the year General Grant was anxious to have Union gunboats patrolling the upper Tennessee, but the vessels which had served so well on the Mississippi and the lower Tennessee could not pass Muscle Shoals. Already Captain Arthur Edwards of the Quartermaster's Department was building transports at Bridgeport, Alabama. Now Meigs responded to Grant's request by instructing Edwards to convert two of these ships into gunboats. Two more followed. The navy supplied the armament, and Meigs turned the finished vessels over to the Navy Department to patrol the Tennessee as far as Knoxville.[13]

The larger and more powerful vessels of the Quartermaster's Department fleet generally were armed; it was impossible to furnish them on every occasion with naval escorts, and early in the war the enemy captured or sank a number of them. The guns subsequently mounted were heavy enough so that the vessels could defend themselves against privateers, and occasionally they might even capture a blockade-runner. In addition, the department maintained through most of the war a number of light-draft armed vessels which were assigned to military commanders of coastal areas. These vessels served not only as transports but also as fighting ships for support of movements on bays and inland waters. As the strength of the Federal navy grew, General Meigs sought to transfer the latter

[13] *Ibid.*, ser. 3, IV, 891; ser. 3, V, 227–28; Q.M.G. Let. B. 71, p. 250; Q.M.G. Let. B. 74, pp. 69–71.

function exclusively to naval flotillas, but progress in with-
drawing quartermaster ships from the task was slow.[14]

George McClellan's movement to the Virginia Peninsula
by sea, begun in March, 1862, with so much fanfare after so
much delay, ended in ignominious failure. General Lee led his
Confederate Army of Northern Virginia out from Richmond
to counterattack against McClellan, and though McClellan's
soldiers fought stoutly, their general lacked the resolution to
stand firm against the enemy's pressure. McClellan abandoned
his advance on the Confederate capital to withdraw to a secure
new base at Harrison's Landing on the James. Particularly because his army turned back Lee's last counterstroke at Malvern
Hill on July 1, McClellan considered the retreat a success; he
had brought out his army in good fighting condition. For all
that, the retreat was the ruin of McClellan's campaign. Losses
were heavy, and the enemy still glared from his citadel in
Richmond. The Lincoln administration could see the event
for what it was. "There is already a great disaster for us,"
wrote General Meigs. "I hope no more such are in store
for us." [15]

No more than after First Bull Run, however, did Meigs
despair of ultimate victory. Like Lincoln he turned his back
on the defeat and looked to the future. But a new harshness
came into the war with the defeat on the Peninsula, and a
growing bitterness emerged in Meigs's reflections on the
defeat.

In the mean time [he wrote] the north must hold this wolf by
the ears until it is exhausted by starvation or destroyed by the
kicks & cuffs which it may yet receive. No peace in compromise

---

[14] *O.R.*, ser. 3, IV, 891; ser. 3, V, 227–28.
[15] Meigs to John Rodgers, July 8, 1862, Rodgers Family Papers, Naval
Historical Foundation Collection, Box 130, L.C.

with the . . . South is possible for our industrious educated democratic people. Death or victory is the . . . necessity of our case,
& I do not the less doubt the ultimate victory that God for our
sins leads us to it through seas of blood.[16]

If the North were to hold the wolf by the ears, still more
troops would have to be gathered into the Federal army. Even
McClellan's awesome force had not been enough to conquer
the Confederacy. For a nation with the population resources
of the North, the answer was to build the army still larger.

As McClellan settled down to idleness at his new base at
Harrison's Landing, a number of governors urged President
Lincoln to call up regiments of the state militia. The President
felt that this method of strengthening the ranks would involve a needless multiplication of regiments. On July 2 he
called instead for 300,000 volunteers, many of whom would
be used to plug holes in existing organizations. But the pressure of the governors persisted, and the war continued to
chew up manpower. On August 4 Lincoln yielded to the
suggestions of the governors and called for a draft of 300,-
000 state militia.[17]

After a year of war General Meigs was incomparably better
prepared to clothe the new recruits than he had been in 1861.
Now he was ready to demonstrate the intelligent planning
and efficient distribution methods of a skillful quartermaster.
He believed that the clothing stores on hand in his depots at
the beginning of July were sufficient to meet the requirements
of the troops already in service for the next six to nine months;
they would be able to fill most of the needs of up to 450,000
recruits. In addition, the Philadelphia depot contained about
3,200,000 yards of uniform cloth, enough for fashioning about
500,000 uniforms. When Lincoln called for volunteers on

[16] *Ibid.*
[17] Randall, *Lincoln the President*, II, 290–91.

July 2, Meigs instructed his subordinates to publish advertisements for contracts which would replenish the stocks. His aim was to gather a new surplus without exciting the market unduly and raising prices.

When Lincoln drafted the state militia, Meigs dispatched cloth from the Schuylkill Arsenal to various points throughout the North. There the cloth was to be fashioned into garments under contracts entered into either by United States quartermasters or the state governments. State contracting was a step backward, but it went hand in hand with the method of raising troops by inducting state forces, and to that method Lincoln had returned only with reluctance. Meanwhile Meigs believed his department should be able to supply all the wants of the new levies before there emerged any reasonable ground for complaint.

After the second call for troops it was apparent that any attempt to replenish the quartermaster stores immediately would create a field day for the profiteers and send prices soaring to unwonted heights. Accordingly, Meigs ordered that the replenishing of stocks be gradual. Commanders of depots were to issue a standing invitation for bids, and they were to contract immediately for articles needed at once and then make further contracts from time to time as the need might arise and as favorable offers were received. Eventually each of the three main depots was to accumulate full equipment for 100,000 men, plus the supplies necessary to meet the ordinary wear and tear of an army of 200,000 men.[18]

Through the rest of the war Meigs attempted to maintain the clothing stocks at that level or higher. In March, 1863, he again instructed each of the principal depots to keep on

[18] O.R., ser. 3, II, 371–73, 732–33. The statement that about 3,200,000 yards of clothing would make some 500,000 uniforms is based on an earlier calculation by Meigs, O.R., ser. 3, I, 608–9.

hand enough clothing to outfit completely 100,000 men, this in addition to materials necessary to fill the current wants of the service. In October, 1863, after the President had sent out a call for the conscription of 300,000 men, the quartermaster general had the New York and Philadelphia depots increase their reserve stock so that each could equip 150,000 men.[19] Accumulation of reserves was aided by a continuing expansion of the Northern textile industry. The army wore chiefly wool, and during the war the sets of cards in the woolen mills of the North rose in number from 3,000 to 5,000. Part of the increase reflected the demand for a substitute for cotton, but much of it mirrored the response to military needs.[20]

Blankets, as we have seen, were the single item of equipage which to the end of the war Meigs had to purchase overseas. In 1862 he felt compelled to urge each volunteer and drafted militiaman to bring with him from home "a good stout woolen blanket." He informed the recruits that the regulation military blanket measured eighty-four by sixty-six inches and weighed five pounds.[21]

For tentmaking the usual material was cotton, so that with cotton in short supply through much of the war, tents became another headache. Meigs stated frankly that he could not supply enough of them for the 1862 recruits, and consequently many of the states erected temporary barracks to house the men as they assembled. Later, troops in winter quarters took to building wooden huts. All soldiers were supposed to receive shelter tents, the "pup tent" that went with them into the field; but even here the scarcity of cotton was a hindrance. With cotton low in quantity and high in price, the Quartermaster's Department turned sometimes to tents made

[19] *Ibid.*, ser. 3, IV, 67.
[20] Emerson David Fite, *Social and Industrial Conditions in the North during the Civil War* (New York, 1910), pp. 83–84.
[21] *O.R.*, ser. 3, II, 483; ser. 3, V, 224.

of a lighter material, particularly linen. This expedient brought a saving in cost but often proved unsatisfactory in service; linen tents were too permeable to rain.[22]

The soldier's care of his clothing as well as of everything else he touched set quartermasters aghast at a spectacle of waste. Early in the war General Meigs learned with horror that as many as 800 overcoats sometimes were picked up behind a regiment on the march. Since few regiments maintained their paper strength of 1,000 men, those who did not discard their overcoats were rare individuals indeed. Inevitably, warm, sunny days gave way sooner or later to chilly, rain-soaked nights; and lest the whole army come down with pneumonia the Quartermaster's Department had to issue new overcoats whether the regulation clothing allowance called for them or not.

The discarding of equipment in battle was even worse than on the march: "Knapsacks are piled," wrote Meigs, "blankets, overcoats, and other clothing thrown off, and whether victorious or defeated, the regiments seem seldom to recover the property thus laid aside." As might have been expected, volunteers were more wasteful than regulars. Appropriations for clothing and equipment for the volunteer army based on allowances for the regular army fell short of the mark. The consequence was added financial difficulty for the Quartermaster's Department during the first year of the war.[23]

For all that, the average Northern soldier was well clad and well protected from the weather. There were, of course, occasional instances of want. "Our reg is purty naked," wrote an Ohio soldier in Alabama early in 1862; "they look more like a reg of secesh than northern troops soom barfootted, soom with out coats soom with a citazens soot on. . . . I have ben bar-

[22] O.R., ser. 3, II, 372; ser. 3, IV, 887.
[23] O.R., ser. 3, II, 804.

footed evry sense we got back from brig porte." [24] But it is significant that the naked Ohioan compared the aspect of his regiment to that of the rebels; it was common for Confederate troops to march in rags, but it was exceptional for Yankees.

Meigs's own favorite illustration of the ultimate success of his clothing supply system concerned General Sherman's march to the sea and thence through the Carolinas. When Sherman's troops reached Savannah at the end of 1864, 70,000 to 100,000 strong, they found a complete new clothing outfit awaiting them. When they reached Beaufort, North Carolina, about three months later the same windfall was in store. These new supplies came from quartermaster's stocks so large that they sufficed to uniform the army for years after the war.[25]

The transformation of the clothing supply system from a chaotic tangle of graft and incompetence to an operation conducted with efficiency and reasonable honesty was largely the work of M. C. Meigs. In this his talent for careful accounting and foresighted planning revealed him at his best. The clothing stores of the Union army were always a wonder to the Confederates, and clothing the army was among the most conspicuous successes of Meigs and the Quartermaster's Department.

The Civil War was the last great war of mounted men and horses. To secure the horses was the responsibility of General Meigs. Thousands of cavalrymen ranged across the South as the eyes and the swift right arm of every army; artillery moved into battle behind teams of horses; great wagon trains drawn by horses and mules followed the soldiers on the march. To the modern observer the numbers of animals with the troops may seem fantastic. At the Federal army's highest peak of

[24] Quoted in Wiley, *Billy Yank*, p. 61.
[25] *O.R.*, ser. 3, V, 225; ser. 3, V, 260–64.

efficiency, in 1864, a group of armies totaling 426,000 men would have with them 221,000 animals, more than one animal to every two soldiers. Of this number, 113,864 were serviceable horses, 87,791 were serviceable mules, and the remainder were oxen plus some unserviceable horses and mules.[26]

All this imposed a tremendous drain upon the horse population of the country, which for the Northern states was 4,688,-878 at the time of the census of 1860. It imposed also a great burden upon the quartermasters charged with securing animals, and particularly cavalry mounts, in sufficient numbers and of satisfactory quality. But unlike the clothing problem, Meigs did not find the task of securing animals for the army acute until the war was well under way.

Largely this result followed because in 1861 and early 1862 the need for animals was not quite so urgent. Troops quartered around Washington could not get along without clothing, but they could make shift with fewer animals than they would require for active campaigning. Futher, the government was slow to seek an increase in cavalry strength. And the available supply of horses was far more adequate than the supply of uniforms. By August 31, 1861, the army included only thirty-one regiments of cavalry and ten of artillery,[27] and the demand created by such a force, even when added to the transportation needs of the entire army, was not especially heavy in a nation which possessed more than four million horses. Purchases from the beginning of the war to the end of September, 1862, totaled about 150,000 horses and somewhat over 100,000 mules.[28]

Indeed, the price of horses actually fell for a time. At the outset a horse delivered at Washington cost $125; on some

[26] O.R., ser. 3, IV, 888.
[27] Williams, Lincoln Finds a General, I, 118.
[28] O.R., ser. 3, II, 799.

occasions thereafter the price reached $100. General Meigs attributed this development to the withdrawal of workers from the farms and to the campaigning in Kentucky and Missouri, states normally rich in horses, where now the marches of armies diminished the security and increased the cost of supporting farm animals, leaving their owners more than usually ready to sell. Later, heavy demand was to produce its inevitable effect; by the close of the war cavalry horses would sell for from $144 to $185. Artillery horses, larger and more powerful animals, would cost in the final year from $161 to $185; mules, from $170 to $195. Whenever possible, Meigs sought to keep prices down by purchasing horses on contract after public notice and competitive bidding. But frequently a demand for instant supply required purchase in the open market.[29]

It was doubtless unavoidable that a number of rundown and sickly nags should have been passed on to the government as good cavalry mounts. That the number had to be as great as it actually was seems less inevitable. The purchase of faulty horses was an ordinary occurrence at the outset of the war, when qualified inspectors and purchasing agents were too few, but the problem of wasting money on diseased and used up animals was one that General Meigs was never able really to solve. What the Van Wyck Committee learned about government horses was one of the things that raised its members' blood pressure. They heard testimony describing new horses whose jaws were swollen with distemper but who were branded with the government's "U. S." and then accepted for the army; how the inspectors held up spavined limbs and then accepted the horses that owned them; how contractors approached various inspectors until they found one who would

[29] *O.R.*, ser. 3, II, 799–800; ser. 3, IV, 888–89; ser. 3, V, 220–21, 255.

accept their beasts; how an individual watching an inspection of horses heard his neighbor remark on the arrival of a horse he had known for twenty-nine years.[30]

In a gesture toward remedying the situation, Meigs had his office issue printed lists of specifications for government animals,[31] but these were not enough to ensure the elimination of unsuitable animals if the inspectors were not qualified judges of horseflesh. Too often they were not, but the Quartermaster's Department could not find men who were. Soldiers who knew horses were already with the cavalry or artillery.

Repeatedly Meigs urged that cavalry and artillery officers disabled in active service be detailed as inspectors of horses, but for months he secured no results. Meanwhile even agents he thought he could trust continued to purchase horses that turned out to be useless.

For all that, Meigs was able until the fall of 1862 to send to the troops in the field a supply of animals sufficient to save him from serious complaints. The late summer and early fall of that year, however, were hard times for the horses of the eastern armies. By the time McClellan stalled on the Peninsula, Lincoln had scraped together the oddments of three corps that were scattered through northern Virginia and the Shenandoah Valley and organized them into a new army, the Army of Virginia, under Major General John Pope, an officer who had won a certain reputation through successes in the West. The original idea seems to have been to make the Army of Virginia a new menace supplementing McClellan's threat to Richmond, but when McClellan settled down to sitting idly at Harrison's Landing, the administration determined to siphon off his troops gradually into the Army of Virginia, in the belief that Pope at least would fight.

[30] 37:2 House Rep. 2 (serial 1142, 1143), p. lviii.
[31] Q.M.G. Let. B. 55, pp. 456, 489–90; Q.M.G. Let. B. 72, pp. 76–77.

Pope did fight, but disastrously; at the end of August he met a stinging defeat near the old battlefield of Bull Run. Moreover, Pope displayed a particular talent for using up cavalry. In the middle of August, just after his first major engagement of the Second Bull Run campaign at Cedar Mountain, he had already asked for 1,500 horses to remount his troopers.[32] This hard service was followed by the long march northward and westward to face Lee along the banks of the Antietam and turn back the Confederate invasion of Maryland. Climaxing it all, in October the cavalry was called upon to chase Jeb Stuart when that daring Southern horseman led his division around the flanks of the Union army in Maryland and northward into Pennsylvania.

The Federal cavalry failed to intercept or to catch up with Stuart, and McClellan, now back in command of a restored Army of the Potomac, sought to turn the consequent newspaper criticism away from himself and onto the Quartermaster's Department by claiming he had not possessed enough horses to handle Stuart. Only 800 mounts, he said, were available to his cavalry command.

On matters such as this, unfortunately, McClellan's testimony was subject to aberrations rooted in his rather oriental disregard for accurate figures. That Meigs and his department had been delinquent is far from certain. The chief quartermaster of McClellan's army, Rufus Ingalls, later reported that the number of cavalry horses with the army at the beginning of October was 8,142; General Meigs reported that McClellan had been issued 5,993 horses in late September and 4,261 in the first eleven days of October.

What does seem to be true is that an epidemic of hoof-and-mouth disease struck the mounts of the Army of the Potomac about this time and put an undetermined number of horses out

[32] Williams, *Lincoln Finds a General*, I, 275.

of action. Beyond that, it is possible that someone involved in
the distribution or care of McClellan's horses might have slipped
up, keeping the new horses from the hands of the cavalrymen
when the troopers most needed them. On the other hand, Ingalls's figures as well as those of Meigs, who was habitually
truthful and a careful accountant, make it appear most likely
that any fault that existed lay with McClellan and his subordinates rather than with officers under the orders of M. C.
Meigs.[33] Serious problems were still to plague the supply of
cavalry horses, but in October, 1862, Meigs was probably
McClellan's scapegoat.

Mont is kept very buzy [Mrs. Rodgers wrote to her son] and
has not slept at home for the last three or four nights. he stayes
at the War Department and gets home at 7 o'clock in the Morning. he says he sleeps on a couch but thinks it is better for him
to be there as telegrams are being received and sent out at all
hours of the night.[34]

So busy was he that the man sometimes seems to have become wholly immersed in the office. Meigs was a tireless machine, signing dispatches, examining accounts, surveying the
needs of widely separated theaters, and calculating the stores
he would require to supply them. But the old Meigs was still
there, behind the office, determined, irascible, conscientious,
unyielding in his integrity, and jealous of his reputation for
being so. He no longer had time nor perhaps the inclination
for prolonged battles with his detractors, battles of the Walter
type, but he would not abide readily an insult or a questioning
of his probity.

So it was that he snapped to attention when in January,
1863, remarks on the Senate floor questioned not only his com-

---

[33] *O.R.*, ser. 1, XIX, pt. 1, 71–72, 97, 422–24.
[34] Mrs. John Rodgers to John Rodgers II, May 27, 1862, Rodgers
Family Papers, Naval Historical Foundation Collection, Box 130, L.C.

petence and honesty but even his loyalty. Henry Wilson rose
in his defense, and he sent to Wilson a letter of deeply felt
thanks; but more than that, he urged Wilson to read into the
*Congressional Globe* a statement which he composed in his
own defense. He wrote to John Sherman and Lafayette Foster
exhorting them to encourage the reading of the document.

Had the accusations [he said] been made in a less high and respectable place, I might have trusted to past service and reputation, and passed them by in silence. But the Senate of the United
States is a part of the Government and every word there spoken
in debate is preserved in the archives of the country long after
the speakers cease to exist. I desire to stand right upon those records.

Wilson did not read Meigs's paper to the Senate. It is a
measure of the continued sharpness of the general's tongue that
the Senator feared his remarks would offend the chamber,
friends as well as enemies.[35]

In debate with generals who thought themselves ill-supplied,
Meigs could yet say all he wished, free from Senatorial deli-
cacy. And if his letters were neither so negative in tone nor
so contemptuous of personalities as those of the Walter period,
they nevertheless were blunt and stinging. They might also
embody good sense.

Such was Meigs's correspondence with Major General William S. Rosecrans, commander of the Army of the Cumberland
in the middle theater of war. Rosecrans assumed command of
the army at the end of October, 1862. Until then, and through
the first two months of Rosecrans's tenure, Meigs had received
no word of any deficiency in the horses of the army. He assumed, since he heard nothing to the contrary, that the supply
of horses moving to the Army of the Cumberland, principally
from the depot at Louisville, was meeting the army's require-

[35] Q.M.G. Let. B. 65, pp. 444–45, 464–65, 468.

ments. With surprise he read in the middle of January a request from Rosecrans for immediate delivery of 8,000 horses;
Rosecrans considered his cavalry too weak and proposed to
mount about 8,000 infantry.

Eight thousand horses could not be gathered overnight, but
in addition to forwarding to Rosecrans all the animals on hand
at the Louisville depot, Meigs had the quartermaster at Indianapolis hurry forward a thousand from that place and take immediate steps to procure and forward a thousand more. He
ordered other depot quartermasters in the West into the market for horses.[36]

The upshot of Rosecrans's sudden request was an acrimonious interchange of letters between him and the quartermaster
general, persisting through most of the first half of 1863.
Rosecrans's horses did not arrive so rapidly as he wished, and
when they did appear many of them were unserviceable. The
army commander repeatedly informed Meigs of this situation,
and he secured no apparent results. He then complained directly to Secretary of War Stanton, and Stanton asked Meigs
what was the trouble. Meanwhile Meigs had been informing
his quartermasters in the West of Rosecrans's dissatisfaction
and reminding them of the standards for army animals established by the department. On April 18 he sent to Louisville
one of his most trusted officers, Colonel Thomas Swords, with
orders to put an end to bribery of the inspectors and to the
acceptance of unsatisfactory mounts and to push the supply of
good horses southward.

But to Stanton and Rosecrans the quartermaster general replied that what Rosecrans was getting was only what he should
have expected when he ordered with no advance warning the
immediate delivery of 8,000 animals and then continued to

[36] Q.M.G. Let. B. 65, pp. 96–97, 432–33.

demand even more. To find so many horses in a limited time, after two years of war, was exceedingly difficult. The natural result of Rosecrans's urgency was that the quartermasters accepted inferior animals that under ordinary circumstances they would never have passed. Moreover, Meigs reiterated his inability to find enough inspectors genuinely qualified to evaluate horses. Several times he telegraphed to Rosecrans suggesting that if the situation were as bad as that general indicated, then it would be a good idea for him to send to Louisville as inspectors a few disabled cavalry officers from the Army of the Cumberland. "Inspection by faithful Cavalry officers," wrote Meigs, "is the only remedy I can devise, unless General Burnside will, under martial law, hang one or two bogus or bribing contractors. That would improve the stock I think." [37]

Thus Rosecrans's inferior horses were chargeable, first, to a genuine defect in the Quartermaster's Department, the lack of qualified inspectors, and second and perhaps more importantly, to the demand that the horses arrive swiftly. Meigs did what he could to remedy the situation, and when his measures failed to halt Rosecrans's complaints to the department, he took time to write the army commander a penetrating critique of his use of the animals he already had. General Meigs was weary of taking the blame for a deficiency of remounts in the Army of the Cumberland when he thought the real root of the trouble was Rosecrans's failure to handle his cavalry astutely.

Nine thousand horses had returned from the Army of the Cumberland to Louisville within a recent period. This, believed Meigs, was evidence that already the army had more horses than it could care for. Rosecrans attributed the high

[37] Stanton Let. B. I, p. 121, Stanton Papers, L.C.; Q.M.G. Let. B. 68, pp. 112, 185–86.

mortality rate among his animals to want of proper forage, which could not be furnished because he did not have enough transportation.

Were there, then [asked Meigs], so many animals in the Department that they would not transport their own food? When an army reaches this limit what is the remedy? Is not every additional horse another subject for starvation?

Meigs noted that in spite of this situation Rosecrans was writing that he wanted ten or twenty thousand horses more. If he already had so many that they could scarcely carry their own food, how did he propose to feed so many more? Here Meigs put his finger upon a difficulty which, on another level, was to appear again in World War II. In the twentieth century it was not horses but motor vehicles that were involved, and not forage but gasoline. Yet in drawing up the tables of organization and equipment for American infantry and armored divisions early in World War II, the army planning staffs had to recognize that there must be a limit to the number of vehicles with which a division ought to be provided, lest the division be immobilized by its own transport; that is, lest the number of vehicles become so great as to render unnecessarily cumbersome the process of moving the division from place to place, or lest the fuel requirements of the vehicles become so great as to approach a point of diminishing returns.[38] When General George S. Patton's armor so far outran its supplies in the autumn of 1944 as to lack sufficient fuel to go on, what was needed for the moment was not more tanks. If Rosecrans had so many horses he could not feed them, he might as well not have had them.

As a matter of fact, Meigs saw no reason why Rosecrans's horses should be starving. Were they not occupying middle

[38] Greenfield, et al., Ground Combat Troops, pp. 281–82.

Tennessee, a good grain country? How did the Confederate cavalry, which Rosecrans considered superior to his own, subsist? The Confederate cavalry must in large measure have been living off the land, and if they could do it, said Meigs, there should have been no reason why Rosecrans's horses could not do likewise.

General Rosecrans in fact had a goodly number of animals. In addition to 11,478 cavalry mounts, he possessed 3,339 artillery horses and enough work animals to raise his total of horses to 19,164. Besides these he had 23,859 mules. Thus the Army of the Cumberland included 43,023 animals, or about one horse or mule to every two men. Rosecrans had received 33,057 animals since December 1 alone.

Asked Meigs:

Is this not a large supply? Except in the first outbreak of War and enlargement of armies, has anything like it ever been done before? These animals cost, by the time they reached you, nearly four millions of dollars.

With such a supply, and so many of them cavalry horses, Meigs thought Rosecrans's cavalry should have been far more active than it was. If there was a single salient shortcoming among most of the Union generals early in the war, it was lack of an aggressive fighting spirit. One gathers they would have done well to share the mettle of the desk-bound quartermaster general.

With great deference to your experience, would not the less costly mode of defending your communications from the Rebel cavalry be to give them some occupation in protecting their own? . . .
Compel your cavalry officers to see that their horses are properly groomed. Put them in some place where they can get forage, near the Railroad, or send them to your rear to graze and eat corn. When in good order start them, 1000 at a time, for the

Rebel communications, with orders never to move off a walk unless they see an enemy before or behind them; to travel only so far in a day as not to fatigue their horses: never to camp in the place at which sunset finds them; and to rest in a good pasture during the heat of the day; to keep some of their eyes open night and day, and never to pass a bridge without burning it, a house without stealing or a telegraph wire without cutting it, a guerrilla without shooting or capturing him, or a negro without explaining the Presidents Proclamation.

Let them go any way, so that it is to the rear of the enemy, and return by the most improbable routes, generally aiming to go entirely around the enemy, and you will put Johnston and Bragg into such a state of excitement that they will attack or retreat to relieve themselves. They will not be able to lie still. You gained a great success at Murfreesboro by your possessing courage and endurance.

The same qualities will enable you to conquer in the next struggle, but this long inaction tells severely upon the resources of the country. The Rebels will never be conquered by waiting in their front.

Operate on their communications. Strike any detached post; rely more upon infantry than upon cavalry, which in the whole war has not decided the fate of a single battle, rising above a skirmish, which taxes the Treasury, and exhausts the resources of the country, and of which we have now afoot a larger nominal strength than any nation on earth. We have over 126 regiments of cavalry, and they have killed ten times as many horses for us as for the Rebels.[39]

William S. Rosecrans was not the man to follow as spirited a plan as this, but he was a skillful general and presently he opened the campaign which captured Chattanooga without a major battle. He made no particularly noteworthy use of his horses, but neither did he continue to plague Meigs with pleas for more. The tough outer shell of the quartermaster general again turned away attack.

[39] Q.M.G. Let. B. 68, pp. 288–92.

If Rosecrans's plaints were often unjust, Meigs's difficulties in finding good horses were nonetheless real. In the middle of 1863 there came to Meigs's desk a series of reports on the animals procured by agents in New York State and reinspected at Washington. In one shipment of forty horses, twenty-five were good; of the others some were too thin, some too young, and the remainder suffered from shoulder injuries or were spavined. One was blind. Of another shipment of thirty-two animals, twenty-one were good, but the rest were listed as too old, too young, wind-broken, or ring-boned. Of a shipment of one hundred sent from New York City only forty-eight were good; the rest suffered from the usual variety of disqualifying ailments, including one characterized simply as "quite used up." [40]

From the beginning of the war, Meigs pleaded for the inspection of potential cavalry horses by qualified cavalry officers. Toward the middle of 1863 his complaints, combined with those of cavalrymen in the field, bore fruit at last in the establishment of the Cavalry Bureau. This was a separate office of the War Department charged with the duty of equipping all the cavalry forces of the army. Under a succession of able commanders it reorganized the remount service and brought it to considerably greater efficiency than before. As Meigs had long advised, it used experienced horsemen as purchasing agents and inspectors. It acted in cooperation with the Quartermaster's Department, and for a time the chief of the bureau was also in charge of related purchases in the Quartermaster General's Office. General Meigs's agents continued to purchase cavalry horses and equipment, but all mounts, remounts, and original equipment bought by quartermasters were turned over to the Cavalry Bureau, and all requisitions for sup-

[40] Q.M.G. Let. B. 69, pp. 216, 225–26.

plies were referred to the Cavalry Bureau for endorsement.[41]

For the collection and training of cavalry horses and for the reception and instruction of cavalry recruits, the Cavalry Bureau established six depots. They were located at St. Louis, Greenville, Louisiana, Nashville, Harrisburg, and Wilmington, Delaware, with the principal depot at Giesboro in the District of Columbia, where the Eastern Branch meets the Potomac. The Giesboro depot was rushed to completion late in 1863; 5,000 men were employed in its construction. By November accommodations were ready for 15,000 horses; by early 1864, 30,000 animals could be cared for. Most of the horses were kept in sheds or corrals, but thirty-two giant stables could accommodate 6,000 of them. There were hospital facilities for 2,650 horses. Altogether, the depot occupied 625 acres and normally employed 1,500 men. With these steps, the horse supply greatly improved.[42]

The 600 tons of supplies which in 1862 moved daily from the supply depots to the advanced positions of a Federal army of 100,000 men may seem a small amount by the standards of our own day. During World War II 600 tons barely met the daily needs of a single American division.[43] Yet to carry 600 tons from railhead to front lines was no minor task when the intervening method of transport had to be wagon and the roads were the sandy tracks of eastern Virginia or the mountain defiles of East Tennessee.

When it lay at Harrison's Landing after the Seven Days Battles for Richmond, the Army of the Potomac had in its

[41] O.R., ser. 3, III, 580–81, 884–86; ser. 3, IV, 229; Q.M.G. Let. B. 71, pp. 224–25.

[42] O.R., ser. 3, III, 884–85; Francis Trevelyan Miller, ed., *Photographic History of the Civil War* (10 vols., New York, 1911), IV, 328. For subsequent achievements, see below, pp. 295–96.

[43] Eisenhower, *Crusade in Europe*, p. 235.

trains 2,578 wagons and 415 ambulances, drawn by 5,899 horses and 8,708 mules. After Antietam, when the strength of the army had grown to about 130,000, its trains included 3,798 wagons drawn by 19,558 animals. At Harrison's Landing the ratio of wagons to men was 26 to 1,000; in Maryland, 29 to 1,000. Two years later, at the outset of Grant's 1864 campaign, there would roll behind the Army of the Potomac 4,300 wagons, with the ratio of wagons to men up to 33 to 1,000.[44]

That the number of wagons following the Federal armies was probably without precedent General Meigs demonstrated by recalling that Napoleon had stipulated a ratio of twelve wagons to every thousand soldiers. What the emperor had had in mind, however, was an army marching rapidly over cultivated country which offered good foraging. As often as not the Union armies were moving through impoverished or devastated areas, and especially in the East they often remained for weeks in a single area. Meigs pointed out that in a region desolate of forage a four-horse team could carry a twenty or thirty days' supply of food only for itself, not for cavalry or artillery horses as well, as Napoleon had intended.[45] Furthermore, campaigning in the American South generally meant campaigning over execrable roads, quagmires in wet weather, fantastically rutted or choked with dust in dry. Drawing the wagons was too tough a job for horses; by the close of the war most of the trains were pulled by mules.[46]

The wagons of the army appear to have been reasonably durable. General Meigs reported after the war that when the eastern and western armies met in Washington for the grand review in the spring of 1865, both forces had with them wagons which had been at First Bull Run and had survived the

[44] O.R., ser. 3, II, 798; Williams, *Lincoln Finds a General,* I, 10.
[45] O.R., ser. 3, II, 798.
[46] O.R., ser. 3, V, 243.

entire war. The standard wagon design profited from the experience of the army on the Western frontier; it had proved itself on the plains and in the passes of the Rockies. Meigs believed there were few or no ways in which it could be improved. To repair damages suffered in the field, portable forges accompanied the wagon trains; they carried spare parts plus wheelwrights', carpenters', and saddlers' tools. Rarely did a good officer have to abandon a wagon.[47]

Little could be done toward improving Southern roads, but it was essential at least to bridge streams, especially in mountain areas. When Federal troops were campaigning in rugged West Virginia, Meigs ordered for them three sets of light and portable equipment for the construction of wire-rope suspension bridges. The same equipment could be used in place of trestlework to support scaffolding in the repair of railroad bridges if the masonry piers of the bridges were still standing, as they usually were even after destruction of a bridge by the enemy.[48]

Closely related to the Seventh Division of Meigs's office, which concerned itself with wagon transportation, was the Fifth Division, whose province was forage and fuel. More than half the supplies forwarded to a field army daily consisted of forage, and the train animals consumed much of this quantity. While a soldier required three pounds of provisions daily, an animal required twenty-six pounds of forage, and the forage generally exceeded subsistence stores for the men as much in bulk as in weight. The total quantities of forage consumed through most of the war were carefully catalogued by General Meigs in his report for 1865, and the figures are staggering. Between December 8, 1862, and June 30, 1865, the Quartermaster's Department purchased and shipped to the depots and

[47] O.R., ser. 3, IV, 888; ser. 3, V, 322–23.
[48] O.R., ser. 3, II, 804.

armies 2,787,758 bushels of corn, 20,997,289 bushels of oats, 43,311 bushels of barley, 269,814 tons of hay, and 8,243 tons of straw. Transportation of the grain by railroad, canal, river, and lake involved 8,567 railroad carloads, 560 barge loads by canal, and 49 schooner, 29 bark, and 20 propeller cargoes on the lakes. The hay traveled by railroad to the depots of distribution in 5,555 carloads. With all this movement, loss by wastage, fire, and at sea amounted to only seven eighths of one percent of the total amount carried.[49]

While the Federal wagon trains had to carry forage month after month, in all seasons, throughout the war, General Meigs diminished the burden of the trains in another respect by curtailing the transportation of shelter materials. At the beginning of the war the Quartermaster's Department introduced the shelter tent—that is, the familiar "pup tent"—and thenceforth each soldier carried half a tent with him on the march. After the first winter of the war, troops in the field generally erected their own winter quarters, constructing wooden huts sometimes roofed with a tent, sometimes with shingles. This practice lifted another burden not only from the cares of the transportation service but from Meigs's purview entirely.

Building semipermanent barracks and hospitals remained a task of the Quartermaster's Department. The quartermasters built both hospitals and barracks cheaply and quickly of wood. By the close of the war army hospitals had a capacity of 127,-821 beds, with the largest of them, at Chestnut Hill, Philadelphia, accommodating 4,000 wounded. The Sixth Division of the Quartermaster General's Office, which after the reorganization of 1864 supervised the construction of barracks and hospitals, also carried on the grim task of preparing, registering, and caring for Federal graves.[50]

[49] *O.R.*, ser. 3, V, 237; ser. 3, V, 305–15.
[50] *O.R.*, ser. 3, V, 239–40; ser. 3, V, 315–22.

# XI

# THE GETTYSBURG CAMPAIGN

GENERAL MEIGS unbuttoned his uniform coat and looked absently out the window toward the old-fashioned brick building of the War Department and the early summer leaves and grasses on the White House lawn. It was morning, but already some of the soldiers and government clerks who walked on Seventeenth Street mopped their brows under the June sun. The general turned to his desk and the day's dispatches, flipping through them impatiently and scanning them in the way that had become routine during the two years since he first entered the Quartermaster's Department.

His attention wandered to the armies below the Potomac. Since Antietam, Lee and his Confederates had twice turned back Federal strikes toward Richmond, once at Fredericksburg in December, again at Chancellorsville in May. Now there floated northward persistent rumors of an impending offensive by Lee's Army of Northern Virginia. There was mysterious Confederate activity along the Rappahannock and westward to the Shenandoah.

At the beginning of June the Confederates had been encamped just south of the Rappahannock near Fredericksburg. On June 4 observers north of the stream with the Army of the Potomac, since April commanded by Major General Joseph Hooker, thought they saw Lee's troops vacating some of their camps. On the 6th Hooker sent a reconnaissance in force across the river, but the sortie met such stiff opposition that the Federal commander remained utterly puzzled as to Confederate intentions. On the 9th Hooker threw his cavalry over the Rappahannock for another look around. They had a sharp fight with Confederate horse and captured orders which instructed the Confederate cavalry to be on the move northwestward. Hooker's cavalry chieftain interpreted the orders as suggesting only a raid, not a prelude to invasion of the North.

The next day the cavalryman was wiring a different story to Hooker: he knew that five or six Confederate infantry divisions were well up the river, in the vicinity of Culpeper. At least a full Confederate corps was still at Fredericksburg, but on June 11 Hooker sent the vanguard of his infantry marching upriver. On the 13th the Federal cavalry sent word from informants in Culpeper that Ewell's Confederate corps had marched north and westward from that place toward the Shenandoah Valley, with Longstreet's corps following. That afternoon the Federals began breaking up their base at Aquia Creek and marching toward the Orange and Alexandria Railroad. Based on this line, Hooker would screen Washington and at the same time follow Lee's advance.[1]

Now Meigs's office began to respond to the new movements, which would occasion more direct intervention by the quartermaster general in the supply of a field army than any other events of the war. To Hooker's chief quartermaster, Brigadier General Rufus Ingalls, the quartermaster general sent word on June 15 urging that he attempt to hold the Aquia Creek depot with a guard and gunboats until the whole of the stores there could be carried away. Meigs understood that 126 railroad cars had been in use between Aquia Creek and Falmouth, and he

[1] For these movements, see especially Williams, *Lincoln Finds a General*, II, 612–29.

advised Ingalls to dump the cars into shallow water where they could be recovered rather than burn them or leave them to the enemy. He wanted no unnecessary burning, of the sort that had occurred when General Ambrose Burnside abandoned the same base the year before. Should the enemy appear at the depot, he said, Federal gunboats could achieve all the required destruction by lobbing shells into the place.[2]

On June 14 the last of the Confederate army moved westward from Fredericksburg, and that same day the enemy vanguard swept down on Winchester, the hub of the lower Shenandoah Valley, where a Union garrison some 5,000 strong had tarried overlong in the face of an order from General-in-Chief Henry W. Halleck to evacuate. By late afternoon a well-conducted attack had won the Confederates the fortifications which commanded the town. The Federals retreated during the night but collided at gray dawn with an enemy division sent northward to cut them off; there was a brief fight which ended in headlong Federal retreat. The Confederates bagged over 3,300 prisoners and twenty-three cannon. News of an enemy army virtually at the banks of the Potomac, with nothing to prevent them from crossing, plunged the North into near-panic. At Pittsburgh the townsmen began digging trenches in the surrounding hills, the governor of Pennsylvania hastened to assemble emergency home guards, and New York rushed some 10,000 militia to Harrisburg because Pennsylvania had not possessed the foresight to organize a defense of her own capital. While the Confederate advance crossed the Potomac near Williamsport on the 15th, President Lincoln called on Pennsylvania, Ohio, Maryland, and West Virginia for 100,000 emergency volunteers.[3]

[2] Q.M.G. Let. B. 69, pp. 315–16.
[3] Williams, *Lincoln Finds a General*, II, 630–31; Freeman, *Lee's Lieutenants*, III, 20–27.

To equip the emergency troops was Meigs's next task. On the 16th his office ordered General Rucker to forward with all speed a number of batteries from the Washington Arsenal to Baltimore and thence to Harrisburg, in order to ensure their reaching the Susquehanna that night. The assistant quartermaster at Harrisburg was directed to purchase the horses he needed in his own neighborhood and to call on the depot at Philadelphia for harness and fifty wagons. After a telegraphic debate with the governor of Pennsylvania, Secretary Stanton authorized Meigs to issue uniforms from quartermaster's stocks to the Pennsylvania emergency troops. "Harrisburg is in a rich district which district should place its resources at the disposal of the commanding General," Meigs told the quartermaster there. "Do not allow speculative prices. With the approval of the Commanding General fix prices and compel supplies." This was an emergency, and the quartermaster general wanted no nonsense such as had accompanied the crisis of 1861.[4]

To General Rucker of the Washington depot Meigs sent instructions to have as many horses as possible shod and ready for instant issue and service. He telegraphed New York, Philadelphia, and Indianapolis to send forward all the horses on hand and to continue purchases and shipments until ordered to do otherwise.[5] The Army of the Potomac was shifting northward in a path parallel to Lee's and between the Confederates and Washington. Hooker's cavalry was knocking at the Blue Ridge gaps in an effort to penetrate the enemy's cavalry shield and pierce the secrecy which still shrouded the strength of Lee's march. Rufus Ingalls's demands for horses would soon be large and urgent.

On June 25 the last of Lee's Confederate infantry reached

[4] Q.M.G. Let. B. 69, pp. 326, 338; Q.M.G. Let. B. 70, p. 21; Stanton Let. B. II, p. 65, Stanton Papers, L.C.
[5] Q.M.G. Let. B. 69, p. 385.

the north bank of the Potomac. The duty of Jeb Stuart's cavalry to hold the line of the Blue Ridge was now done. The task had been a vital one, but it was too prosaic, too routine a job to satisfy Jeb Stuart. He was thirsting for an opportunity to win glory, and in two amazing orders which came to him from Lee he saw his chance. What Lee was thinking of when he sent these dispatches to Stuart is difficult to imagine. They authorized Stuart, if he thought he could do it without hindrance, to enter Maryland by riding around Hooker's army—a feat which would win all the newspaper notices Stuart craved, but which would deprive Lee of the eyes of his army at the time when, advancing into hostile country, he needed them most. On June 25 Stuart led three mounted brigades eastward from Salem, Virginia; his third ride around the Federal army had begun.

The time was especially ill chosen. Hooker was fast closing in on Lee. Three Federal infantry corps crossed the Potomac at Edwards Ferry on June 25. By evening of the next day most of the Federal army had forded the river, and Hooker's headquarters were at Poolesville, Maryland.[6]

Meigs's wagon trains for the army now moved out the Rockville Pike toward Frederick. The quartermaster general had given strict orders against sending trains unescorted during Lee's earlier invasion of Maryland, and he assumed that General Rucker and his subordinates would have the presence of mind to follow the same procedure now that the enemy was north of the Potomac again. He assumed too much. On June 28 at Rockville, Fitzhugh Lee's brigade of Stuart's cavalry descended upon a train of 900 mules and 150 wagons, bound for Hooker's army with oats, corn, and even some ham and whisky. The principal result was to slow Stuart's march, since

[6] Freeman, *Lee's Lieutenants*, III, 54–58; Williams, *Lincoln Finds a General*, II, 641.

the Confederates took the train with them. But Meigs could not know how severely Lee was suffering from lack of reconnaissance, and on no grounds could he excuse the loss of the train.[7] He got off a stiff message to Rucker:

Gen. Ingalls asks that 10,000 pairs of shoes and as many socks, (Ten Thousand) be sent to Head Quarters Army of Potomac, for issue to the corps as they pass that place.

Send them whenever a safe route is open, or a sufficient escort. Last fall by positive orders, I put a stop to the sending of trains without escort from this District to the Army about Frederick. My orders in the present circumstances are similar, [have] been neglected and to day we have lost 900 mules and 150 wagons sent without escort, while only yesterday morning 400 cavalry, which could have taken care of the train, marched for Frederick.

Take measures to prevent a repetition of this gross violation of all military rule. The orders of last Sept. & October should not have needed repetition. It is impossible for me to reach each Quarter Master and as Chief Quarter Master of the Dept., I wish you to assume control of all the officers of the Department forwarding supplies to the army from this District and to prevent any more such disasters if possible. The present disaster could have been prevented.[8]

More than a wagon route was needed to keep the Army of the Potomac supplied as it should be with a crucial battle impending. Meigs could use the tracks of the Baltimore and Ohio Railroad as far as Frederick, but as Hooker pushed northward into Pennsylvania, reliance on that line would necessitate a long wagon haul from the railhead. The Confederate vanguard around Harrisburg and York was astride the Northern Central, which normally linked Baltimore with Harrisburg. The situation left as the nearest railroad to the army the line from Baltimore to Westminster, Maryland, but the road was a pathetic little line with only a single track and not so much as one sid-

[7] Freeman, *Lee's Lieutenants*, III, 66, 70–71.
[8] Q.M.G. Let. B. 70, p. 28.

ing long enough to pass a full-length train. It had no telegraph line. It did not even have water stations and turntables. The best effort of which it seemed capable was to run three or four trains a day, while the Army of the Potomac would demand about thirty.

Fortunately, Herman Haupt, the genius of the railroads, was available. He arrived at Westminster on July 1 with orders from Meigs and Stanton to put the Westminster road and the Northern Central to the maximum use possible. Immediately Haupt requested 400 men of the Quartermaster's Department Railroad Construction Corps, a goodly number of full train crews, and plenty of rolling stock. The enemy had now pulled westward from Harrisburg in order to concentrate on the path of the Army of the Potomac, and Haupt put the Construction Corps to work rebuilding bridges and repairing track on the Northern Central to Hanover Junction and thence along the York and Cumberland toward Gettysburg, which was held by part of the Federal 1st Cavalry Division. The crews and the trains he sent rolling along the Westminster line. Since there could be no passing, the trains were to run in convoys of five each. They would depart from Baltimore every eight hours, affording each convoy time to unload at Westminster and return before the next got under way. Haupt informed General Meigs that from here it was up to the Quartermaster's Department to get the trains loaded and unloaded rapidly enough to make his schedule work.[9]

Meanwhile Meigs assured Rufus Ingalls that his requisitions would be met. Early on July 1 he informed Ingalls that 20,000 pairs of shoes and socks as well as other stores had gone forward to Union Bridge, just west of Westminster; a duplicate order was on its way to Frederick. These shipments should go far toward refitting the army after the long hike from the

[9] Turner, *Victory Rode the Rails,* pp. 278–79.

Rappahannock. Grain also was moving to Frederick, and the Construction Corps was on its way to repair the Northern Central. Meigs enjoined Ingalls to guard well the Monocacy Bridge on the B. & O.: "if lost there will be six days break on the R. Road." [10]

From Ingalls that same day Meigs received important word of the activities of the army, which he passed on promptly to Rucker:

A despatch just received from Gen. Ingalls. Enemy just appeared in force near Gettysburg driving in our cavalry pickets. Attack and pitched battle expected very soon. Gen Ingalls thinks he has plenty of supplies to last till after the battle, and can then better tell where to receive them. All his trains ordered on the Rail Road between Union Bridge and Westminster—none to Frederick. He wishes therefore the forage sent to Union Bridge, but that nothing be sent for the present to Frederick. Matters will culminate very quickly, and they doubt not victoriously for the Army of the U. S.[11]

The battle was opening, and Ingalls had testified that the Quartermaster's Department had done its part to ready the army. The army had marched from the Rappahannock to the Monocacy, and at each new position it found a supply line functioning behind it. Meigs awaited the outcome hopefully:

Our army is strong I have no doubt stronger than Lee's. If properly handled it will defeat & most seriously cripple & damage him. . . .

Arms men provisions ammunition guns horses mules wagons tents all the material of war he [the commander of the Federal army] has had to the extent of the capacity of the government & he has now as many men as have been placed under one commander in very few . . . fields since the dawn of European civilization. . . .

The history of men is the story of "tendencies" We tend toward

[10] Q.M.G. Let. B. 70, pp. 51, 54.
[11] Q.M.G. Let. B. 70, p. 59.

liberty We were three years ago tending towards universal slavery
—a wrong tendency & therefore arrested before it became too
strong—[12]

While the battle raged around Gettysburg and inconclusive
reports filtered into Washington, Meigs made his preparations
for the aftermath. To Colonel G. H. Crosman, assistant quartermaster at Philadelphia, he telegraphed:

Report the number of wagons you can supply at once and to
meet expected losses increase your stock largely.

If horses for army service are to be had in the neighborhood
of Philadelphia, purchase them and forward them to this city. The
present campaign will necessitate large remounting.[13]

Similar word flashed to Harrisburg:

If Col. Crosman cannot supply immediately wagons enough for
present needs you will be obliged to hire or purchase country
wagons about Harrisburg.

Purchase all the horses suitable for army wagons you can get
and forward any surplus horses thus obtained to Washington.

Show capacity and energy by calling out the resources of the
rich country in which you are operating.[14]

On the hills around Gettysburg, Lee failed on July 2 to dis-
lodge the Union soldiers, commanded by George G. Meade
since June 28, from the wooded slopes which anchored their
flanks. On the 3rd the Confederate commander surmised that
his attacks of the day before had impelled Meade to weaken
the Union center and he determined to send a column of 15,000
Confederate troops smashing directly against the core of
Meade's line in an effort to split the Army of the Potomac
in two. The result was the glory, gallantry, and futility of
Pickett's charge. Late on July 4 Lee's Army of Northern Vir-

[12] Meigs to Charles D. Meigs, June 27, 1863, Meigs Misc. Papers.
[13] Q.M.G. Let. B. 70, pp. 62–63.
[14] *Ibid.*, p. 63.

ginia began its retreat toward the Potomac. On the 5th Meigs wrote to his father of the results and of Washington's hopes that Meade's good work was not yet complete:

The rebels are in full retreat. This is the latest news. Lee has failed in his invasion of the North has broken his waves upon the rock of the Army of the Potomac & shattered & broken his sullen stream of rebellion is flowing down the Cumberland valley to find the ponton Bridge which he had left across the Potomac destroyed, & it is hoped a rising river to put a stop to his flight.

What a stubborn fight? [*Sic.*] Three days of repeated assaults. And yet neither army is destroyed. If Meade can overtake or press him hard in the retreat we may put an end to the career of the hitherto victorious army of Lee, & if it is destroyed one great step towards pacification will have been taken.

. . . Repulsed in so many desperate assaults his loss must have been greater than that of the victorious army which has defeated him & which will after a days sleep hurry in his rear pick up his stragglers & cut off his trains & perhaps press him to a decisive trial of arms on the banks of the swollen Potomac. May it be his destruction.[15]

Already Meigs had taken steps to ensure that Meade's army would not fail through want of supplies. On the 4th he had telegraphed Ingalls:

To improve the victory you will need doubtless many remounts. Stand on no ceremony, but by purchase or impressment of all serviceable horses within the range of your foraging parties—refit the cavalry and artillery in the best possible manner.

By order of the Secretary of War.[16]

To Haupt on the Westminster railroad Meigs sent the injunction: "Let nothing interfere with the supply of rations to the men, and grain for the horses." [17]

[15] Meigs to Charles D. Meigs, July 5, 1861, Meigs Misc. Papers.
[16] Q.M.G. Let. B. 70, p. 112.
[17] *Ibid.*, p. 113.

To the assistant quartermaster at Baltimore went a plea for remounts:

All horses shipped for Washington or for the army passing through Baltimore should for the present be sent to Frederick Md. no matter what their address may be. It is of utmost importance to remount the cavalry.[18]

On July 6 Meigs wired again to Harrisburg:

The moment the Northern Central is repaired send by that route via Baltimore. Urge speed in forwarding horses upon the Rail Road. The speedy refitting of the cavalry may have a most important effect upon our operations.[19]

The same day Meigs advised Ingalls that 1,600 horses and over 2,000 cavalry just mounted or remounted were on their way from the capital to Frederick. Several trains of 100 to 275 horses were moving westward from Washington on the railroads. By five that afternoon Meigs was able to wire that not less than 5,000 horses would be traveling toward Frederick the next morning from depots throughout the East and the Northwest. They would arrive as rapidly as the railroads could carry them. He urged that the detention of rolling stock at Frederick cease: "No such detention should occur unless under a necessity greater than that for forage food and ammunition and horses." In the emergency, and with Lee in retreat, Meigs was willing to send supplies even without escort if necessary. On the 12th he directed Rucker to send one hundred wagons and teams to Frederick immediately: "If an escort can be obtained it should accompany the wagons—if not, under the circumstances, the risk must be taken, and the wagons dispatched as requested." [20]

That evening Meigs wrote again to his father, rejoicing at

[18] *Ibid.*, p. 97.
[19] *Ibid.*
[20] *Ibid.*, pp. 100, 106–7, 117, 152.

word of the fall of Vicksburg and awaiting important news from the Potomac:

Meade's success has been great—& sudden. To morrow there is every prospect of a great battle. Lee is by this time entrenched but it is likely that Meade has twice his numbers and they are flushed with victory & will fight strenuously. The rebels have their best troops their best leaders & all moved by desperation to contend for existence. The battle will be . . . bloody God grant the victory to the right.[21]

Once again the Quartermaster's Department had done its part. The losses of the campaign had left Meade still short of horses, but Meigs had done everything possible to hasten remounts to him. And it was not a scarcity of horses which most delayed Meade's pursuit of the Confederate retreat. At one time Meade had explained a delay in the pursuit by saying he would move as soon as he could supply the army with subsistence and ammunition, but Ingalls was to report that so great a quantity of supplies accumulated at Westminster that they had to be shipped back to Washington when the army changed its base. It was not for want of supplies that Meade failed to engage Lee once more in battle north of the Potomac, but he failed nevertheless. The Confederates reached the Potomac at Williamsport and Falling Waters on July 7. Finding the river flooded and impassable, they prepared a defensive beachhead. On the 12th Meade's infantry at last began to appear before their lines; on the 13th the Federal army would be in position to attack. But Meade hesitated. On the night of the 12th he called a council of war; his corps commanders voted caution. Many of them thought their regiments too thin for an offensive role. Meade was not sure—Lee had been damaged too. But he postponed action and sent the news to General-in-Chief Halleck at Washington.

[21] Meigs to Charles D. Meigs, July 12, 1863, Meigs Misc Papers.

Halleck replied by enjoining him not to heed a council of war: "It is proverbial that councils of war never fight." Halleck's advice came too late. The Potomac had receded. Shielded from Meade's observation by new rains, the Confederates crossed into Virginia all through the 13th. Next morning Federal cavalry drove forward to discover only a rear guard of Lee's army still in Maryland.[22]

The campaign ended on a note of disappointment, but Meade had driven the enemy from Northern soil, and never would the Army of Northern Virginia be strong enough to try in full force again. When Confederate soldiers observed the Capitol from the Seventh Street Road in 1864, they would only be on a raid, without hope of maintaining themselves in Washington. Nor did Meigs believe that the outcome which he had always prophesied could longer stand in doubt. In August Secretary Seward asked him for an appraisal of the military situation. Viewing the successes of the Union army in the West, crowned by the opening of the Mississippi, and the manpower, industrial, and financial status of both North and South, Meigs concluded:

The rebels are a gallant people & will make a desperate [?] resistance but it is exhaustion of men and money that finally terminates all modern wars, and in their case that exhaustion rapidly approaches[.] As their country decreases they lose their manufactories of arms, & they will find it impossible to replace the heavy artillery & arms of which they have lost such large quantities[.] The situation may be summed up in a few words. The National Government enjoys the highest credit—with abundant resources in money in men & in material. Its armies every where outnumber the rebel forces who are all in retreat. Every rebel port is blockaded besieged or possessed by the national arms. The Confederacy is divided by the Mississippi; all whose fortresses are

[22] Williams, *Lincoln Finds a General*, II, 730–54; Freeman, *Lee's Lieutenants*, III, 166–67.

in our hands & whose waters are patrolled by abundant war Steamers. Missouri, Kentucky Maryland Delaware all slave states are entirely in our possession[.] Four fifths of Tennessee one half of Virginia the coast & sounds of North Carolina one half of Mississippi . . . one fourth of Arkansaw, part of Alabama & the whole sea coast of Georgia & South Carolina with part of Florida held by our troops.[23]

This was it. Relentlessly, the iron fist of the North was closing on the Confederacy. The South could not save itself. Only if the resolution of the North weakened could the doom of the Confederacy be averted.

All the more inflexible was the North for the growing bitterness with which she fought. Few could read the casualty lists of Fredericksburg, Chancellorsville, Vicksburg, and Gettysburg without feeling anger as well as pity; certainly not General Meigs, the God of whose family was a stern Old Testament God of war.

Nothing new [he wrote in August], except the crumbling under Gilmores batteries of the walls of Sumter. I hope to hear in a few days that the rebel flag has bit the dust in the place where it first triumphed over the Stars & Stripes. But after this I fear there will be a long tedious unhealthy work before the city of Charleston the nest of treason to free government & civil & personal liberty to human rights gets its deserts which are those of Ninevah & Babylon—& Jerusalem. The place ought to be plowed up & sowed with salt.

Did I command the army which will take it I should be sorely tempted to go through the ancient ceremonial & literally plow up its foundations & sow them with salt.[24]

The anger became more acute, the bitterness deeper still, when the grief of war became personal. Late in August came

[23] Meigs to W. H. Seward, Aug. 1, 1863, Q.M.G. Consolidated Correspondence File, Box 653.
[24] Meigs to Charles D. Meigs, Aug. 23, 1863, Meigs Misc. Papers.

news of the death of Louisa Meigs's kinsman Captain George
W. Rodgers of the U.S.S. *Katskill* in Charleston harbor:

> Another hero has gone to his rest before Charleston [wrote
> Meigs]. . . . No better truer braver gentleman & Christian has
> died since Sidney.
> And so goes on the work; one after another, the nations dearest
> jewels are laid upon the altar of sacrifice, & from time to time
> while hecatombs in the great battles of liberty lay down their
> lives, Can all this devotion this sacrifice this courage, this patriotism
> be wasted? Will God allow this sacred blood to be poured upon
> the ground & not accept it as an expiation of the national sins?
> Not call the authors of this bloodshed this strife, this war against
> humanity, against the Christian brotherhood of our race, to a
> strict account?
> Will Floyd & Cobb & Brown & Thompson & Davis escape?
> Yancey is dead, Twiggs has escaped the hangman; but will they
> escape that omniscient & omnipotent judge who, in the next
> world, makes even the false balances of this one?[25]

To Meigs, the war was a fight against evil men; but it was
also an expiation for the nation's sins, and particularly for the
sin of slavery. To the Protestant mind of nineteenth-century
America, standing in direct descent from the Bible Common-
wealths of seventeenth-century New England, there could be
no other explanation, no other justification, for the horrors of
the Chickahominy bottomlands and the wilderness of Chancellorsville. But for God so to chastise America for the wicked-
ness of slavery was only right and just. Will not God accept
our sacred blood as an expiation, Meigs had asked. The general
did "not doubt less the ultimate victory that God for our sins
leads us to it through seas of blood." Or as he wrote at the
time of Gettysburg: "God does not intend to give us peace
again until we expiate our crime. . . . Until the last shackle is

[25] Meigs to Charles D. Meigs, Aug. 25, 1863, Meigs Misc. Papers.

stricken from the wrist of the black man." [26] One day Abraham Lincoln would express with greater eloquence the same idea.[27]

The war was an expiation for sins, and so it was also a purging and purifying process from which the nation would emerge cleansed and strengthened, that from its shores the light of freedom might shine more brightly throughout the world. This too was Lincoln's conception of the war, and it was also Meigs's. Meigs had begun to formulate the idea as early as 1861, while he waited to assume the post of quartermaster general.

> The world will be better [he had written]. Liberty in all climes will take a leap forward & future ages will rejoice in the advance of liberal ideas, in the proof, the signal proof, that the people the true democracy is capable of self government.
> It is a great & holy war. God is with us who shall be against us.[28]

The cause of the North, then, was just, its material power was great, and its people were strong in character. In the long run the American Union could only grow mightier. When Meigs's father worried even after Gettysburg how the republic was to meet the threat of French invasion of Mexico, the quartermaster general urged him to have no fear:

> If the Almighty desires to use us for the humbling of the infidel Emperor and his atheistic soldiers, He will in his own good time brg it about. If he means only to chasten us for our sins & establish again our state with a more perfect freedom with intelligence & education in the blighted regions from which come up Jeff Davis' deluded victims he will do so. . . .

[26] Meigs to Charles D. Meigs, June 27, 1863, Meigs Misc. Papers.
[27] In his Second Inaugural. See Roy P. Basler, ed., *The Collected Works of Abraham Lincoln* (9 vols., New Brunswick, 1953), VIII, 333.
[28] Meigs Let. B. 1861, pp. 87–88.

Look at the prosperity of the North! Even in this time of war agriculture manufacturers labor; all have their rewards for industry. In the field die the patriots . . . who are reforming the nation's character. We are not a nation of shopkeepers & pedlars. We believe in courage generosity devotion to right, & love of country. . . . Have we not done much to raise the name of this people! Do you not remember the jeers of the European press at the bloodless battles of the Yankees. now changed the same unfriendly spirit never complains of the waste of blood, of the dreadful carnage. We lose some hundreds of thousands, whose death is put forward a few years; but the nation is purified & strengthened, & when in forty years we number perhaps 60 millions, perhaps 100 millions, will any European Monarch or Emperor venture to disregard our notice to quit his . . . seat on this continent? . . .

. . . I see a great future before us. Two fresh & vigorous nations one in the East, the other in the West. Russia will rule the Eastern as we shall rule the Western continent & England & France, having done their work must take their positions as subject vassal nations. Do not trouble yourself with the future of your country, it has a bright destiny, & while it is working out, man will live & eat & think & toil & be happy or unhappy as he does his duty[.] [29]

Thus Meigs encouraged his father, with confident vision and remarkable prophecy.

[29] Meigs to Charles D. Meigs, Aug. 25, 1863, Meigs Misc. Papers.

# XII

# THE FIERY GOSPEL

AT THE CLOSE of August, General Meigs rode into the camps of the Army of the Potomac north of the Rappahannock to present to General Meade, the victor of Gettysburg, a ceremonial sword awarded by the governor of Pennsylvania. The next morning Meigs began a four-day tour of the camps and trains of the army, viewing the broad fields dark with horses branded "U. S.," the long lines of canvas-topped wagons, the blacksmiths' and carpenters' and wheelwrights' shops, the seventy-six glistening guns of the Artillery Reserve and the horses that moved them. This was also the first stop in an extensive inspection of the armies and particularly the quartermaster facilities in the field.[1]

A month later the quartermaster general reached William S. Rosecrans's Army of the Cumberland, besieged in Chattanooga after its defeat at Chickamauga. The enemy occupied the high ground which commanded the town; worse, he commanded and closed the railroad and wagon road which followed the coiling of the Tennessee into Chattanooga from Bridgeport, Alabama. Rosecrans probably would be able to hold his position against Confederate attack, but he might not be able to hold it against hunger.

Therefore on his second day in Chattanooga Meigs tele-

[1] Meigs Diary, Aug. 28–Sept. 1, 1863.

graphed to Secretary Stanton to send ships' carpenters to
Bridgeport. The first step toward conquering famine, thought
the quartermaster general, might well be to get supply boats
into the Tennessee. Even if they could not steam all the way
to Chattanooga through the narrow gap just below the town,
they might reach Kelley's Ford at the mouth of the gorge. In
the end they did so, to form an essential part of the "cracker
line" which saved the army.[2]

Saving the Army of the Cumberland by provisioning it
opened the way to its reinforcement by the Army of the Tennessee and two corps from the Army of the Potomac. Meigs
watched at the end of November when the combined Union
forces moved out from their camps to break the Confederate
lines that held them and strike the final crushing blow against
the Confederacy in the West. He witnessed Joe Hooker's
fight on Lookout Mountain and named it "the battle above the
clouds." [3] He stood on Orchard Knob to watch the Army of
the Cumberland go sweeping up the face of Missionary Ridge.
"The slave aristocracy is broken down," he wrote afterward in
his tent. "The grandest stroke yet struck for our country." [4]

The victorious commander at Chattanooga was Ulysses S.
Grant, and the accomplishment won him promotion to the
command of the Armies of the United States and to the full
rank of lieutenant general, vacant since George Washington
held it. In early 1864 Grant established himself in the East,
turning command in the West over to William Tecumseh
Sherman. Meade would remain at the head of the Army of the
Potomac, but Grant would accompany that army and determine the general lines of its movements. Returned to Wash-

[2] *Ibid.,* Sept. 27, 1863.
[3] In a special report to Stanton. Meigs to Charles D. Meigs, July 24,
1865, Meigs Let. B., 1864–1865; *O.R.,* ser. 1, XXXI, pt. 2, 77–78; Meigs
Chattanooga Journal, Nov. 24, 1863.
[4] Meigs Chattanooga Journal, Nov. 25, 1863.

ington, Meigs spent the early spring accumulating supplies for a massive offensive by all the armies, scheduled for the beginning of May. The gathering of stores proceeded smoothly and quietly, and other preparations with it. In the green of late April the armies began to move, Meade's forces toward the Wilderness beyond the Rapidan, Sherman's toward Buzzard Roost Gap and the railroad to Atlanta.

The momentum of Sherman's drive after he turned the enemy out of Dalton and Resaca depended on the maintenance of the railroad behind him and upon the rebuilding of the road as its twisted rails and ruined bridges were recovered from the Confederates. Without the railroad, Meigs's department could scarcely have funneled sufficient supplies southward from Chattanooga. The Atlanta campaign was the supreme test of the Quartermaster's Department Railroad Construction Corps.

Eleven bridges had to be rebuilt on the way from Chattanooga to Atlanta, seventy-five miles of completely new track laid, and mile after mile of additional track worked back into usable shape. The Railroad Construction Corps met every challenge. When Federal troops found the Oostenaula River bridge destroyed, "The work of reconstruction commenced while the old bridge was still burning, and was somewhat delayed because the iron rods were so hot that the men could not handle them to remove the wreck." Nor did Confederate raids sweeping around Sherman's flanks to the railroad in his rear long disrupt traffic. When Confederate General John B. Hood destroyed thirty-five and a half miles of track and 455 feet of bridges, the railroad construction men were rebuilding even before Hood had left the road. The biggest single break, over twenty-seven miles long, they repaired in seven and a half days, despite the fact that destruction of supply depots compelled

them to cut new ties in nearby woods and to bring new rails
200 miles from Nashville. As Sherman pressed toward Atlanta,
the repair of tracks never fell more than five days behind the
vanguard of the army.[5]

The advance brought into the Federals' possession scorched
and twisted heaps of rails which even the Railroad Construction Corps could not readily straighten. Early in Sherman's
campaign General McCallum of the United States Military
Railroads suggested that this iron could be put to good use,
and the Railroad Construction Corps enabled to rebuild track
in the wake of the armies more cheaply, if the government
would complete a rolling mill begun by the Confederates at
Chattanooga and operate it.

This was the sort of unorthodox but highly practical idea
that appealed both to the quartermaster general and to General-in-Chief Grant; both officers approved it. Major General
George Thomas suggested to McCallum that the mill would
be safer if he moved it from its original site to a place within
the defenses of Chattanooga. The movement helped raise the
cost of the mill far above McCallum's first estimate, but eventually the project more than paid for itself. McCallum did not
get it into operation until April 1, 1865, but thereafter the
Quartermaster's Department operated it until its sale in October.

From the fiery depths of the mill came rails to rebuild the
Chattanooga-Atlanta line after the coming of peace, for Sherman destroyed that route in the fall of 1864 when he cut off
from Atlanta to march to the sea. Thus the mill helped set
on the road to economic reconstruction an important area
of the South. Using the ruined rails picked up by Federal

[5] Weber, *Northern Railroads*, pp. 198–204; Turner, *Victory Rode the
Rails*, pp. 319–36. The quotation is from the chief engineer of the
Railroad Construction Corps and appears in Weber, *Northern Railroads*,
p. 201.

troops, the mill was able to reroll fifty tons of iron per day. The cost was $35.42 per ton, considerably cheaper than Mc-Callum's estimate of $50 per ton, cheaper still than what the government was paying Northern manufacturers for rails. Even including the cost of moving and finishing the mill, the government saved over half the cost of new iron rails at the prevailing rates.[6]

At the end of the summer of 1864 Sherman bogged down before Confederate entrenchments outside Atlanta, but up to this time his advance had been rapid and his casualties slight compared with the slow and costly progress of Grant and Meade. After the Army of the Potomac plunged into the Wilderness, it tore at the throat of its rival for two days; wounded men lay helpless in the flames of dry leaves burning, and finally Grant was beaten much as Hooker had been beaten on nearby ground the year before.

Grant took his beating with a difference: he was a man who did not know when he was whipped. When the army marched out from the Wilderness on the night of May 6 and reached that famous fork where one road turned north toward the fords of the Rapidan and safety, while another turned south toward the clearing of Spotsylvania Court House—then Grant sent the army southward, and in doing so he brought all the scintillating tactics of R. E. Lee to nought.

From the Wilderness and Spotsylvania in those early days of May the wounded came back to Fredericksburg, where they crowded into public buildings because the houses would not open to them and suffered because the Medical Bureau had failed to send enough doctors and medicines. "O God! such suffering it never entered the mind of man or woman to think of!" said a nurse who had seen the hospitals after Gettysburg. Thousands lay in the open streets, and it was said that cavalry

[6] *O.R.*, ser. 3, V, 234.

patrols could not go about their business for fear of stepping on the wounded. The doctors and the volunter workers carried them into buildings as rapidly as they could, but after the first day or two there was never enough room, and one badly wounded man considered himself fortunate to lie on a closet shelf. When a wounded soldier was sent out of Fredericksburg to one of the big hospitals at Washington or farther North, he had to endure a jarring ride of ten or twelve miles in a springless wagon over corduroy roads to the landing at Belle Plain on Aquia Creek, which was where the boats docked. Sometimes rebel bushwhackers attacked the wagons. Soon the rains came, and the teams stalled in the mud. Neither at Fredericksburg nor on the road did anybody in particular seem to have charge of things, and confusion and disorder added their trials to all the other plagues.

Edwin Stanton did not especially cotton to the idea of females trotting around on battlefields, and this spring he had denied Clara Barton a new pass to the front. When the great tide of the wounded poured into Fredericksburg he relented, but Miss Barton took only one look at what was happening in that town before she scurried back to Washington. It was not that she had lost her nerve, but this situation was more than one woman could handle on the spot. She stormed into the office of Senator Henry Wilson, and when she had finished her story Wilson got up and stormed into the War Department. Miss Barton understood him to say that he told the department they had better have someone on the way to straighten things out at Fredericksburg that night, or the Senate would send someone next day.[7]

The faithful quartermaster general was already at Belle Plain to look after transportation, and on May 17 he received

[7] Bruce Catton, *A Stillness at Appomattox* (Garden City, N. Y., 1954), pp. 102–7; Leech, *Reveille*, pp. 322–25.

orders from the Secretary to consider himself the commanding officer in Fredericksburg and to give such orders for justice and safety as he thought proper. Meigs responded by directing that the private houses of Fredericksburg be opened to the wounded, which did much to solve the problem of space, and he made new arrangements for them to receive adequate food supplies. Soon the river banks were cleared of guerrillas, and quartermaster's steamers began to come upstream to Fredericksburg. The worst of the Fredericksburg tangle was over.[8]

But the flow of casualities did not cease. The war had changed now that Grant had come to the East. The era of brief battles of a day or two followed by several weeks or months of recuperation had ended, and the fighting went on almost without a break from the Wilderness through Spotsylvania to the North Anna and Cold Harbor and the crossing of the James, until finally Grant found himself brought up short in the trenches of Petersburg. The casualty lists shortened somewhat then, but what followed was nerve-straining trench warfare in which the soldier at the front had to reckon that a shell or a bullet with his name on it might come hurtling into the lines at any hour of the day or night. Worst of all, there no longer seemed to be any progress. The explosion of the mine under the enemy lines at Petersburg at the end of July was a bloody fiasco, and autumn came on to find the Army of the Potomac tightening the noose around the throat of the Confederacy but doing it so slowly and imperceptibly that to most newspaper readers it may have seemed the army was doing nothing but suffering casualties.

Never were the demands upon Meigs for replacements of equipment and animals so great. During the first nine months of 1864, for example, the Quartermaster's Department and the

[8] Meigs Diary, May 16–18, 1864; *O.R.*, ser. 1, XXXVI, 854–66; Leech, *Reveille*, p. 325.

Cavalry Bureau purchased 87,825 cavalry horses, an average of 500 per day. This was the measure of destruction of the animals in service. During the first eight months of the year the cavalry of the Army of the Potomac was completely remounted twice, that is, it received nearly 40,000 horses. The evidence of the success of the reorganized horse supply service lies in the testimony of Rufus Ingalls that he never received better horses than now.[9]

Unhappily, attrition among men was even greater than among the animals. So many died in the hospitals at Washington that the cemetery at the new Soldiers' Home filled up, and a site had to be found for a new military cemetery near the capital. Federal soldiers had long since occupied General Lee's estate at Arlington, and the government finally had come into possession of the property through somewhat dubious default-of-taxes preceedings. It was the duty of the Quartermaster's Department to provide for interments, and Meigs chose the Arlington grounds as a suitable site. He recommended the place to the Secretary of War, and the order for the establishment of Arlington Cemetery passed from Meigs to General Rucker on June 15.[10]

On July 4, 1864, the day Meigs's reorganization bill for the Quartermaster's Department became law, the heat smothered most of the capital's enthusiasm for Independence Day. Congress adjourned at noon. Northwest of the city an enemy force captured Harpers Ferry; the chief of staff, General Halleck, was not alarmed by this event.

He should have been mightily alarmed. By the 6th the enemy was reported in Maryland around Hagerstown. The situation was clearly developing as a possible Confederate raid

[9] *O.R.*, ser. 3, IV, 889; ser. 3, V, 221; ser. 3, V, 254–60.
[10] Q.M.G. Let. B. 77, pp. 332–33.

on Washington, and although the capital was virtually defenseless, Halleck had just turned down an offer from Grant
to send up an army corps from Petersburg. Major General
Christopher C. Augur commanded the Military Department
of Washington and nominally had on hand the XXII Army
Corps of 31,000 men. But only about 20,000 of these troops
were actually near the capital, and most of them were green
recruits or guards of bridges and buildings. In the ring of
fortifications around the city there were in fact only 9,600
troops, and these would be next to useless if they had to fight
a veteran enemy, since most of them were semi-invalids or
Ohio militia. The leader of the enemy's column, it was learned,
was crusty and profane General Jubal Early from the Army
of Northern Virginia. Estimates as to his strength reached
50,000. Numbers aside, nearly all were veterans of Lee's
battles.[11]

At Baltimore the Union commander—who like Augur at
Washington commanded little more than a mirage—was General Lew Wallace. Wallace made the wise decision to lead his
2,500-odd men out the road toward Frederick to meet the
enemy. He could not hope to defeat Early, but he might delay
him, and a delay might prove of value. Chief of Staff Halleck
had been stoutly denying the need for reinforcements since
the rebel raid began, but General Grant now happily decided
to ignore him and ship to Washington from the Army of the
Potomac the 3rd Division of the VI Army Corps. Landing in
Baltimore, these veterans set out on Wallace's trail. On the
morning of Saturday, July 9, Wallace was able to draw up
about 9,000 men on the banks of the Monocacy River where
the road from Frederick forked toward Washington and
Baltimore.[12]

[11] Leech, *Reveille*, pp. 331–33; Meigs Diary, July 7–10, 1864.
[12] Leech, *Reveille*, p. 334; Catton, *A Stillness*, pp. 259–60.

That morning General Meigs saw his wife and daughter Loulie, along with Mrs. Rodgers and one of Louisa's sisters, off on the train for a summer at Rye Beach. He then proceeded to rout from their posts and desks most of the soldiers and civilian employees of the Quartermaster's Department in and around Washington and to form them into regiments. He had established a Quartermaster's Brigade for the defense of Washington during the previous summer, but while he was absent at Chattanooga somebody decided that all the drilling going on was a waste of time, and his organization fell into disrepair. Still, the preparations of the year before saved him from starting from scratch, and before the day was over he had an armed and uniformed brigade which at least looked somewhat like a body of soldiers.

Impatient for at least one opportunity in this war to lead troops in the field, Meigs went to see General Halleck to persuade that gentleman to find a use for his brigade. The musty Halleck disappointed him; he said Meigs's soldiers would be of no value in the entrenchments, and he advised Meigs simply to direct some of his men to relieve the guards of the depots and corrals. The quartermaster general was unwilling to rest with this advice. When Meigs made up his mind to do something, he generally did it, let the authorities be damned. He went in search of General Augur and found him more than eager to accept the 2,000 men he offered. He next approached Stanton, and the Secretary gave him an order to report with the Quartermaster's Brigade for duty in the field.[13]

On the Monocacy, Lew Wallace's scratch force spent the late morning and early afternoon fighting a delaying action before the power of Early's numbers swept them from the

[13] Meigs Diary, July 9, 1864; Meigs to John G. Barnard, Dec. 6, 1869, Meigs Misc. Papers; Leech, *Reveille*, pp. 336–37.

field and back toward Baltimore. Wallace had accomplished all he could have hoped. The delay imposed on Early by the need to deploy for and fight a battle, and the added caution with which he advanced after meeting troops of the VI Corps, cost the Confederate commander a full day, which was to make all the difference as far as the safety of Washington was concerned.

Early's men resumed their advance on Sunday morning and by night were near Rockville, about ten miles above the District line. That night and on Monday a handful of Union cavalry skirmished with them between Rockville and Tenally-town. On Monday morning General Meigs rode out to Fort Stevens, which commanded the important Seventh Street Road from Silver Spring. When he heard the crackle of small arms from the direction of Tenallytown he wheeled his horse and hurried back to Washington to order out his brigade. His men were assembled when an order arrived telling him to report with them to Major General Alexander McCook. This was the same McCook whom Meigs had met at First Bull Run as colonel of the 1st Ohio. He had since made a name for himself in the Army of the Cumberland, but a cloud had fallen over his reputation after the defeat at Chickamauga. Now he was in the capital, fresh from exoneration by a court of inquiry, looking for a new command. Augur put him in charge of the threatened northwestern defenses.

The Quartermaster's Brigade marched out Fourteenth Street at five in the afternoon. When they reached McCook's headquarters he directed them to occupy about a mile of trenches west of the Seventh Street Road, and he placed Meigs in command of a division consisting of the Quartermaster's Brigade and a brigade of Veteran Reserves, holding the line between Fort Stevens and Fort Totten. On Meigs's right McCook improvised another division under Major General Quincy Adams

Gilmore, on his left a third under Brigadier General Martin
D. Hardin. The quartermaster men filed into the trenches as
night was falling and bivouacked on the ground. By the time
Meigs looked for a place to sleep it was so dark he found
himself stumbling into a haystack, and he decided simply to
rest under that.[14]

By now Washington had completely shaken its summer
lethargy. Refugees had burst into the city from the western
suburbs to tell of hordes of unkempt men in butternut prowling through Maryland houses. Confederate sympathizers in
the capital were said to be preparing rebel flags to break out
when Early entered the city, and the mayor was strenuously
engaged in calling out the District militia, which was principally a figment of his imagination. Meigs's was the only one
of the government departments with anything resembling an
existing military organization and the only one able to throw
men into the lines. Even the Quartermaster's Brigade probably
was not good for anything much beyond giving a section of
the front the appearance of being held, and the same could be
said for most of the rest of the men in the fortifications. A
serious attack by Early's battlewise soldiers from the Army of
Northern Virginia would brush them away as easily as it had
Wallace.[15]

Early did not know it. During the night word had reached
him of the arrival of two Federal corps from the Army of the
Potomac. For all he knew, these troops might already be in
the trenches. His force actually numbered little more than
10,000, and he dared not risk attack.[16]

It was only one corps that was coming from Grant's forces

[14] Meigs Diary, July 10–11, 1864; Meigs to John G. Barnard, Dec. 6,
1869, Meigs Misc. Papers; Q.M.G. Let. B. 78, p. 148; O.R., ser. 1,
XXXVII, pt. 1, 231–32, 254–56.
[15] Leech, Reveille, pp. 337–38.
[16] Freeman, Lee's Lieutenants, III, 564–65.

around Petersburg, and as yet it was still far down at the Sixth
Street wharf in Washington, but it was enough. "It's the old
Sixth Corps! The danger is over now! It's the Sixth Corps!"
shouted the people who watched the corps land, and veterans
wearing white Greek crosses on their soiled kepis began tramping toward the defenses.[17]

General Meigs spent the morning straining his eyes toward
the enemy position and directing his men while they improved
their trenches and cleared away all wood within cannon shot
that might protect a hostile advance. Toward noon he and a
colonel rode toward the right to discover the cause of smoke
they saw in that direction, and they found merely some burning railroad bridges. Then they heard musketry and cannon
fire off to the left and returned to their outfit. They arrived
in time to see a brigade of the VI Corps moving out from the
entrenchments to drive enemy sharpshooters from two houses
up the Seventh Street Road beyond Fort Stevens. There was
a brisk little fight, and the enemy gave way. That evening
Early drew back toward the northwest. The civilians were
right: the VI Corps had saved the city.[18]

Meigs was still in the trenches the next morning when a
courier brought him a letter of appointment as brevet major
general, United States Army, "for distinguished and meritorious service during the present war." He felt especially gratified to receive the honor while he was in the field, and hoped
his prompt response in raising the Quartermaster's Brigade to
meet the Confederate invasion had something to do with it.[19]

Next day McCook informed him that the War Department
had ordered the Quartermaster's Brigade relieved; the men

[17] Leech, *Reveille*, pp. 338–39; Catton, *A Stillness*, p. 263.
[18] Meigs to John G. Barnard, Dec. 6, 1869, Meigs Misc. Papers; *O.R.*,
ser. 1, XXXVII, pt. 1, 256–60; Catton, *A Stillness*, pp. 264–66; Leech,
*Reveille*, pp. 342–44; Meigs Diary, July 12, 1864.
[19] Meigs Diary, July 13, 1864.

were to return to their usual occupations. Meigs was still pleased with himself and his men, and he rewarded his amateur soldiers for their brief service with a high-flown proclamation that would have done credit to some of his more pompous brother generals of the line.

The Rebel Army [he said], under tried and skilful leaders, has looked at, and has felt of the Northern Defences of Washington. They looked ugly and felt hard. They left their dead unburied, and many of their wounded on the way by which they retired.
They will not soon again insult the majesty of a free people in their National Capital.[20]

Under the warm evening sun the brigade marched back into town, enjoying something of a holiday mood now that it was all over. They were doubtless overjoyed to learn that henceforth they would be subjected to regular weekly drills, so that in another emergency they would be better prepared. Meigs instituted a similar system in all quartermaster depots which by any chance might some day be attacked. He was proud at the close of the year to report that quartermaster troops held a portion of George Thomas's line at the battle of Nashville.[21]

Nor would he ever forget that for a few days at least, M. C. Meigs had commanded a division in the field. When he was an old man, the "battle of Washington" would be a memory to warm his heart.

Before it ended, the nation's tragedy became a personal tragedy for General Meigs.

In June, 1863, Louisa and her two daughters journeyed to West Point to see John R. Meigs graduate first in his class and receive his commission as second lieutenant in the Corps of

[20] Q.M.G. Let. B. 78, p. 164; Meigs Diary, July 14, 1864; Meigs to John G. Barnard, Dec. 6, 1869, Meigs Misc. Papers.
[21] Q.M.G. Let. B. 78, pp. 164–65, 325, 344–45; O.R., ser. 3, V, 247–49.

Engineers. General Meigs was too busy to make the trip, but in his diary he recorded his satisfaction: "My son has graduated with honor. God protect him in his career & make it useful to his country." [22]

John's first orders called him to the Army of the Tennessee around Vicksburg. But this was the month of Lee's invasion, and a new directive sent him to Baltimore and the headquarters of the threatened Middle Department, the state of Maryland. While Lee's infantrymen flowed back in defeat from the guns on Cemetery Ridge, John was in the party which captured the Confederate pontoon bridge at Falling Waters and made possible Meade's great opportunity when Lee halted before the flooded Potomac. In the aftermath of the raid on the pontoon bridge John barely escaped capture near Harpers Ferry, and he had to borrow money from his father to replace the horse he lost there.[23]

Before he left Baltimore, the young lieutenant devised an armored railway car for use on the B. & O. against the attacks of guerrillas and bushwhackers. Then he was transferred to West Virginia, to serve on the staff of General Benjamin F. Kelley in the uninspiring but necessary work of preserving order on the upper Potomac and along the line of the Baltimore and Ohio through the mountains. Alert, intelligent, self-reliant, and reliable, he won the confidence of his commander, and when Kelley visited Washington in August he could tell the quartermaster general he was highly gratified to have his son under his command. The chief surgeon of Kelley's department told General Meigs he had never seen such a young man: "There was no discount on him at all. Why, he had not even the gentlemanly vices." He had a certain boyish simplicity about him, but unquestionably he had also strength of

[22] Meigs Diary, May 23, June 11, 1863.
[23] Meigs Diary, June 16, 20, July 18, 20, 1863.

character. "The Doctor spoke most warmly," Meigs recorded, "congratulated me & predicted if Johns health & life are spared a high destiny for him in the service of his country. All this is very gratifying." [24]

In December, John roamed too much through the mountain snow, and he ended with a case of frosted feet. At least this gave him a short leave at home over the holidays, with visits from neighboring young ladies and sociable evenings marred only by the necessity of learning what he considered a stupid game of cards. By late February he was back at Harpers Ferry with General Kelley.[25]

When spring brought renewed campaigning to the Shenandoah Valley, John joined the Federal forces there. His father felt some concern for his safety when Early defeated General David Hunter near Lynchburg, but John escaped unscathed. After Early raided to the suburbs of Washington in the middle of July, as just described, and advanced across the Potomac again at the end of the month to burn Chambersburg, Pennsylvania, the administration decided that this sort of thing had gone too far. Scraping together three corps to form a new Army of the Shenandoah, they put Phil Sheridan at its head and turned it loose with orders to crush Jubal Early and put a definite end to Confederate use of the Shenandoah as a highway of invasion. John was among the men assigned to the new force, and no more need be said of his military ability than that he quickly won the favor of General Sheridan. Presently he was chief engineer of the Army of the Shenandoah. His prewar vacations in the Valley had left him acquainted with nearly every road and stream, and as a topographical engineer he was invaluable. To his services in planning the

[24] Meigs Diary, Aug. 1, 1863; Meigs to Charles D. Meigs, Aug. 25, 1863, Meigs Misc. Papers; New York *World*, June 9, 1886, clipping in Meigs Misc. Papers.

[25] John R. Meigs Diary, 1864, Meigs Misc. Papers.

campaign against Early he soon added gallantry under fire at Opequon and Fisher's Hill in late September.[26]

Fisher's Hill seemed pretty well to have completed Sheridan's Valley assignment. On that rolling knob which crosses the Valley Pike just south of Strasburg he smashed Early's line to tatters and captured twelve guns and a thousand prisoners. The Army of the Shenandoah was able to march southward up the Valley practically at will, and Lincoln and Grant wondered whether Sheridan should not bring his troops to the trenches around Petersburg. But Jubal Early was regrouping his forces and planning his revenge, and beyond that there was an ugly outbreak of guerrilla warfare within Sheridan's lines.

The war had changed since the days of the gentlemen's militia companies of 1861, and a lot of people besides Sherman held that war is war, not a popularity contest, and that there was not much point in trying to prettify it. David Hunter had gone through the Valley with a torch in June, and Early had repaid in kind when he reached Maryland and Chambersburg. Now Sheridan was burning out everything that struck him as having the slightest military value, including barns. And more of the angry farmers of the Valley who seemed peaceable enough by day took to spending their evenings harrying the fringes of the Union army with those grim guerrillas who took their orders from Colonel William S. Mosby.

An electric tension descended upon the once pleasant Valley. The personable soldiers in blue who waved to the little boys when they marched through Kernstown or New Market one day might be out burning haystacks the next, and the

[26] Philip H. Sheridan, *Personal Memoirs of P. H. Sheridan* (2 vols., New York, 1888), I, 467; Richard O'Connor, *Sheridan the Inevitable* (Indianapolis, 1953), p. 193.

bluecoats themselves could never be sure when they stopped
to talk to a local rustic that he had not whiled away the previous night by cutting a Yankee throat. The war was becoming a nasty business, and this was the atmosphere of the Valley
when Lieutenant John R. Meigs and two orderlies rode out
from Sheridan's headquarters on a routine scouting mission in
the morning of October 3, 1864.[27]

Late September had brought bright blue days to Washington. On the 21st General Meigs rejoiced to welcome Louisa,
Montie, and Loulie home from their summer trip. On the
24th the city echoed to a salute of 150 guns for Sheridan's
victory at Fisher's Hill; John's name was not on the casualty
lists. Most of the fighting in the Valley seemed to be over,
and probably he would be comparatively safe for a time.
Louisa was feeling so carefree that on the evening of the 27th
she went riding with Mont—the first time she had done so,
they thought, in several years. "We used to ride on horseback
much," the general wrote in his diary. "I hope to renew her
habit." [28]

On October 3 General Meigs had to take the seven-thirty
train in the morning to inspect the quartermaster's depot at
New York. There had been some ugly talk of frauds there,
and the uniforms and equipment shipped out of the place
lately were not quite up to snuff. The general observed operations as closely as he could, and he visited other installations
such as hospitals and a prisoner-of-war depot. He left New
York on the evening of the 5th, spent most of the next day in
Philadelphia, and reached home early on the evening of the
6th. Louisa told him their son was dead—"our noble son." [29]

The story they heard was that John had ridden away from

[27] Sheridan, *Personal Memoirs*, II, 99; Catton, *A Stillness*, pp. 303–5.
[28] Meigs Diary, Sept. 21–27, 1864.
[29] Meigs Diary, Oct. 3–6, 1864.

headquarters on the morning of the 3rd accompanied by two orderlies. The three of them were riding down the Swift Run Gap Road, toward the Valley Pike and about four hundred yards from the Dayton Pike, when three men emerged suddenly from the roadside brush, pointed pistols at them, and demanded that they surrender. John plainly said he surrendered, but one of the men shot him in cold blood. In the confusion one of John's orderlies jumped his horse over a fence and escaped; it was he who told the story.

The next morning Sheridan's chief of staff, Colonel James W. Forsyth, heard of the incident and set out from General George A. Custer's headquarters with a party of Custer's men to find the scene. They met a sergeant of the provost guard, who said he had just stumbled upon a Federal officer lying dead in the road a few hundred yards farther on. Forsyth hurried forward. In the roadway he found the body of Lieutenant Meigs.

John's body lay extended at full length, one arm partially raised, the other extended at his side. His face was looking upward. His hat and cloak lay under him. He had been shot just under the right eye and in the left breast. The sergeant of the provost guard had recovered his revolver and his papers. One chamber of the revolver was empty; apparently John had had time for one shot before he fell to the ground.[30]

To General Meigs this seemed not a death in war, at the hands of an honorable enemy; it was murder. Phil Sheridan

[30] Meigs Diary, Oct. 3, 1864; Q.M.G. Let. B. 81, p. 139. Mystery shrouds the death of John R. Meigs to this day; Confederates who claimed to be witnesses later said that John died resisting capture. For additional information see subsequent entries in Meigs Journal; Meigs Diary, especially Aug. 19, 1865, and April 24, 1876; James A. Carrington (one of John's orderlies) to Meigs, March 20, 1871, Meigs Misc. Papers; Washington *Sunday Herald and Weekly National Intelligencer*, Sept. 7, 1873, clipping in Meigs Misc. Papers; Walter McFarland to Joseph H. Taylor, April 17, 1876, Meigs Misc. Papers.

thought so too. He ordered the burning of every house within five miles of the body.

So they ended—all the dreams General Meigs had cherished for this finest of sons.

And so has perished my first born, a noble boy—gallant generous gifted who had already made himself a name in the land At the age of 19 he had fought with distinction at the first battle of the war Bull Run 21 July 61 [while on summer furlough from West Point]. He had been in most active service since he graduated in July 63, & had passed thru many battles unscathed. A martyr in the cause of liberty.[31]

John's pocket diary came back to Washington, and it remained for Louisa to make the final entries. She tried to be matter of fact:

Oct. 3. Lt. J. R. Meigs was killed by guerrillas on the 3$^d$ of October about 7 oclock in the eveng, returng to camp at Genl Sheridans H$^d$. Quarters He was Chief Engineer of the Army of the Valley of the Shenandoah & aid to Genl Sheridan.

She did not entirely succeed:

Oct. 7. Was brought home this day, the loving remains of my noble precious son.[32]

They held the funeral on the 8th, and the President and the Secretary of War came to pay their tribute. For the time being John lay in the chapel of Oak Hill Cemetery in Georgetown. But they would bury him beside his brothers Charles and Vincent and the little nameless child of their first days in Washington, and they would plant an ivy at the foot of the oak under which he lay. Meigs would order a monument with a bronze representation of the body lying on the Swift Run

[31] Meigs Diary, Oct. 3, 1864.
[32] John R. Meigs Diary.

Gap Road. On New Year's Day, Louisa would be unable to make the usual rounds of visiting, and Mont would leave her weeping. For a long time to come these anniversaries would remind her of her son.[33]

But in time the sharpness would pass from their grief. They would learn of John's posthumous brevets: the rank of captain, to date from September 19, 1864, for meritorious service at the battle of Opequon; the rank of major, to date from September 22, 1864, for meritorious service at the battle of Fisher's Hill.[34] They would visit the grave on the anniversary of the death:

I went last evening with Louisa to visit the graves of our children. The monument of our eldest son is completed & the ground about it restored.

Louisa placed a garland at the head & we spent some time in meditating upon the short but faithful career of our eldest son. Today is the anniversary of his death. It finds the country restored to peace & entering upon a career of safety & prosperity & glory to open which he gave his life. His memory & his acts are one of the leaves of the chaplet of glory & honor that America now proudly wears.

There is much consolation in the memory of good deeds faithful service heroic endeavor patriotic self-sacrifice but many bitter thoughts will arise in the presence of his . . . monument The murderer is not yet certainly known various stories have reached my ear More than one person is self accused & in time it may be that justice will yet have its course.[35]

"The murderer"—in these words was a sting that signified General Meigs could never again feel quite the same toward the South and his old friends of the South. Mrs. Rodgers thought he bore up manfully under the loss,[36] and it is true

---

[33] Meigs Diary, Jan. 1, 1865.

[34] *Ibid.*, May 23, July 30, 1866.

[35] Meigs to Charles D. Meigs, Oct. 3, 1865, Meigs Let. B., 1864–1865.

[36] Mrs. John Rodgers to John Rodgers II, Nov. 18, 1864, Rodgers Family Papers, Naval Historical Foundation Collection, Box 130, L.C.

that he went about his daily work with scarcely a break and in the old way. But not quite the old way: he returned to the war with a cold anger, and by the autumn of 1864 thousands of other men in the North were feeling the same anger.

# XIII

# THE QUARTERMASTER'S DEPARTMENT COMPLETES ITS WAR

THE LAST YEAR of the war was a harsh and ghastly year. The wounds and the deaths mounted as they never had before, but the blue armies trudged onward because enough men were angry to make it certain that this war would never end short of complete victory.

"Tomorrow the most momentous election of this countrys history takes place," Meigs wrote in his diary on November 7. "God inspire the hearts of his people with wisdom and patriotism to do right." Meigs's loyalty to the Democracy had passed in the turmoil of war, and that of his family too. In his father's house the Union League of Philadelphia was organized, and his brother John Forsyth Meigs was among the founders. "*Mr. Lincoln Reelected*," Meigs chronicled the returns.

A great spectacle a great people in the midst of civil war quietly voting the Chief Office of the Government to the man of their choice & thus determining the policy whether of war & maintenance of national life & support of liberty or base surrender to traitors.[1]

[1] Meigs Diary, Nov. 7–8, 1864; Winnifred K. MacKay, "Philadelphia during the Civil War, 1861–1865," *Pennsylvania Magazine of History and Biography*, LXX (1946), 26–27.

The election drove a knife into the vitals of the Confederacy; William Tecumseh Sherman turned the knife when he marched from Atlanta to the sea. Meigs exulted at the spectacle of a great army demonstrating at last the validity of the dictum he had long urged on commanders more timid—or less ruth-less—than Sherman: that far more than they had been doing, the Union forces could subsist off the Southern countryside, could make war nourish war. From Sherman himself he was to receive a gratifying letter:

As you say, my marches have demonstrated the great truth, that armies even of vast magnitude are not tied down to bases. In almost any quarter of the South, armies of from thirty to forty thousand may safely march, sure to find near their route forage of some kind or other for their animals. It is a physical impossibility to supply an army with forage, and you do perfectly right in demanding that each army should provide itself with long forage and a large proportion of its grain. . . .

I beg to assure you that all my armies have been admirably supplied by your Department, and I am sometimes amazed at the magnitude of its operations. I think I have personally aided your Department more than any General officer in the service, by draw-ing liberally from the enemy, thereby injuring him financially and to some extent helping ourselves. And you may always rely upon my cordially cooperating with any system you may establish.[2]

All through the fall Meigs's ocean-going transports were busy shuttling along the coast to supply the detachments scattered from Texas to the Carolinas and, most important, to keep in the field the huge army with which Ulysses Grant was strangling Richmond and Petersburg. This latter task alone was so formidable that on an average day forty steamers, seventy-five sailing vessels, and one hundred barges would be unloading at Grant's base at City Point. Here the wharves lined the James River for more than a mile and then swung up

[2] Q.M.G. Let. B. 82, pp. 178–79.

the Appomattox; City Point was one of the great seaports of the world.[3]

December brought a new task for Meigs's fleet, as well as bad weather at sea. As Sherman's armies approached Savannah and tidewater, Meigs began to prepare for the extensive refitting they would require, including a complete change of uniforms. He considered the slight possibility that in order to stop Sherman the Confederacy might abandon its eastern positions and throw the Army of Northern Virginia across Sherman's path. In order to be ready for an emergency movement southward by Grant's armies around Petersburg, Meigs ordered that a supply depot be prepared and partially stocked at Pensacola.

Meanwhile he assembled a great fleet of transports at Port Royal on the Carolina coast, loading the ships with everything that Sherman's armies conceivably might need. "Clothing, shoes, shelter tents, forage, provisions, spare parts of wagons, wagons complete, harness, leather, wax, thread, needles, and tools for all the trades which were plied on the march and in the camp were collected in the harbor of Hilton Head." When on December 13 the naval vessels off Savannah sent word that the blue infantry of the West had stormed Fort McAllister to open the city, the quartermaster fleet moved at once to the mouths of the Ogeechee and the Savannah.

The Confederates had closed the port of Savannah with underwater obstacles: "These for four years," learned General Meigs, "seemed to have employed all the ingenuity and mechanical skill of the people, who had torn up the pavements of their commercial streets to supply material to obstruct the channels of the harbor." The quartermaster general ordered a wrecking party from the coast of Florida to clear the way. In a few days the passage was open, and the quartermaster vessels anchored off the dilapidated wharves of Savannah to discharge

[3] *O.R.*, ser. 3, V, 225; ser. 1, XL, pt. 1, 270–71.

their burdens for Sherman's waiting soldiers and then to sail away northward laden with captured cotton.[4]

Meigs regarded the provisioning of Sherman as perhaps the greatest of all the accomplishments of the quartermaster fleet:

All this was done in the dead of winter. Light-draft, frail river-steamers trusted themselves, under daring Yankee captains and crews, to the storms of the stormiest coast of the world, and all arrived safely at their destination. And here let me pay tribute to those gallant seamen of the merchant shipping of the Nation, who in war entered its transport fleet. No service has been so difficult or so tedious—none so dangerous as to discourage or daunt them.

No call for volunteers has ever failed to meet a ready response, whether to tempt the shoals and storms of a tempestuous coast, the hidden and mysterious danger of the dark bayous of the South, strewn with torpedos by the devilish ingenuity of deserters from our own military and naval service, or to run in frail river-steamboats the batteries of the Potomac, or the James, or the Pamlico, or the still more dangerous batteries of Vicksburg. Urged by the spirit of adventure, supported by the patriotism of freemen, they have always stood ready, and have cheerfully obeyed every order, incurred every risk.[5]

Meigs and Secretary Stanton journeyed to Savannah to visit Sherman before the armies of the West turned northward through the Carolinas. Meigs found the troops "a splendid body of soldiers with muscles sinews hardened by 2000 miles of marching & nerves strong & steadied by fifty battles. Such troops as would have made Napoleon ready to encounter the world." [6] The quartermaster general enjoyed being with these hard veterans of the West—they seemed to transmit to him

[4] *O.R.*, ser. 3, V, 214, 225–26.
[5] *O.R.*, ser. 3, V, 214–215.
[6] Meigs to Louisa Rodgers Meigs, April 24, 1865, Meigs Let. B., 1864–1866; Q.M.G. Let. B. 1880D, pp. 1975–77.

an electric exhilaration—and he returned to them again in March as they regrouped at Kingston for their last stride into Virginia.

Moving with Sherman's armies through the Carolinas was a detachment of the Railroad Construction Corps, which had traveled to the scene from Tennessee by crossing the Appalachians in midwinter. The transport fleet carried locomotives and rolling stock into the harbor of Beaufort, North Carolina, and the Construction Corps opened the railroad from Beaufort toward Sherman's headquarters at Kingston. In January the long awaited fall of Fort Fisher opened the Cape Fear River to Meigs's transports. The fleet brought in Major General John Schofield's XXIII Corps to reinforce the troops that had taken the fort; together the two forces pushed on up the Wilmington-Goldsboro Railroad, rebuilding as they went, to unite with Sherman. Cars and locomotives continued to come in from the sea. When Sherman reached Goldsboro from Kingston he found Schofield and a store of provisions and supplies already awaiting him.[7]

Now the Confederacy was more than tottering. Already Sherman had whipped at Bentonville the force hastily assembled under Joe Johnston to block his path. Meigs was with Sherman at Goldsboro on March 30 when he heard a report that Grant was breaking at last out of the Petersburg lines, marching with 80,000 men toward Dinwiddie Court House while 45,000 remained in the trenches. Sheridan was said to be ranging ahead with 15,000 cavalry, and the aim was to cut the South Side and Danville Railroads, Richmond's last lines of supply. The next day Lee evacuated Richmond and Petersburg. The Virginia deadlock was broken; the race to the west was on, Lee striving to curl around Grant's left and move southward

[7] *O.R.*, ser. 3, V, 214–15, 226–28.

to a junction with Johnston, Grant trying to head him off and trap him.[8]

On April 3 Meigs visited the supply docks at Morehead City. On the 5th he journeyed to Wilmington, where he sketched the ramparts of Fort Fisher, so long the bane of Union amphibious operations and of his brother-in-law, John Rodgers. That day he learned of the fall of Richmond.[9]

At seven P.M. on the 8th Meigs embarked from New Berne for Grant's base at City Point on the James. "News from Grant better & better," he recorded. His ship anchored off Old Point Comfort at 9:30 on the evening of the 10th; the garrison of Fortress Monroe was jubilant with the news that on Sunday, the 9th, Lee had surrendered with 27,000 men at Appomattox Court House.[10]

Meigs landed at City Point on April 12. He ordered construction on the Seaboard and Roanoke Railroad to cease at once. He suspended the purchase of horses, mules, and wagons and all contracts for clothing and equipage. "Every thing indicates the submission of Va.," he felt. "Lee," he was told, "has gone to see Davis & Johnston & urge surrender & pacification." [11]

With the surrender of Lee, only mopping-up activities remained to complete the victory of the North. In the Quartermaster General's Office at Washington, the accountants of Meigs's Ninth Division could begin reviewing the total costs of quartermaster operations for the war.

In the first quarter of the calendar year 1861, the last full quarter of peace, the expenditures of the Quartermaster's Department totaled $982,555. If this figure was somewhat low

[8] Meigs Diary, March 30, 1865.
[9] *Ibid.*, April 3–5, 1865.
[10] *Ibid.*, April 8–11, 1865.
[11] *Ibid.*, April 12, 1865.

even for peacetime, since in each of the last two quarters of 1860 expenditures had topped the million mark, it was nevertheless not far from typical. A mushrooming of the budget began with the second quarter of 1861, a period during which the expansion of the army barely got under way; expenditures for that quarter totaled $3,582,601. This spurt during April, May, and June raised the total expenditures of the department for the fiscal year July, 1860 to June, 1861 to $8,066,118. Even the spring of 1861, however, provided only a meager inkling of what was to come.

For the fiscal year 1861–1862 expenditures soared to $40,631,-147, so far as accounts had been analyzed by the time General Meigs issued his report for the year. After being thus quintupled in one year, the department budget nearly tripled its first advances during the following year; for 1862–1863 it reached $118,463,312. From that point expenditures more than doubled in the next year, skyrocketing to $284,809,697 for the fiscal year 1863–1864. Here at last they stabilized themselves; for the final fiscal year of the war, including the first months of peace, they totaled $226,119,362. The contribution of inflation to rising costs should not be forgotten, but the expansion of the budget was nevertheless a significant measuring rod of mounting activity.[12]

The Quartermaster's Department accounts for the fiscal year 1863–1864 furnish a reasonably typical record of the distribution of expenditures among the various activities of Meigs's department. The highest bill was that for purchase and preparation of clothing and related camp and garrison equipage; it amounted to slightly more that $98,000,000. About half as high as these items were expenses for "regular supplies"—fuel, forage, straw, stationery—which totaled approximately $43,-

[12] O.R., ser. 3, I, 680–82; ser. 3, II, 786–88; ser. 3, III, 1118–20; ser. 3, IV, 874–77; ser. 3, V, 282.

000,000. Cavalry and artillery horses cost the department about
$27,000,000. Following in order were expenditures for bar-
racks and quarters at $8,000,000, construction and maintenance
of the gunboat fleet at $2,000,000, and a host of lesser items.[13]

During the financial crisis of January, 1862, General Meigs
had addressed to Secretary of War Stanton a message in which
he sought to explain why estimates of expenditures had fallen
so far short of actual needs. His words are those of an interested
party, but they sum up as well as any both the difficulties and
the achievements of the Quartermaster's Department in the
first frenzied months of the Civil War:

The Army is said to far exceed in number that intended to be
raised. It was raised irregularly upon the spur of extreme danger.
It was impossible for the officers of this department, few in number and overburdened with duties, to provide all the supplies
needed as rapidly as the army grew. The State authorities, the
efforts of patriotic committees and citizens, all were by the force
of circumstances called into play, and the result has been an army
of great size, well equipped in a marvelously short time, but at
great cost.[14]

Equally worthy of attention are words written by Rufus
Ingalls, who grappled with the difficulties of a supply service
in the field as chief quartermaster of the Army of the Potomac
from the Peninsula to Appomattox. Ingalls was writing in 1863
and recalling the problems of the first days of the war:

It must be borne in mind that war on a scale inaugurated by
this rebellion was decidedly new to us, if not to the civilized
world.
Easy as it may seem now, after the lapse of two years, to
organize the transportation of a great army, and to provide for
its supplies with the known means we now have, there were few

[13] *O.R.*, ser. 3, IV, 876–77.
[14] *O.R.*, ser. 3, I, 867.

men at that day in the republic who could have accomplished the task sooner than it was. It required the united abilities and exertions of our whole department, aided by the loyal producers and manufacturers of the country, to meet the public wants; and, if there were temporary failures, the department should stand excused, for its labors have been unparalleled and gigantic. Perhaps the failures in our department have been fewer than in fighting the troops.[15]

It is easy to find corruptionists and incompetents among the supply agents of the Federal army in the early months of the Civil War, and it is easy to find instances of deplorable mismanagement leading to pointless suffering for the troops. Yet if the historian is obliged to call stupidity by that name when he sees it, and to present a failure as a failure and not as something else, at the same time he should be obliged to observe the characters of his drama with a certain sympathy for their situation as human beings; that is, he should not expect from them unlikely prodigies of achievement and then castigate them when they fall short of his expectations, nor should he require that they apply the knowledge and attitudes of his own day to their problems of the past.

This may seem elementary enough, but its obviousness has not always prevented extravagant criticism of those who organized and supplied the Union armies in the Civil War. In the two world wars we assembled our armies in accordance with a certain amount of previous planning, and after a more or less extensive study of the mobilization problem had given us some notion of what difficulties we might anticipate. In the Civil War we mobilized with no previous planning and did it more rapidly than in 1917 or 1940. The remarkable fact is not that a few sentries were tramping about Washington in their drawers, but that a substantial part of the Union army was not similarly clad.

[15] *O.R.*, ser. 1, XIX, pt. 1, 100.

Once the Quartermaster's Department of the Union army had had time to discover what it was doing and how to go about it, it performed by and large so efficiently that a general review focused upon its commander in Washington makes its activities appear to have been largely matters of routine. The striking feature that emerges from a study of the operations of the department is the magnitude of those operations. The Federal government before the Civil War had been an organ of severely limited functions, to an extent that it is difficult for our own minds to appreciate. Then suddenly there was thrust upon the government the task of feeding, clothing, and transporting about the country an army of 500,000 to 1,000,000 men. The government at Washington necessarily became a huge business organization.

One effect of this development was to transform the national capital from a sleepy country town into a busy city.[16] Another was to change men's attitudes toward the Federal government, to call its existence to the attention of many who hitherto had scarcely felt a need to look beyond their state capitals, and to impress upon men's minds the idea that in the government at Washington there lay an instrument of potentially tremendous power, for personal or for group advancement, for good or for evil.[17] In more ways than one, it was a new America that rode in upon the lightning of the terrible swift sword.

[16] See Leech, *Reveille*.
[17] For the growth of Federal power in relation to state power during the war, see William B. Hesseltine, *Lincoln and the War Governors* (New York, 1948).

# XIV

# BITTER FINALE

MEIGS hoped to visit Richmond on his return trip northward from the sojourn with Sherman, but he gave up the visit in order to leave City Point for Washington with Grant on the evening of April 12. The quartermaster general and the general-in-chief reached the capital at 2:30 the next afternoon and reported promptly to Stanton. Meigs visited also his old friend Secretary Seward, whose team had run wild a few days before while he was riding in his carriage, and who now lay painfully in his bed, a double iron brace around his jaw and neck, his broken right arm hanging over the bedside. He was no longer young or healthy, and his family were not wholly confident of his recovery. Meigs gave him what news and consolation he could and then returned home. He had been absent since March 22.[1]

That night the city was illuminated in celebration of victory, as it had been for several nights before. Candles shone from every window of the government buildings, including the eleven structures into which the War Department had over-flowed from its little headquarters on Seventeenth Street. The Lee Mansion across the river was gleaming, and on its lawns freedmen danced to *The Year of Jubilo*. From the Capitol

[1] Meigs Diary, April 13, 1865.

shone the words, "This is the Lord's doing; it is marvelous in our eyes." [2]

The next day, April 14, was Good Friday. General Meigs went to his office for a few hours, then to St. John's. In the afternoon he wrote to his father and to a friend who had sent him a book on the war powers of the government. He received a visit from the chief quartermaster of the Army of the Tennessee. Victory celebrations continued in the evening despite the religious holiday. "The country is drunk with joy," Meigs wrote as he closed his diary for the day.[3]

He was sitting quietly with Louisa some time after ten that evening when an excited messenger knocked at the door and shouted that Secretary Seward had been murdered in his bed. It was a walk of only three blocks to Seward's house on Lafayette Square, and Meigs slipped on his uniform coat and hurried into the night. The streets were coming alive with people, and they said that young Frederick Seward was dead or dying as well as his father. As Meigs approached F Street he probably heard vague rumors that the President had been assassinated too. A crowd was gathering around and even entering the Seward house, which was a shambles. Seward was not dead, but how long he could live was questionable; he lay groaning and bleeding on his bedroom floor, gashed with knife wounds. Frederick Seward was in a coma, also badly knifed. A State Department messenger was gagging with blood. A damp red spot was growing across the coat of a male nurse. Miss Fanny Seward lay bruised and unconscious on the floor.[4]

Soon Stanton and Gideon Welles appeared, and Stanton said it was true about the President: he had just talked with a man who had come from Ford's Theater, where Lincoln had gone to see *Our American Cousin*. Stanton ordered Meigs to

[2] Leech, *Reveille*, pp. 378–83.
[3] Meigs Diary, April 14, 1865.
[4] *Ibid.*; Leech, *Reveille*, pp. 394–96.

clear the Seward house of sightseers, which Meigs did. The Secretary announced that he was going to Ford's Theater, and Meigs tried to dissuade him; murder was in the streets. Stanton hesitated, then shrugged impatiently and followed as Welles led the way out the door and into a carriage. Meigs hurried after them and called for a cavalry escort.

They rode through swarming streets, and now the crowds were ceasing to move aimlessly. Everyone was turning toward Tenth Street and the theater. They discovered that someone had ordered Lincoln moved to a narrow house across the street, and there he lay in a small first-floor bedroom under the stairway. Mrs. Lincoln was sobbing in the front parlor. The Lincoln family physician arrived, probed the bullet hole in the back of the President's head, studied the bloodshot eyes, and announced that the case was hopeless. Lincoln would die.

General Meigs spent the long night at the President's bedside, with cabinet members and Congressmen gliding in and out and Stanton conducting a belated and ill-conceived inquisition in the parlor. At 7:22 in the morning the President expired. Rain was beating on the windows, and Gideon Welles went out to find strong men crying in the streets.[5]

On Tuesday, Lincoln lay in state in the East Room of the White House. On Wednesday, General Meigs rode at the head of the quartermaster deputation in the funeral procession. They moved slowly to the Capitol, where Meigs had charge of arrangements for another day of lying in state, this time under the Capitol dome. At six the next morning the cabinet, General Grant, General Meigs, General Rucker, and the honor guard moved the body to the railroad depot. "The last of our great & good Presidt left the city. He will live in history with Washington. The one connects his name with republican Liberty. The other with personal liberty & emancipation." [6]

[5] Meigs Diary, April 14–15, 1865; Leech, *Reveille*, p. 396.
[6] Meigs Diary, April 16, 1865.

Scattered Confederate forces now surrendered, and the war was over. The war—but not the bitterness it had engendered, nor the memory of the departed President, nor Meigs's memory of his dead son. At the end of June, the Mr. Myers who had been Meigs's assistant engineer on the Aqueduct called upon the quartermaster general: he had been one of Meigs's closest friends. He was a Virginian who had served the Confederacy, and he worked now as chief engineer of the Richmond, Fredericksburg and Potomac Railroad.

He was not [wrote Meigs] a states rights man not a secessionist but says had he known his family were going to be overwhelmed in the Red Sea he would have felt compelled not to separate himself from his blood. . . . He is a Hebrew Christian. A noble fellow. Yet he went South & be[in]g there took up arms against his country & helped stay her patriotic defenders—!

I told him that old feelings of friendship stirred within me at sight of him but that what had passed must ever be a barrier between us[.] [7]

At the close of the year Alfred Rives visited Meigs's office; he had been one of the general's friends and an assistant on the Aqueduct and the Capitol. But like Myers he had served the Confederacy, and Meigs declined to receive him. He told him "that I could not see any of those gentlemen who had deserted their country & joined the party who murdered my son with any satisfaction." [8]

Another visitor was Gustavus Woodson Smith, West Point, '42, a prewar officer of the Corps of Engineers, and a former major general of the Confederacy. Smith had business with the Quartermaster General's Office and said that he wished also to see Meigs again:

[7] *Ibid.*, June 29, 1865; Meigs to Charles D. Meigs, July 1, 1865, Meigs Let. B., 1864–1866.

[8] Meigs Diary, Dec. 23, 1865.

Looked confident & assured of a cordial greeting as thgh no dead sons shut loyal hearts against those who fought against the flag they had dedicated themselves to support & sped the bullets of assassins in bushes & in theatres.

I think he understands now that I for one have no pleasure in association with such as he.

Hemp or salt water should be offered to all such had I the power.[9]

Often during the war Meigs's thoughts had turned to Jefferson Davis, once his close friend and staunch supporter, once the man for whose health Meigs prayed, for the country's sake and his own. At the end of June, 1865, Mrs. Jefferson Davis addressed a letter to Meigs from Savannah, appealing to him as an old friend of her husband. She asked that Meigs plead for her, that the Secretary of War might allow her to come northward to communicate with her husband in his prison cell at Fortress Monroe and to bring her children out of the unhealthy climate of the Georgia coast. Meigs showed the letter to Stanton, who declined to advise him whether it would be proper to reply. "He thinks," wrote Meigs of the Secretary, "of the starvation of 10 000 men at Andersonville under the orders of Jeff Davis."

Meigs considered the case for himself:

Poor woman she has been guilty of great crime  She set on this husband of hers, but I feel pity for her present condition. A tigress who has lost her whelps is an object of commiseration & a woman thogh the Chief of Rebels who is separated from her husband in such conditions is to be pitied. Even the blood of my son slain by her husbands hired murderers does not shut up my compassion.

But he reflected that Davis was said to be in good health and that Mrs. Davis would read of this in the newspapers. In the end, he could not bring himself to write a direct reply.

[9] Meigs to Charles D. Meigs, no date (about Sept., 1865), Meigs Let. B., 1864–1866.

He merely asked the commanding general at Savannah to have Mrs. Davis informed that he had learned her husband's health was better than when she parted from him.[10]

Sometimes Meigs found irksome the business of settling claims for property damage on behalf of Southerners who professed to be loyal citizens. In October he consumed nearly a whole day with President Andrew Johnson at the White House discussing the claim of a Mrs. Randolph of Virginia, a claim being pressed for settlement by the wife of Surgeon General Joseph Barnes, whose aunt Mrs. Randolph was. Mrs. Randolph wanted payment for several thousand cords of wood cut from her 3,000-acre plantation near Warrenton for the military railroads. She had taken the oath of loyalty and thus, under Johnson's Reconstruction program, had won amnesty before the wood was carried from her farm, although it had already been cut.

The next day Mrs. Barnes called on Meigs to tell him that Johnson had decided her aunt should be paid. Meigs vented his anger in his diary:

This mother of . . . rebels one of them among Mosby's Hellhounds gets them the money of the loyal people to compensate her in part for destruction . . . of property wrung from the unrequited labor of generations of slaves[.] A mother whose two sons have given their lives to our cause who has won her food by working as a nurse in the hospitals of the army called the same morng to ask help to brg the body of her son starved by these conspirators tyrants & vultures at Andersonville[.] I had no right to spend the money won from taxation for this sacred purpose but it goes to the mother of Virginia hellhounds! One of Mosbys men murdered my own gallant son[.] [11]

The bloodshed of war had passed, but the hatred had not; and the hatred would be a long time dying.

[10] Meigs to Charles D. Meigs, June 28, July 5, 1865, *ibid*.
[11] Meigs Diary, Oct. 12–13, 1865.

# PART FOUR

# THE POSTWAR YEARS

# XV

# RECONSTRUCTION

TOWARD the end of May Meigs's house on H Street filled with relatives from Philadelphia, and by nine A.M. on the 23rd the general had them all in their places to hear the booming of the signal gun and await the march down Pennsylvania Avenue of General Meade and his staff, heading the grand review of the Army of the Potomac. All day the troops passed by, the drums beat, bands played, and colors dipped as the regiments filed past the reviewing stand. The next day it was much the same, with four corps from Sherman's armies of the West marching down the avenue. Again the capital cheered, and even the absence of the martyred President was almost forgotten in the gaiety of the victory celebration.[1]

For a few nights the campfires of the army continued to circle the capital, but on the 27th the Quartermaster's Department commenced the task of dispersing the troops to their homes. In 1861 the states had arranged the transportation of most of the regiments to their points of rendezvous; now it was the Federal Quartermaster's Department that was seeing them to their homes, and the change was one measure of the shift in the balance of Federal power which had accompanied the war.

[1] Meigs Diary, May 22–24, 1865.

During the forty days following May 27 Meigs put on the trains of the Washington branch of the Baltimore and Ohio 233,200 men, 12,838 horses, and 4,300,850 pounds of baggage. At Relay House just south of Baltimore the tracks forked; here some trains headed westward, others north into the city. In Baltimore itself there was a further divergence into two streams: some moved up the Northern Central toward Harrisburg, others along the Philadelphia, Wilmington, and Baltimore line. Meanwhile ninety-two steamers were carrying men homeward by water. Most of them were on the Western rivers, where they met the trains at Parkersburg and continued the journey into the West at a cost less than half as great as that of rail transportation. By the end of the year Meigs was able to report that a total of about 800,000 men had been carried home from the South on the railroads and navigable rivers of the country. In the fiscal year 1865–1866 the department paid $22,593,818.17 in transportation fees.[2]

While the armies dispersed, the Quartermaster's Department began reorganizing itself and its holdings and disposing of its surplus property. General Grant was recommending the maintenance of a peacetime army of 100,000, and for such a force Meigs made his plans. Quartermaster's officers scoured the South for department property in order to concentrate it in a few large depots, principally New York, Philadelphia, Washington, Cincinnati, and Jeffersonville, Indiana. At these places nonperishable property such as clothing and harness would be stored. The stock of clothing on hand would be large enough to support the army for many years to come; it was so large, in fact, that Meigs planned to sell much of it as soon as the market was less overstocked than it was immediately upon the close of the war. Damaged and irregular clothing he sometimes sold immediately, sometimes transferred to the

[2] O.R., ser. 3, V, 231–33, 301–5.

Freedmen's Bureau to aid in relieving distress among the refugees.[3]

Horses and mules had to be sold promptly. Meigs issued advertisements advising farmers of the opportunity to secure work animals at prices far cheaper than usual, and he conducted sales at auction at depots scattered throughout the country. Sometimes broken down and unserviceable animals he retained briefly in depot in order that they might recuperate and bring in a better price. Between May 1, 1865, and August 2, 1866, the department sold at public auction 104,474 horses and 102,954 mules; these animals, along with others whose exact numbers were not yet reported when Meigs drew up his annual report for 1866, afforded the department a total return of $15,-269,075.54. The average price received per horse was $53.89; the average price per mule, $74.64. Some of the horses sold for as little as fifty cents; these were the kind likely to die almost as soon as they left the department's hands. The highest price secured for a single horse was $280; for a single mule, $325. On June 30, 1865, the army contained 59,303 cavalry horses, 9,843 artillery horses, 97,358 mules, and 22,460 unserviceable animals. A year later the totals were down to 8,891 cavalry horses, 566 artillery horses, 15,362 mules, and 1,528 unserviceable animals.[4]

During the war the United States Military Railroads as part of Meigs's department had operated fifty different lines, with an aggregate length of 2,630.5 miles and with 433 engines and 6,605 cars. The total expenditure of the Military Railroads for repairs, equipment, and operation had been $45,367,480.27. Now Meigs proceeded to dispose of the roads by returning them to the prewar owners, to private corporations, or to the boards of public works of the states in which they were located. The policy of the government was to charge the old owners the

[3] *Report of the Secretary of War, 1866,* pp. 107–8.
[4] *Ibid.,* pp. 105–7.

amount spent by the Quartermaster's Department on improvements and repairs. The authorities recognized the financial impoverishment of the South and of the railroad owners, and they extended liberal credit terms to the roads. Most of the railroads then met promptly their engagements to the United States, but some proved utterly incapable of doing so. The Nashville and Chattanooga, for example, had an original debt to the government of $1,566,551.73. After charging interest and crediting all payments and earnings of the road to June 30, 1866, the debt remained $1,493,204.07.[5]

On July 1, 1865, the Quartermaster's Department still owned or employed 590 ocean and lake transports, with an aggregate tonnage of 193,936. It maintained this fleet at an estimated daily cost of $82,405. A year later only 53 vessels remained, with a tonnage of 14,163 and an estimated daily cost of $3,000. Sales of vessels during the year totaled $1,767,844.69. Meigs conducted the sales at auction, and he believed that generally he secured a fair commercial value for his ships, allowing for the severe deterioration of steamships under military service. By the end of 1866 the Quartermaster's Department was generally carrying on transporation by sea on the established commercial lines; only occasionally did Meigs continue to secure special charters, and at a few places on the Southern coast the department continued to operate its own transports.[6]

A lesser but still important sum was realized by Meigs's department from the sale of its wagons and related equipment. In the fiscal year 1865–1866 sales of such items totaled 12,534 regular wagons, 1,457 two-horse wagons, 441 spring wagons, 1,459 wagons of irregular models, 3,432 ambulances, 63 carts, harness for 112,607 animals, and 810 traveling and portable forges.[7]

[5] O.R., ser. 3, V, 233–35; Report of the Sec. of War, 1866, pp. 111–12.
[6] Report of the Sec. of War, 1866, pp. 109–10.
[7] Ibid., p. 117.

The rolling mill completed by the Quartermaster's Department at Chattanooga Meigs transferred to a buyer from Plymouth, Massachusetts. At the buyer's request he did not sell the mill outright, but on a two-year lease renewable for another two years. The mill stood on land which Meigs regarded as held by the United States by military right; but the old owners were likely to challenge that right, and the buyer of the mill felt safer as a mere lessee, with the United States still claiming the land.[8]

Probably the most tedious duty of the Quartermaster's Department in the aftermath of war, and to Meigs the most exasperating, was that of adjudicating claims upon the United States for property seized by Federal troops from persons claiming to be loyal citizens. By the end of 1867 the department had received 24,417 claims for compensation for the seizure of horses, mules, forage, fuel, and the like, aggregating over $13 million; and although two and a half years had passed since the close of the war, 12,496 of the claims still awaited attention. Throughout the border states, whence most of the claims emanated, claim agents sprang up, making a business of filing claims upon the government in return for a share of the award. It was impossible to send an officer to the home of every claimant, and opportunities for imposing upon the Treasury were abundant. Still, of the first 11,921 claims acted on, less than half were accepted as legitimate; 6,513 were not allowed.[9]

Between claimants seeking personal attention and Southern railroad officials negotiating for the return of their roads and the settlement of their debts, Meigs had to deal with a steady stream of visitors from the Southern states. He found the chore a trying one:

[8] Q.M.G. Let. B. 87, pp. 439–40.
[9] *Report of the Sec. of War, 1867*, p. 535; Q.M.G. Let. B. 94, pp. 212–13.

I have been very much occupied lately Southern Rail Road men
& all sorts of men with claims who are now being let out of the
Southern prison house overrun us here. I recoil with disgust from
those who make it appear that they have been active rebels &
feel some sympathy with those who can show that they have
desired to remain loyal but of these the number is small. Others
who say nothg on the subject transact business without calling
up these feelings[.] [10]

What annoyed and angered General Meigs was that the
Southerners did no more than regard themselves as subjugated.
They were not repentant. From Meigs's point of view they
were both sinners and criminals: sinners, because they had
maintained human slavery; criminals, because they had committed treason. Yet none of the Southerners he met had the
remotest consciousness of this, for him, obvious truth. He
spoke to Seward about it; and the shrewd Secretary informed
him, rightly enough, that he was expecting the impossible.
Thousands on thousands of men who had risked their lives and
fortunes for a cause they held to be just and sacred were not
going to reverse themselves in defeat and in dust and ashes
regard all that they had done as wicked. The most that could
be expected of the present generation of Southerners was submission. Seward's hope was for a later generation, little touched
by the bitterness of war, which would come to accept the
outcome as beneficial even for the South.[11]

The less tolerant Meigs could not so easily reconcile himself to Southern attitudes. Sin was sin, and the unrepentant
sinner was a sinner still, even though restrained from crimes
by physical force. Meigs was particularly infuriated by his
correspondence with his brother Henry, who had served as a
quartermaster captain in the Confederate army. Henry was

[10] Meigs to Charles D. Meigs, Sept. 27, 1865, Meigs Let. B., 1864–1866.
[11] Meigs to Charles D. Meigs, July 24, 1865, *ibid.*

completely without regret for his course; he considered himself a Southern patriot. The only concession of opinion he made to the outcome of the war was to say that now a Southern convention not overawed by Federal bayonets might of its own volition agree to a law for gradual emancipation. For a time Henry considered going to Brazil, and this to General Meigs was the final proof of his brother's unfitness for respect: he was not even a republican, he was willing to offer his allegiance to an emperor. When General Meigs's efforts to make Henry realize the error of his ways proved unavailing, the correspondence closed. Henry wrote to their father that Montgomery was among those permanently excluded from his affections. General Meigs concluded, "It will be only when the confiscation commissioners commence proceedings against his house & lot & mill & farm that he will begin to feel & see clearly that he is not the innocent patriot he now holds himself to be." [12]

In Meigs's view it came down to this. The leaders of the South would have to be punished severely, even harshly, not merely out of a desire for revenge—although this was part of it, for Meigs could not forget the vision of his son lying in the dust of the Swift Run Gap Road—but in order to create some realization in the Southern mind that loyal and Christian men considered the conduct of the South traitorous and sinful. The men of the South, he came to believe, would not recognize that they had gone wrong "till a dozen are hanged. This will make them not martyrs but criminals & may have a good effect on public opinion on this subject on which it is all wrong south & too loose north." [13]

Meigs was glad that the decision on the fate of Jefferson Davis lay not in his hands; but if it had, Meigs felt he would have thought it necessary to hang him. "Perhaps if I had to

[12] Meigs to Charles D. Meigs, July 1, 5, Aug. 20, 21, 1865, *ibid*.
[13] Meigs to Charles D. Meigs, July 1, 1865, *ibid*.

act or vote & appeals for mercy came right to me I should act as they [the government] do. But I feel still some bitterness towards the murderers of my kin & more towards the chiefs than the subordinate actors, more towards the head & hand than towards the knife." This meant that Meigs would execute that "traitor & murderer" R. E. Lee as well as Davis. "Read Lees letter to Mosby," Meigs enjoined his father, "thankg him for his efficient service. It was a party of Mosbys men that killed your grandson." [14]

A personal thirst for revenge, then, was an inextricable part of Meigs's feelings toward the South. But more than that, there was in Meigs's attitude a recognition of the true state of Southern feeling and a conviction that only by treating the principal ex-Confederates as criminals could a step be taken toward convincing the South that its course had been morally and criminally wrong:

It is whipped rebellion not repentant rebellion, & to whipped rebellion not repentant I believe that we ought to have measured out more justice than mercy.

I have no faith in all that we hear of the loyalty &c of the South. They are beaten, they are cowed, they have been treated with trustg condescension instead of the severity that justice & policy both demanded & they will revenge themselves for their defeat upon the North & upon the black in every mode which may be safe.[15]

Particularly Meigs feared that the South would turn as soon as it had the power to reduce the Negro to a status as close to slavery as possible. Therefore the North should have exerted itself not only to punish the former leaders of the Confederacy, but also to ensure as nearly as it could that the Negro would be treated as a human being and not as dirt underfoot

[14] Meigs to Charles D. Meigs, Sept. 5, 1865, *ibid*.
[15] Meigs to Charles D. Meigs, Oct. 10, 14, 1865, *ibid*.

when Federal bayonets left the South. Meigs was no extremist who regarded the Negro as simply a white man who happened to have black skin, and who should immediately take a place in American society equal in every respect to that of the white man. Meigs tended to subscribe in a limited way to the racialist doctrines of his time and to regard the white race as unique in its superiority. He was not sure that the emancipated Negro should immediately be granted the suffrage; he suspected the ability of illiterate field hands to exercise it intelligently. Steps should be taken to educate the next generation of Negroes, and when they became adults it would be time enough to grant the suffrage. Meanwhile the North should have been stirring itself to protect the Negro from reduction to the status of a chattel.[16]

The general concerned himself especially with ensuring the economic emancipation of the Negroes; in failing to secure such emancipation he thought the North was committing its principal blunder in its attempt to secure a better life for the freedmen. The South was an agricultural society. In an agricultural society, Meigs asked himself, who is it that controls the economic life of the society and thus the lives of its inhabitants? His answer was the owners of the land. If in a society almost totally dependent upon agriculture a man owns no land he cannot really be free, for he will be dependent upon the owners of the land. In the South the former slaveholders still owned the land; and thus they were still in fact the masters of their former slaves, and the freedmen were not fully free.

The emancipation of the negro slave is incomplete as long as, being without land, he is at the mercy of his former master, who may drive him from the acres on which his cabin is built, his family sheltered, and which, by mixing with them his own and his father's labor, he has acquired a natural right to possess.

[16] Meigs to Charles D. Meigs, Oct. 5, 1865, *ibid*.

Sometimes Meigs's phrases took on the flavor of a Henry George:

How does man acquire a right to exclusive possession and control of land?
This question goes to the foundation of the rights upon which civilized society is constructed.
Who has the stronger claim to the land, the man whose own and whose family's yield has reclaimed it from a state of nature, has compelled it to yield its fruits, or he who has enjoyed their fruits won by the unrequited toil of others?

He recalled that in the recent emancipation of Russia's serfs by Alexander II, emancipation had been accompanied by a transfer of land ownership.

It is believed that in all other countries great emancipations have accorded a grant or a recognition of the right of the freed serf to a portion of the soil he has labored upon.
So long as the black man is at the mercy of his former master, the only available employer, he is a slave. . . .
It is for statesmen, as the military power is dying out, to meet this question; and to me it seems more important than the question of suffrage, which, in its ultimate results, it involves.[17]

How were the Negroes to receive land? Meigs did not believe that reliance could be placed upon the Homestead Act. Obviously, Southern Negroes lacked the resources to transport themselves and their families to the free lands of the West and to establish themselves there. Nor did he favor the idea of aiding the Negroes by colonizing them by communities in the West. To establish separate Negro communities would create an *imperium in imperio*; the communities were too likely to become enclaves isolated from the general stream of American life, like the German communities of Pennsylvania. In particular, all-Negro settlements were likely to remain back-

[17] Meigs to Charles D. Meigs, July 20, 1865, *ibid*.

ward. Land for the Negroes, then, would have to be found in the South.[18]

Meigs did not follow Thaddeus Stevens's scheme of confiscating entirely the land of the great holders of the South and distributing it among the slaves. For one thing, Meigs recognized the legal objection to this idea. The Constitution forbade the forfeiture of real estate as punishment for treason beyond the life of the person attainted; and Congress, in a curious and superfluous proceeding, had attached to the Confiscation Act of 1862 an explanatory resolution reaffirming the principle of the Constitution. Furthermore, Meigs feared the effects of complete confiscation upon the over-all prosperity of the South. He thought it likely to reduce the South to a region of subsistence farmers. Some holdings of considerable size must endure in order to make possible the commercial growing of staple crops such as cotton, without which the South would find it difficult to secure manufactured goods and other items she herself did not produce.

In fact, Meigs did not carry his advocacy of land reform to any startling lengths. He proposed merely that heads of Negro families be given five acres of land. This plan would enable most families nearly if not entirely to subsist themselves, and thus it would grant them that measure of economic independence essential to genuine freedom. The males of the family could labor on those acres when not otherwise employed; the women and children could help them. But since five acres could scarcely afford more than a mere subsistence, there would exist an incentive for the Negro to hire his surplus labor to the larger landholder, and the production of commercial crops could continue. The Negro should receive his five acres in fee simple, but with some provision discouraging

[18] Meigs to Charles D. Meigs, no date (about July, 1865), *ibid.*

alienation during his lifetime. Meigs did not wish to establish a system of entail, so that he would not have restricted the ownership of the land to the freedman's family beyond the lifetime of the first owner. But he did wish to ensure that the ignorant and perhaps gullible freedman would not be bamboozled into transferring his land to some unscrupulous operator.[19]

But by what right was the government to confiscate Southern lands? The nation had rejected the course of regarding all ex-Confederates as traitors, and thus it had rejected the possibility of declaring their property forfeit. But Meigs pointed to the fact that President Johnson had excepted from his general amnesty proclamation of May 29, 1865, persons who owned property of a value greater than $20,000. Such persons could be pardoned only upon making special application to the President. Such persons were the principal landowners. Why not, said Meigs, make the distribution of five acres of their land to each head of family among their former slaves a condition of their receiving amnesty? Why not, in short, base land reform upon the presidential pardoning power? [20]

Meigs presented his plan to Congressmen, cabinet members, and influential citizens. Through Major General Oliver O. Howard, commissioner of the Freedmen's Bureau, who liked the idea, it reached the desk of President Johnson. But Johnson turned his back on it. "The truth is," wrote Meigs, "that he is not from early education disposed to favor or raise the blackmen. . . . Nothing more will be given by the President,

[19] Meigs to Charles D. Meigs, July 20, Aug. 22, Sept. 12, 1865, *ibid.*; Meigs to O. O. Howard, Aug. 27, 1865, *ibid.*; Randall, *Lincoln the President*, III, 119–24.

[20] Meigs to O. O. Howard, Aug. 27, 1865, Meigs Let. B., 1864–1866; James G. Randall, *The Civil War and Reconstruction* (Boston, 1937), 711–12. To Meigs's plan could still be raised the constitutional issue of the forfeiture of property beyond a single lifetime.

& we must do the best practicable under the circumstances." [21]

Meigs feared that the best practicable now would not be good enough.

God has punished us for allowg slavery & oppression in the South & has more severely punished the South for it[s] greater & more active guilt. He lifted his hand from them for a time & they are returning like dogs to their vomit. They can not enslave but they will outrage & oppress. Their hearts are not changed. We are guilty again. We permit this oppression they are guilty again they enact it. God will surely visit both sections of the Union until the foul spot is wiped off our escutcheon & it blazes with unsullied brilliance as altogether free.[22]

Probably Meigs's Reconstruction plan is most significant in what it suggests about Northern attitudes during Reconstruction. General Meigs could be as vindictive as the fiercest of the Congressional Radicals; his talk about hanging Jeff Davis was not spoken in jest, and comparatively few other Northerners called General Lee a murderer. But Meigs, like all but perhaps a handful of the Congressional Radicals, was thinking of more than revenge, and of more than establishing the Republican party in the South. The war which had begun as a struggle to preserve the Union had ended with a double aim; it had become a war for emancipation as well. Meigs hoped to ensure that the sacrifices of the war had not been in vain, that the South should not nullify by subterfuge the results won by Northern arms, and that the Negro should have more than a superficial freedom, that he should enjoy genuine liberty to carve his own future as a human being.

[21] Meigs to Charles D. Meigs, Aug. 22, 31, Sept. 8, 15, 1865, Meigs Let. B., 1864–1866; Meigs to Charles Sumner, Sept. 16, 1865, *ibid.;* Charles Sumner to Meigs, Sept. 18, 1865, Meigs Misc. Papers; Andrew Johnson Papers, LXXV, 6537–38, L.C.; O. O. Howard to E. M. Stanton, Sept. 4, 1865, Meigs Misc. Papers.
[22] Meigs to Charles D. Meigs, Feb. 23, March 2, 1866, Meigs Let. B., 1864–1866.

On New Year's Day, 1867, General Meigs trudged through the usual calls on the President, the Secretary of War, and General Grant. But beyond these courtesy calls he stopped at the homes of only a few neighbors. For several weeks he had not been feeling well. His symptoms were heightening: a swelling of the legs, dyspepsia, a quickened pulse on the slightest exertion.

On January 2 he went to his office as usual, but he was unable to remain long. He tried again on the 3rd and found himself greatly tired by only a minor exertion.[23]

Through the four long years of war Meigs had found himself tied to a desk with long hours, little exercise, and much worry. In quick succession at the close of the conflict came the death of his son John, the emotional shock of watching the President's life ebb away through the ghastly night in the Peterson house, and within a month of that the death of Meigs's own mother.

With the coming of peace Meigs's work continued to be tedious and tiring, but without the stimulation of feeling involved in a great enterprise. The business at hand, chiefly the settlement of claims, was important to those involved but scarcely challenging to the mind. "Its decision," wrote Meigs, "is too easy. It is only fatiguing because of the multiplicity of cases which leave no rest. Each requires a distinct & separate & different thought & action & as shaking hands with a crowd is physically fatiguing so acting on a crowd of cases quickly disposed of is mentally exhausting." Already a visit to his brother John had brought a warning that his health demanded a long and thorough rest.[24]

His unsuccessful attempt to accomplish something at the

[23] Meigs Diary, Nov. 13, 28, Dec. 24, 1866, Jan. 1–3, 1867.
[24] Meigs to Charles D. Meigs, July 10, 1865, Meigs Let. B., 1864–1866; Meigs Diary, Nov. 13, 1866.

office on January 3 convinced him he had better stay home a few days in the hope of recovering his strength. He amused himself by preparing plans for a new home which he wished to build, but he felt no better. By the 6th he had to stay in bed all day with a feeble pulse, a cough, and a headache. His physician diagnosed the trouble as a mild attack of typhoid fever. The next day Meigs finally wrote the Secretary of War that he was ill and advised him to detail General Rucker as acting quartermaster general.[25]

By the end of the month Meigs was finally out of bed and feeling improved, but his physician advised a long vacation and a change of scene. He traveled to Philadelphia, and both John and his father concurred in the advice of the doctor at Washington. John believed the general was suffering from emphysema, an enlargement of the air cells of the lungs; Charles Meigs said Montgomery suffered simply from over-work and advancing age. In either case the prescription was care, attention, and rest.

Meigs settled down for several months of ease at the family summer place, Hammanassett, in Delaware County. When he was well enough to travel his father and brother urged a trip abroad; his father would help with the finances. At the end of May he secured from the War Department an extended sick leave, and within a few days he and Louisa, his son Montie, his daughter Loulie, his sister Emily, and a niece and nephew were aboard the *Bremen* sailing for Europe. What followed was a grand tour; they did not return to New York until May 19, 1868.[26]

[25] Meigs Diary, Jan. 4–7, 1867.
[26] *Ibid.*, Jan. 8–Feb. 6, Feb. 23–25, March 22–23, 1867.

# XVI

# THE REGULAR ARMY

THE HUNDREDS of thousands of men in blue who fought the Civil War were volunteers and drafted men, volunteers mostly, with only a handful from the regular army. Not even the greatest national trial by fire could impel Congress to forsake the national antimilitarist tradition. In 1861 the authorized strength of the regulars increased to 34,000, but the regular army never attained even this limit during the conflict. The regular army continued small. When the war ended and the volunteer forces melted away, it was upon the small regular army that the defense of the nation, the occupation of the conquered South, and the patrolling of the vast Western frontier again devolved.

In the early seventies it was a force of about 25,000, organized into ten regiments of cavalry, twenty-five of infantry, and five of artillery.[1] Much of it lay scattered in driblets of battalions and companies in half isolated outposts in the West, and to send wagon trains rolling from railhead through often dangerous territory with adequate supplies was no mean task of organization and planning for the Quartermaster's Department. But it was almost child's play compared with the problems of the Civil War.

[1] *Report of the General of the Army, 1874,* pp. 3–18.

Meigs's duties, more than in wartime, tended toward the advisory and clerical. Once again supplies for the troops of one of the geographical military departments were secured through advertisement by the chief quartermaster of the department upon the orders and approval of the commanding general of the department. Again if Meigs disapproved the departmental contracts his chief recourse was simply that of protest to the Secretary of War. Meigs himself remained responsible, under the Secretary of War, for maintaining stocks in the general depots and for transportation over the long routes which crossed departmental lines. It was he who prepared the estimates to be submitted to Congress for the annual expenses of supplying the troops. It was he who battled with economy-minded legislators to keep both the appropriations and the staff of his department large enough to meet in more or less adequate fashion the demands upon them; usually in this era of military retrenchment he did not quite succeed.[2]

The general depots of the Quartermaster's Department now numbered four. At New York warehouses sheltered the stores of the troops along the Atlantic coast until in response to demand the stores were shipped to their destination by sea. At Philadelphia the Schuylkill Arsenal continued to carry on limited manufacturing operations, and in the early postwar years it housed the surplus clothing and equipage held over from the conflict and intended to be issued to the troops as the need for it arose.

The presence of the surplus allowed Meigs to proceed without requesting new clothing appropriations until the end of the sixties, and even later goodly quantities of certain items remained on hand. The larger clothing sizes tended to dis-

[2] *Reports of the Quartermaster General, 1866–1882;* Q.M.G. Let. B. 1873C, pp. 737–47.

appear first, since soldiers preferred to have the tailors cut down their uniforms to as nice a fit as possible; knapsacks and forage caps eventually became useless because of chemical changes in the paint which coated their leather surfaces.

Additional war surplus materials reposed in a general depot at Washington. At Jeffersonville, Indiana, the fourth depot, provided with a fireproof building only during the seventies, stored still more surplus property and facilitated the supplying of the troops in the West. Beyond the Mississippi, Fort Leavenworth, though not a general depot, served as a focus for supply operations on the plains. In 1878 the Quartermaster's Department completed a new depot at San Antonio, since in Texas could be found as much as one sixth of the strength of the army.[3]

Before the transcontinental railroads snaked across the plains, four great wagon routes carried military supplies to the posts on the frontier. In 1867 Route No. 1 took off from the Omaha branch of the Union Pacific Railroad to reach posts and depots in Nebraska west of longitude 102 degrees, in southern Montana, in western Dakota, in southeastern Idaho, and in northern Utah and Colorado. Across the route Wells, Fargo and Company carried freight at $1.64 per hundred pounds per 100 miles from April 1 to August 31, 1867, at $1.99 from September 1 to December 31, 1867, and at $2.50 from January 1 to March 31, 1868, their rates varying according to the severity of the seasons. Route No. 2 led from Fort Riley or other posts on the eastern division of the Union Pacific to southern Kansas and Colorado and to Fort Union, New Mexico. From Fort Union Route No. 3 departed for other posts in New Mexico. Route No. 4 led from St. Paul, Minnesota to the Minnesota posts and to Dakota east of the Missouri.[4]

[3] *Report of the Quartermaster General, 1869*, pp. 18–19; *1870*, p. 8; *1871*, pp 9–10; *1878*, pp. 16–17.
[4] *Report of the Secretary of War, 1867*, pp. 533–34.

Route No. 1 was the first of the wagon routes to fall to the transcontinental railroads; in 1869 its work passed to the Union Pacific. The extension of the railroads diminished Meigs's costs, but financial relations with the federally subsidized lines were to offer a continual source of contention. At first the subsidized lines were paid half in cash, half in credits on the bonds issued by the United States in their favor. Then, by laws of June 16, 1874 and March 3, 1875, Congress prohibited payment for military transportation to land-grant railroads whose grants provided for free use of their roads by the government. Only nine of the forty-nine land-grant lines were found to fit this category, but these nine were not eager to cooperate. In some cases the roads refused to give up property committed to them until they were paid in the usual way; sometimes military officers avoided writs of replevin only by taking upon themselves the payment of railroad charges.

Two of the nine roads brought suit for payment in the Federal courts, and the Supreme Court reversed the judgment of Congress and the executive, ruling that the land-grant roads despite their charters were not bound to transport troops and military materials without compensation. Difficulties continued until Congress after much delay produced legislation to implement the judicial decision; not until March 3, 1879, did a Sundry Civil Bill appropriate $300,000 for meeting fifty percent of the arrears owed for army transportation. The $300,000 proved insufficient to meet fifty percent of the arrears; not until the early eighties did additional legislation finally bring the problem toward resolution.[5]

General Meigs enjoyed little discretion in fixing his estimates of expenditures. The strength of the army was author-

[5] *Report of the Quartermaster General, 1868,* pp. 6–7; *1873,* p. 12; *1874,* p. 10; *1876,* p. 12; *1878,* pp. 11–12; *1879,* p. 7; *1880,* pp. 7–9; *1881,* pp. 8–9; *1882,* pp. 14–15.

ized by law. Most contracts for quartermaster's supplies were made by the commanders of geographical departments. The requirements of supplies and transportation depended largely upon what movements the line commanders ordered and upon the decisions of the War Department on changes in the allowances of officers and men. Because Congress failed to vote military appropriations commensurate with the authorized strength of the army, Meigs repeatedly had to request deficiency appropriations. The remedy was not in his hands. When one set of laws stipulated allowances for the troops which involved relatively fixed expenses, while another set failed to supply enough funds to meet those expenses, he could only recommend that the strength of the army be reduced from the maximum authorized to a level which within his appropriation he could supply.[6]

Financial stringency reached absurdity in 1876 when a new fiscal year began with no military appropriation on hand whatever, and Meigs was prevented by recent legislation from applying in the new year any surplus which he might have retained from the old. The quartermaster general was reduced to contriving measures for eking out the stocks on hand, to foregoing the cutting of grass and the care of trees and shrubs in the national cemeteries, and to recommending the gradual suspension of nearly all civilian employees and their replacement as far as possible by specially detailed personnel.[7] But this was only the climax of constant financial difficulties, a climax brought on when the issue of Reconstruction became entangled with the Congressional demand for military economy.

Economy was the watchword when postwar Congresses

[6] Q.M.G. Let. B. 1873C, pp. 737–47; *Report of the Quartermaster General, 1869*, p. 19.
[7] Q.M.G. Let. B. 1876B, pp. 1268–70.

turned toward the army, and the Quartermaster's Department suffered with the rest. Never did Meigs possess a force adequate to fulfill the responsibilities of his department. By 1874 the number of officers regularly attached to the department had shrunk to sixty-six. Year after year Meigs's annual reports complained of the high turnover and consequent slipshod work among post quartermasters. Because the department was not large enough to provide quartermasters for every post in the country, lieutenants of the line generally filled the role. Bearing heavy responsibilities for money and property, they received no special compensation in return. In the fiscal year 1869–1870 the average number of line officers acting as assistant quartermasters at a given time was 150, but the total number who served at one time or another during the year was 433. Thus the positions changed hands too often to allow their holders to become sufficiently acquainted with their duties.

Meigs believed substantial economies could be achieved in the cost of military equipment and buildings, the length of service of animals and wagons considerably increased, and the health and efficiency of the soldiers furthered if the post quartermasters were responsible men thoroughly familiar with their duties. In order to hold such men at their stations, he recommended that post quartermasters receive an allowance of $100 a year; this would increase by $15,000 annually the expenses of the army, but the resulting improvements in supply could easily offset that small sum. Meigs's advice continued to go unheeded.[8]

The army was in its doldrums, and the Quartermaster's Department with it. The troopers and infantrymen who fought the Indians on the Western plains may well have been man

---

[8] *Report of the Quartermaster General, 1870*, pp. 4–5; *1874*, p. 8. Meigs's request for compensation for post quartermasters was repeated annually.

for man or company for company as good as any soldiers in the world, but in total they did not add up to a modern army. They were simply a collection of regiments, or even of companies, without tactical or logistical organization for the sort of expansion which a war with a foreign power would have entailed; this fact the Spanish War was to demonstrate all too well. What was worse, even the most astute of the commanders appear to have had little appreciation of the decline of the army, beyond recognition of the obvious fact that it was notoriously small. They were content to rest on the achievements of the army in the Civil War, and General Meigs was no exception.

I have had experience [he wrote] in the management of what is embraced in the Quartermaster's Department at least as extensive as any other living man, and I do not hesitate to say that there is no other organization in the military forces of the world at this time, which has better accomplished the objects for which it was created than our Quartermaster's Department.

The elasticity and pliancy and power of adapting itself to varying circumstances of our Quartermaster's organization properly conducted, is certainly unrivalled. Its conduct during the late war, a war more difficult than that of Germany against France, was satisfactory to the people, to the soldiers, and to their commanders.

It has grown up in the course of many years, is adapted to the genius and habits of our people, it admits of expansion at the outbreak of war, while able to teach new officers their difficult duties, and an arm which has served so well should not be experimentally broken or thrown aside.[9]

In his last sentence Meigs was referring to proposals to fuse the Quartermaster's Department with the Subsistence Department (a step finally taken in 1912). "Two such perfect machines," he wrote, "should be preserved distinct in readiness for the call of war. You will remember how both expanded

[9] Q.M.G. Let. B. 1876B, p. 1222.

in a moment at the touch of war in 1861." [10] Had he forgotten the confusion and delays of the first months of war? Had he forgotten his inability to supply McDowell with transportation on schedule before First Bull Run? Had he forgotten the sentries freezing in their drawers?

Meigs's conduct of the quartermaster generalship in the postwar years was marked by no great achievement. He continued to be honest and competent, but little more can be said. His spark of imagination was burning low, or transferred to other things. Like so many of the generation which won the Civil War, he had succumbed to the nemesis of creativity, the idolization of an ephemeral technique. The military methods of the United States Army had succeeded gloriously in the past; therefore they were sacrosanct, whether or not they continued to be relevant to the present.

Meigs would never be forty-five again, he told himself, as he had been at the outbreak of the war, but the decade of the seventies was a pleasant one nevertheless. Both he and Louisa returned from their first European trip much improved in health (they were to visit the continent again in 1875); and if at first on their return they had to live in a stuffy house at 225 H Street, a place which kept Meigs depressed and lacking in appetite, on May 21, 1869, they were able to move at last into the home which the general himself had designed for their old age.[11]

The house stood at the corner of N Street and Vermont Avenue. Its architecture was typical late nineteenth-century eclectic, mostly Italian and French in inspiration. It was comfortable, large, and roomy, three stories high to the mansard roof, with a wide, airy hallway leading to a twelve-foot porch.

[10] *Ibid.*, pp. 1222–23.
[11] Meigs Diary, May 21, 1869.

Here a hammock and half a dozen easy chairs looked over a
lawn, a fountain, and shrubbery. The solid, erect General
Meigs had built a solid, substantial house. There was little
woodwork in the place; the home of his declining years was
not going to burn as so many wooden quartermaster's depots
had burned. The stairways were brick and stone, the floors
brick and mortar. Not only was the house sturdy, but it was
comparatively cool in summer; Meigs was pleased to note that
when the thermometer stood at one hundred degrees on the
north side, in the parlor it was eighty-six.

Inside, the parlor was flanked by the general's library, with
his three to four thousand books on military affairs, science,
and history, plus the clutter of his diaries and the photograph
albums wherein he stored his collection of hundreds of Civil
War scenes. In the basement was a billiard table, at which
the general relaxed though his game was awkward, and a
workshop where he liked to spend a few hours each morning
before going to the office, tinkering at some new gadget which
might add to his list of patents.[12]

The care of the house was Louisa's task; once he had designed it, the general's primary interest lay in enjoying it.
He left to his wife even the difficulties of finding good serv-
ants. "The servant question is a very vexed one with me,"
Louisa would write. "I do not seem able to manage them &
Mont never says a word to them, *good, bad* or *indifferent*
which as we have two *men* makes a greater difficulty for
me." [13]

On June 22, 1869, the general was summoned to Philadelphia; his father had died in his sleep during the night. Dr.
Meigs was found lying "upon his side with calm & peaceful

[12] Clipping in Meigs Journal from *The Republic,* 1880; Meigs Sealed
Diary, July 16, 1874.
[13] Louisa Rodgers Meigs to Mrs. John Rodgers, Oct. 22, 187[?], Rodgers
Family Papers, Box 2, L.C.

expression. Evidently he had passed away as he had so often prayed in sleep without a struggle or a pang." He had always been close to his sons, and the general unfailingly had turned to him for guidance. Now there would be no one to whom General Meigs could write quite the same sort of letters he had so long addressed to his father. "A good man has finished his course & is at rest." [14]

During the war the general's daughter Mary had married Lieutenant Colonel Joseph H. Taylor, the son of Commissary General Joseph Taylor and nephew of Zachary Taylor. Meigs's son Montgomery was now a graduate engineer; he had studied both at the Lawrence Scientific School and at Stuttgart, and now he worked on improving the channel of the Mississippi at Rock Island, where his father had helped make the initial surveys with young Captain Lee so many years before. The general's daughter Louisa was still at home, unmarried, pretty, but a somewhat temperamental young lady whose presence was not always soothing to her mother's nerves. Mary and Colonel Taylor were presenting Meigs with grandchildren to hold in his lap, and for much of the decade the colonel was stationed in the capital. In the earlier years of the seventies Meigs could write that his wife was "merrier & better than I have seen her for years. She seems to have recovered her spirits & elasticity & looks well." Surrounded by his family, Meigs enjoyed now his quiet Sundays at home:

Spent a quiet day of rest with my dear wife in the new & beautiful home which God has at length enable[d] me to provide for our old age I pray that he may allow us to enjoy it in thankfulness & in peace— A refuge for ourselves & children & grandchildren.[15]

[14] Meigs Diary, June 22, 1869; Meigs Journal, July 26, 1869.
[15] Meigs Journal, July 26, 1869; Meigs Sealed Diary, July 16, 1874; Meigs Let. B., 1879, pp. 6–7; Meigs Diary, May 23, 1869.

Yet the general had not given himself wholly over to advancing years and idle rest. He still enjoyed traveling. When the Centennial Exposition opened at Philadelphia in May, 1876, he took the train to the hills above the Schuylkill: "All the world & Congress is going It is curious to note in the car the delicate beauty of the American girls—2 or 3 are prettier than any I ever saw of European nations." [16] As quartermaster general he occasionally took extensive swings around the country. In the winter of 1872–1873 he visited the Northern Pacific Railroad as far as the Red River of the North, then dipped southward to Cheyenne and Denver, and returned east by way of Fort Leavenworth. In 1871–1872 and 1873–1874 he traveled as far as the Pacific coast, reaching both San Francisco and Los Angeles and crossing the Arizona desert.[17]

At home Meigs busied himself beyond his quartermaster's duties by keeping his hand in as an architect. He submitted designs for a fireproof museum building to the University of Michigan, and he prepared for Dickinson College in Pennsylvania a study for a fireproof building to contain chemical and physical laboratories, a library of twenty to thirty thousand volumes, and a scientific museum collection. His principal project was the designing of the National Museum behind the Smithsonian Institution in Washington—the present Old National Museum. To this somewhat depressing brick pile he gave careful attention; on his behalf it probably can be said that the defects of the building lay as much or more in the materials and the limitations of concept within which he had to work as in Meigs's design.[18]

Abruptly in the summer of 1877 Louisa began to complain

[16] Meigs Diary, May 9–10, 1876.
[17] There are delightful descriptive letters from the Western trip of 1871–1872 in Meigs Misc. Papers.
[18] Meigs Let. B., 1879, pp. 301–2, 265–80; 1879–1880, pp. 30–34.

that she could not bear the fatigue of walking, and that exertion left her with discomfort in the region of the heart. Thereafter she was never able to move as freely as before. On the night of March 20, 1879, she awoke with a violent seizure of congestion of the lungs, and for hours she hung between life and death. She was an invalid through the summer, though Meigs still hoped for a substantial recovery. Even the slightest exertion of walking in her room was likely to send her to bed for two or three days. On the night of November 20 she suffered another attack, and at 1:15 the next morning she died.

And thus my dear Louisa left us!

A more noble true generous . . . woman never blessed a man. . . . Growg more beautiful as time allowed the good & great soul to stamp itself on the features she never looked more beautiful than at the eveng chimes of the day at the end of which she left us.[19]

[19] Meigs Let. B., 1879, pp. 27–28, 256–58, 281–84; Meigs Diary, Nov. 21, 1879.

# XVII

# TWILIGHT

GENERAL MEIGS had just reached his office when a note arrived from the adjutant general of the army. That officer had just received from the President an executive order placing Meigs's name on the retired list as of the present date. It was February 6, 1882.[1]

The retirement law allowed the President to retire any officer of forty-five years' service, or who was sixty-two years of age, if in his judgment that officer needed rest or was incapable of discharging his duties. Congress from time to time received proposals to stiffen these provisions in order that younger officers might enjoy a better opportunity to rise. Meigs consistently argued against such schemes. He pointed out that the German army, reputedly the best in the world, had no law of compulsory retirement, that Moltke had been seventy when he conducted the Franco-Prussian War and continued in high command at seventy-eight; that Zachary Taylor had been sixty-three at Monterrey and Winfield Scott sixty-four when he entered Mexico. For his own part, Meigs felt no diminution of his mental capacities, and he saw no reason why the country should not continue to benefit from his long experience as quartermaster general.[2]

Unfortunately for him, two officers had long been waiting

[1] Extract from Special Orders No. 29, Adjutant General's Office, Feb. 6, 1882, Meigs Misc. Papers; Meigs Diary, Feb. 6, 1882.
[2] Q.M.G. Let. B. 1877B, p. 1514; 1878B, pp. 830–32.

to succeed him, both knew they must do so soon or never, and both had access to high influence. One was Colonel D. H. Rucker, the Civil War commander of the Washington quartermaster's depot; the other was Colonel Rufus Ingalls, the wartime chief quartermaster of the Army of the Potomac. Rucker was the father-in-law of Lieutenant General Sheridan, now commander of the Military Division of the Mississippi. Ingalls enjoyed the special friendship and backing of Ulysses Grant.

Of the two, Rucker was pressing his claims the more insistently. The trouble was that he was seventy, while Meigs was only sixty-five. To retire Meigs on grounds of age only to make room for someone five years older would be somewhat odd. Nevertheless, Rucker seemed determined to add to his name the titles of quartermaster general and permanent brigadier, and his son-in-law applied all the influence he could bring to bear. Meigs himself was generous enough to tell Secretary of War Robert Lincoln that if he must retire, in justice Rucker, his second in rank, should have his place long enough to retire as a brigadier general. Rucker's partisans began to say that their candidate would be willing to vacate the post as soon as he received it; he wanted only the honor and the advance in rank which he considered due him. President Chester Arthur and Secretary Lincoln yielded to the pressure. Meigs's name went onto the retired list, and amidst outraged cries from a part of the press the older Rucker became quartermaster general. The Philadelphia *Evening Telegram* pointed to Rucker's relationship with Phil Sheridan and commented: "A good many features of the Grant era have been revived of late, but the feature of nepotism has hitherto lingered in the background. Now, it seems, we are to have this too, with the other elements of 'Stalwartism.' " [3]

[3] Meigs Diary, Jan. 23, 1882; clippings, Feb. 2, 9, 1882.

Rucker had the grace not to retain the office long. At the end of February Rufus Ingalls's name went to the Senate in nomination for the quartermaster generalship. For this consummation General Grant had labored long.[4]

Meigs could retire with the satisfaction of duty faithfully performed, and he could read with gratification the letters which now reached him from great and small. From an ordinary clerk in the Quartermaster General's Office came a letter of grateful thanks for Meigs's kindness and confidence since 1865 and an offer to put his pen at Meigs's disposal whenever the old general might wish to use it. From the regimental quartermaster of the 16th Infantry in far-off Texas, a lieutenant who had seen Meigs but seldom, came an expression of regret "at the deprivation the corps must sustain at the loss of such a Chief. By the measure of pride we have been accustomed to point to you as Quartermaster General of the Army, must we weigh our sorrow at your retirement." Other persons scarcely known to Meigs addressed him their tribute. So did old army officers whom he had known well, and one friend sent him a clipping from the Pittsburgh *Post:* "Of the many millions of money which he handled during his long service as Quartermaster General, friend and enemy alike admit that none of it stuck to his hands." [5]

The general-in-chief, William Tecumseh Sherman, added the final note: "We all feel like orphans losing the Quartermaster General." [6]

[4] Meigs Diary, Feb. 25, 1882. For the efforts of Grant in 1874 to persuade Meigs to become American minister to Russia so that Ingalls might succeed him as quartermaster general, see Meigs Sealed Diary, July 20–24, Aug. 7, 22, Sept. 1, 6–7, Oct. 21–22, 29, 1874; Allan Nevins, *Hamilton Fish: The Inner History of the Grant Administration* (New York, 1936), pp. 726–30.

[5] Letters from L. F. Randolph, Edward Stabler, J. G. C. Lee, W. S. Rosecrans, Irvin McDowell, John J. Bowen, Addison Barrett, W. V. Richards, *et al.*, Meigs Misc. Papers.

[6] Meigs Diary, Feb. 14, 1882.

Thus terminates [wrote Meigs in his diary], my command of the Qur Mrs Dept after over 20 years of control in which I have seen great events pass. In June next I shall accomplish if I live to that time 50 years of service as cadet Lt—Capt. Col. & Brig & Brevet Major Gen. I signed & handed to chief Clerk a farewell letter to officers of my Dept dated today.[7]

The last years were quiet years, rich with a sense of fulfill-ment, unshadowed by pain and tragedy such as that which dimmed the last days of General Grant at Mount MacGregor.

Meigs did not wish to retire to complete inactivity. When he left the Quartermaster General's Office, Congress was mov-ing toward the erection of a Hall of Records in which to house the archives of the government and particularly of the late war. The sponsors of the plan favored General Meigs, the builder of the Capitol, as the man to construct the hall.[8] But the idea did not move beyond the floor of Congress.

Pressure for a building to house the Pension Office, that dispenser of unexampled largesse to the veterans of the war, was understandably greater, and in the summer of 1882 Gen-eral Meigs began work as architect and supervising engineer. His memories of his Italian tour having impressed themselves upon his initial leaning toward the classical and classical de-rivatives in architecture, he planned a structure in the manner of the Palazzo Farnese in Rome. But budget restrictions strait-ened his schemes, the dome he intended did not materialize, and the end was that dreary red brick edifice which Washing-tonians came to call "Meigs's barn." If nothing else the place was huge; even in semifinished state it was seized upon in 1885 for the inauguration ball (somewhat ironically) of Grover Cleveland. Meigs's chief pride among the ornamental features was the terra-cotta procession of Federal soldiers which end-

[7] *Ibid.*, Feb. 6, 1882.
[8] *Report of the Quartermaster General, 1881,* pp. 15–16.

lessly encircles the building, rank on rank of infantry, cavalry, and artillery. The figures in relief are at least realistic in a literal sense: Meigs had the Boston quartermaster's depot parade before the artist American soldiers in unifrom—not parade dress, Meigs stipulated, but marching and fighting dress.[9]

When the Pension Office was finished in 1886, Meigs could find no similar work. He had failed in his attempt to become supervisor of the new Aqueduct extension, so that he might complete as an old man what he had begun in his first years in the capital. He settled down to tinker in his basement workshop, but he produced no more inventions such as his reflecting candlestick of the late seventies and his improved valve for gas lamps of the early eighties, from which, after much haggling with the licensees, some royalties were flowing into his hands.[10] He continued interested in politics—a staunch bloody-shirt Republican now, obsessed as so many of his generation were with the fading issues of the Civil War. "Today will be decided," he wrote in his diary on election day, 1884, "the policy of the Govt for 4 years Republican or Democratic Blaine or Cleveland Progress or regression Protection & prosperity or Free foreign trade & damage to our indsutry & . . . which is 10 times the greater Loyalty or rebellion in the saddle?"[11] Only with the coming of the free-silver issue did he reveal flickerings of his old independence of thought; he favored free silver.[12]

In 1886 the general's daughter Louisa entered into a marriage of which the old soldier did not particularly approve, to a

[9] Meigs Let. B., 1882–1883, esp. pp. 17, 72, 205–7, 310–11, 314, 351–54, 486–87, 603, 623–24; 1885–1887, pp. 286–87; *Report on Pension Office*, copy in Meigs Misc. Papers.

[10] Meigs Let. B., 1882, 1882–1883, 1885–1887, *passim*.

[11] Meigs Diary, Nov. 4, 1884.

[12] Meigs Let. B., 1885–1887, pp. 265–66, 410–13.

famous English newspaper correspondent considerably older than she, Archibald Forbes. Her departure did not leave Meigs alone in the house on N Street; Mary's husband, Colonel Taylor, had died, and Mary and her children returned to live in Washington. Into a house next door moved Colonel John Macomb and his wife, friends of the general's and Louisa's early married years. It was a quiet and pleasant society in which General Meigs found himself as the eighties came to their close.[13]

3d May . . . 1891 . . . This is my 75th Birthday. I have good health except the rheumatism in my Knee . . . which lames me & prevents active exercise or walk g except about the house. I feel twinges in other parts of the body which seem to be best regulated & prevented from becomg too troublesome by common Steam Baths. I find that I sometimes see double which I presume is some failure in the power of coordination in the nervous centers. Otherwise I am able to enjoy the good things which God has provided me The love of my family & descendants & with fine appetite & books & papers & some mechanical amusements & occupation I do my duty & wait the end.[14]

It was his last birthday. On January 2, 1892, he died.

[13] Meigs Let. B., 1885–1887, *passim.*
[14] Meigs Diary, May 3, 1891.

# BIBLIOGRAPHY

The principal source for a biography of Lincoln's quartermaster general must be the M. C. Meigs manuscript collection in the Library of Congress. Meigs's pocket diaries provide a record of his day-to-day activities from his years as supervisor of Aqueduct and Capitol until his death; unfortunately, they are not rich either in introspection or in reflective comments on public affairs. For such material, a more fruitful source is the collection of letter-press copies of Meigs's outgoing correspondence. The collection is most complete for the 1850's, and for that period it contains almost weekly letters from Meigs to his father, consistently detailed, expressive, and apparently candid.

It is the period of the fifties that is covered by the famous shorthand volumes of Meigs's longer diaries, or journals. The shorthand journals have not been used for this biography; the author's time and resources did not permit a translation of the four large volumes, nor did his purposes seem to make it essential. The shorthand is a form of Pitman, modified and rendered more difficult of translation by Meigs's abominable handwriting characteristics. Deciphering the shorthand journals will be a major undertaking and ought to have at least the assistance of a stenographic expert. While a translation is desirable, its importance is diminished by the fact that the period of the shorthand journals is also the period of the frequent and revealing letters from Meigs to his father.

Personal sources are more scanty for the Civil War years than for any other period of Meigs's life after 1850. The shorthand journals cover the episodes of the Florida forts, the appointment as quartermaster general, the First Bull Run campaign, and the visit to Fremont's headquarters in St. Louis. Happily, there exists a translation of this section of the journals, deposited in the John G. Nicolay collection in the Library of Congress, used by Nicolay and Hay in writing their *Lincoln*, and according to Meigs's later diaries apparently prepared in large part by Meigs himself. After the fall of 1861, however, the shorthand journals virtually cease. There are few letters for the war years, and principal reliance has to be placed upon the generally laconic pocket diaries.

The nucleus of a history of Meigs's official career as quartermaster general is, of course, his annual reports to the Secretary of War. For the war years these reports are bound in the third series of the *Official Records*. Supplementing the reports are the letter, decision, and report books of the Quartermaster General's Office deposited in the National Archives. These manuscript documents are disappointing. For the most part they deal in minutiae and reveal little of Meigs's administrative methods and thought processes. The particularly important area of procurement and contracting methods is undocumented; the materials which would have been pertinent apparently were among those that have been destroyed. The result is that the *Official Records*, for all their relative neglect of supply problems, remain the source of first importance on the Quartermaster's Department in the Civil War.

## MANUSCRIPT SOURCES

Alexander Dallas Bache MSS, Library of Congress (hereafter L.C.)
James Buchanan MSS, Historical Society of Pennsylvania
Joseph Holt MSS, L.C.
Andrew Johnson MSS, L.C.
Abraham Lincoln MSS, L.C. (The Robert Todd Lincoln Collection)
M. C. Meigs MSS, L.C.
    Meigs Journals (large diaries, chiefly in shorthand)
    Meigs Diaries (pocket diaries, chiefly in longhand)
    Meigs Sealed Diary (in separate envelope, formerly sealed, deals
       mainly with offer of ministry to Russia)
    Meigs Notebooks (jottings made in the field)

Meigs Chattanooga Journal (an account of the battle of Chattanooga)

Meigs Letter Books (letter-press duplicates of outgoing correspondence and one volume of bound originals)

Meigs Miscellaneous Papers (various incoming correspondence, outgoing originals, newspaper clippings, miscellaneous mementos)

Meigs Sketchbooks

Meigs Photograph Albums

John G. Nicolay MSS, L.C. (including longhand transcription of Meigs Journal, March–September, 1861, prepared for the Nicolay and Hay *Lincoln* with the aid of Meigs)

Quartermaster General's Office, Documents, National Archives
Consolidated Correspondence File
Decision Books
Letter Books
Report Books

Rodgers Family MSS, L.C.

Rodgers Family MSS, Naval Historical Foundation Collection, L.C.

Winfield Scott MSS, L.C.

Edwin M. Stanton MSS, L.C.

Gideon Welles MSS, L.C.

## PRINTED SOURCES

Annual Reports of the General of the Army

Annual Reports of the Quartermaster General

Annual Reports of the Secretary of War

Basler, Roy P., editor. The Collected Works of Abraham Lincoln. 9 volumes, including Index. New Brunswick: Rutgers University Press, 1953; Index, 1955.

Carter, William H. Creation of the American General Staff. 68:1 Sen. Doc. 119 (serial 8254)

Congressional Documents
32:2 Sen. Ex. Doc. 48 (serial 665)
33:1 House Rep. 191 (serial 743)
36:1 Sen. Ex. Doc. 20 (serial 1031)
36:1 Sen. Misc. Doc. 29 (serial 1038)
36:1 House Rep. 566 (serial 1070)

Congressional Documents (*continued*)
    37:2 Sen. Ex. Docs., II (serial 1118)
    37:2 House Rep. 2 (serial 1142, 1143)
    37:3 Report of the Committee on the Conduct of the War
    38:1 Sen. Rep. 39 (serial 1178)
    58:2 House Rep. 646 (serial 4585), Documentary History of the
        Construction and Development of the United States Capitol
        Building and Grounds
    68:1 Sen. Doc. 119 (serial 8254)
*Congressional Globe*
Documentary History of the Construction and Development of the
    United States Capitol Building and Grounds. 58:2 House Rep.
    646 (serial 4585).
Donald, David, editor. Inside Lincoln's Cabinet: The Civil War
    Diaries of Salmon P. Chase. New York: Longmans, Green, 1954.
Grant, Ulysses S. Personal Memoirs of U. S. Grant. New York:
    World Publishing Company, 1952. First published in 2 volumes,
    1885–1886.
"Interesting Historical Letter, An" (recommendation of John R.
    Meigs for appointment to West Point), *Pennsylvania Magazine
    of History and Biography*, XXV (1901), 77–79.
Johnson, Robert Underwood, and Clarence Clough Buel, editors.
    Battles and Leaders of the Civil War. 4 volumes. New York: The
    Century Company, 1884–1888.
Keyes, Erasmus Darwin. Fifty Years Observation of Men and
    Events, Civil and Military. New York: Scribner's, 1884.
McClellan, George B. McClellan's Own Story. New York:
    Webster, 1887.
Meigs, M. C. Extracts from Journal
—— Material in *American Historical Review*, XXVI (1920–1921),
    285–303.
—— "The Relations of President Lincoln and Secretary Stanton to
    the Military Commanders in the Civil War"
Moore, John Bassett, editor. The Works of James Buchanan. 12
    volumes. Philadelphia: Lippincott, 1908–11.
*Pennsylvania Magazine of History and Biography*, XXV (1901),
    77–79. "An Interesting Historical Letter" (recommendation of
    John R. Meigs for appointment to West Point).

Porter, David Dixon. Incidents and Anecdotes of the Civil War. New York: Appleton, 1885.

Revised Regulations for the Army of the United States, 1861. Philadelphia, 1861.

Schofield, John M. Forty-Six Years in the Army. New York: The Century Company, 1897.

Sheridan, Philip H. Personal Memoirs of P. H. Sheridan, 2 volumes. New York: Webster, 1888.

University of Pennsylvania. Catalogue, 1831.

War of the Rebellion, The: A Compilation of the Official Records of the Union and Confederate Armies. 4 series, 70 volumes in 128. Washington: Government Printing Office, 1882–1900.

War of the Rebellion, The: A Compilation of the Official Records of the Union and Confederate Navies. 26 volumes. Washington: Government Printing Office, 1894–1922.

Welles, Gideon. Diary of Gideon Welles. Edited by John T. Morris, Jr. 3 volumes. Boston: Houghton Mifflin, 1911.

## GENERAL LITERATURE

Adams, Henry. The Education of Henry Adams. New York: Modern Library Edition, 1918.

Boynton, Edward C. History of West Point. New York: Van Nostrand, 1863.

Brown, Glenn. History of the United States Capitol. 2 volumes. Washington: Government Printing Office, 1900–1903.

Bryan, W. B. A History of the National Capitol. 2 volumes. New York: Macmillan, 1914–1916.

Buley, R. Carlyle. The Old Northwest: Pioneer Period, 1815–1840. 2 volumes. Indianapolis: Indiana Historical Society, 1950.

Burt, Maxwell Struthers. Philadelphia, Holy Experiment. Garden City, N. Y.: Doubleday, 1945.

Catton, Bruce. Mr. Lincoln's Army. Garden City, N. Y.: Doubleday, 1951.

—— A Stillness at Appomattox. Garden City, N. Y.: Doubleday, 1954.

Coulter, E. Merton. College Life in the Old South. New York: Macmillan, 1928.

Cullum, George W. Biographical Register of the Officers and Graduates of the U. S. Military Academy. 3 volumes. Boston: Houghton, 1891.

Curtis, W. T. S. "Cabin John Bridge," *Collections of the Columbia Historical Society,* II, 299.

Dictionary of American Biography. 21 volumes. New York: Scribner's, 1928–1937.

Dupuy, R. Ernest. Men of West Point: The First 150 Years of the United States Military Academy. New York: William Sloane Associates, 1951.

—— Where They Have Trod: The West Point Tradition in American Life. New York: Frederick A. Stokes Company, 1940.

Eisenhower, Dwight D. Crusade in Europe. Garden City, N. Y.: Doubleday, 1948.

Elliott, Charles Winslow. Winfield Scott, the Soldier and the Man. New York: Macmillan, 1937.

Fairman, Charles E. Art and Artists of the Capitol of the United States. . . . Washington: Government Printing Office, 1927.

Fite, Emerson David. Social and Industrial Conditions in the North during the Civil War. New York: Peter Smith, 1910.

Forman, Sidney. West Point: A History of the United States Military Academy. New York: Columbia University Press, 1950.

Freeman, Douglas Southall. Lee's Lieutenants: A Study in Command. 3 volumes. New York: Scribner's, 1946.

—— R. E. Lee: A Biography. 4 volumes. New York: Scribner's, 1934.

Gosnell, H. Allen. Guns on the Western Waters: The Story of the River Gunboats in the Civil War. Baton Rouge: Louisiana State University Press, 1949.

Greenfield, Kent Roberts, and others. United States Army in World War II: The Organization of Ground Combat Troops. Washington: Historical Division, Department of the Army, 1947.

Hesseltine, William B. Lincoln and the War Governors. New York: Knopf, 1948.

Kamm, Samuel Richey. The Civil War Career of Thomas A. Scott. Ph.D. thesis, University of Pennsylvania, 1940.

Knox, Dudley W. A History of the United States Navy. New York: G. P. Putnam's Sons, 1936.

Kreidberg, Marvin A., and Merton G. Henry. History of Military Mobilization in the United States Army, 1775–1945. Washington: Department of the Army, 1955 (Department of the Army Pamphlet No. 20–212).

Larkin, Oliver W. Art and Life in America. New York: Rinehart, 1949.

Leech, Margaret. Reveille in Washington. New York: Harper, 1941.

Lewis, Lloyd. Sherman: Fighting Prophet. New York: Harcourt, Brace, 1932.

Long, A. L. Memoirs of Robert E. Lee. New York: Stoddart, 1887.

MacKay, Winnifred K. "Philadelphia during the Civil War, 1861–1865." Pennsylvania Magazine of History and Biography, LXX (1946), 26–27.

Meigs, Henry B. Record of the Descendants of Vincent Meigs. . . . Philadelphia, 1901.

Meigs, Return J. Register of the Descendants of Vincent Meigs. . . . Westfield, N. J., 1935.

Meigs, Wm. M. Life of Josiah Meigs. Philadelphia, 1887.

Meneely, A. Howard. The War Department, 1861: A Study in Mobilization and Administration. New York: Columbia University Press, 1928.

Miller, Francis Trevelyan, editor. Photographic History of the Civil War. 10 volumes. New York: Review of Reviews, 1911.

Murdock, Myrtle Cheney. Constantino Brumidi, Michelangelo of the United States Capitol. Washington: Monumental Press, 1950.

Nevins, Allan. The Emergence of Lincoln. 2 volumes. New York: Scribner's, 1950.

—— Fremont, the West's Greatest Adventurer. 2 volumes. New York: Harper, 1928.

—— Hamilton Fish: The Inner History of the Grant Administration. New York: Dodd, Mead, 1936.

—— Ordeal of the Union. 2 volumes. New York: Scribner's, 1947.

Nichols, Roy F. The Disruption of American Democracy. New York: Macmillan, 1948.

Nicolay, Helen. Our Capital on the Potomac. New York: The Century Company, 1924.

Nicolay, John G., and John Hay. Abraham Lincoln: A History. 10 volumes. New York: The Century Company, 1890.

O'Connor, Richard. Sheridan, the Inevitable. Indianapolis: Bobbs-Merrill, 1953.

Osterweis, Rollin G. Three Centuries of New Haven, 1638–1938. New Haven: Yale University Press, 1953.

Randall, James Garfield, and Richard N. Current. Lincoln the President. 4 volumes. New York: Dodd, Mead, 1945–1955.

Raymond, Henry J. The Life and Public Services of Abraham Lincoln. New York: Derby, 1865.

Repplier, Agnes. Philadelphia, the Place and the People. New York: Macmillan, 1898.

Scharf, J. T., and Thompson Westcott. History of Philadelphia, 1609–1884. 3 volumes. Philadelphia: L. H. Everts and Company, 1884.

Shannon, Fred Albert. Organization and Administration of the Union Army. 2 volumes. Cleveland: Arthur H. Clark, 1928.

Smith, William Ernest. The Francis Preston Blair Family in Politics. 2 volumes. New York: Macmillan, 1933.

Swinton, William. Campaigns of the Army of the Potomac. New York: Richardson, 1866.

Thomas, Benjamin Platt. Abraham Lincoln. New York: Knopf, 1952.

Tryon, Walter S., editor. A Mirror for Americans; Life and Manners in the United States 1790–1870 as Recorded by American Travelers. 3 volumes. Chicago: University of Chicago Press, 1952.

Tucker, Glenn. Poltroons and Patriots. 2 volumes. Indianapolis: Bobbs-Merrill, 1954.

Turner, George Edgar. Victory Rode the Rails. Indianapolis: Bobbs-Merrill, 1953.

Twain, Mark. Life on the Mississippi. New York: Author's National Edition, Harper, 1917.

Upham, Cyril B. "Arms and Equipment for the Iowa Troops in the Civil War." Iowa Journal of History and Politics, XVI (1918), 27–51.

Ward, Christopher. The War of the Revolution. 2 volumes. New York: Macmillan, 1952.

Weber, Thomas. The Northern Railroads in the Civil War. New York: King's Crown Press, 1952.

Wiley, Bell Irvin. The Life of Billy Yank: The Common Soldier of the Union. Indianapolis: Bobbs-Merrill, 1951.

Williams, Kenneth P. Lincoln Finds a General: A Military Study of the Civil War. 4 volumes to date. New York: Macmillan, 1950–1956.

Williams, T. Harry. Lincoln and His Generals. New York: Knopf, 1952.

—— Lincoln and the Radicals. Madison: University of Wisconsin Press, 1941.

# INDEX